Global Statement

Beginning Phase

In this phase, children use the language of the home and community to communicate with familiar others. They often rely on non-verbal cues to convey and comprehend spoken language. Their speech may be characterised by short utterances and they may require support in unfamiliar settings.

Key Indicators

USE OF TEXTS
- Responds to spoken texts in own personal way.
- Communicates in own personal way.
- Understands simple and familiar questions, e.g. Are you hungry? Where would you like to play?

CONTEXTUAL UNDERSTANDING
- Communicates to meet own needs.
- Assumes a shared background between speaker and listener.
- Recognises meaning from familiar language, tone of voice and facial expression in familiar situations.
- Is understood by familiar adults in supportive or predictable situations.

CONVENTIONS
- Uses a small range of vocabulary.
- Responds to spoken language in ways appropriate to home language or culture.
- Attends to spoken texts that are personally significant.
- May ask many questions.

PROCESSES AND STRATEGIES
- Relies on personal experience as a stimulus for speaking and listening.
- Uses a limited range of processes and strategies when speaking, e.g. uses repetition.
- Uses a limited range of processes and strategies when listening.

Major Teaching Emphases

ENVIRONMENT AND ATTITUDE
- Provide opportunities for relevant, challenging and purposeful communication.
- Create a supportive environment which values the diversity of students' speaking and listening development (in their home languages).
- Encourage students to see the value of effective listening and speaking for community, school and family life.

USE OF TEXTS
- Expose students to a range of functional spoken texts composed in Standard English.
- Provide authentic opportunities for students to participate in unplanned and planned speaking and listening.
- Provide opportunities for students to participate in extended talk.
- Teach students to share personal comments after listening.
- Build knowledge of common topics to which students can relate, e.g. toys, families, community.
- Teach students the metalanguage associated with speaking and listening and encourage its use, e.g. speak, listen, hear, speaker, listener, take turns, word, think.

CONTEXTUAL UNDERSTANDING
- Discuss speaking and listening, referring to the audience and purpose.
- Provide effective feedback to students about their speaking and listening.
- Model and discuss how to include relevant information when speaking.
- Draw students' attention to the way ideas and feelings are communicated through speaking and listening.
- Encourage students to use verbal and non-verbal devices to create meaning.

CONVENTIONS
- Develop and extend children's vocabulary for different purposes.
- Model speaking for different purposes, e.g. making requests, seeking information.
- Model speaking and listening behaviours, maintain a conversation.
- Model listening behaviours, e.g. responding to requests, questions, looking at the person.

PROCESSES AND STRATEGIES
- Model language to describe thinking.
- Involve children in conversations with family members and others.
- Model the language and behaviours of listening, e.g. Let's listen to the music. Would you like to hear this story?
- Model ways to improve communication, e.g. adjusting volume, respond to comprehension checks.

In this phase, students use the
questions. They understand sp
They are becoming aware of a

USE OF TEXTS
- Makes sense of spoken texts
- Uses a range of brief unplan
- Participates with support in
- Recalls personally significant

CONTEXTUAL UNDERSTAND
- Beginning to adjust speaking
- Will often assume a shared b
  information to orientate the li
- Is aware that people talk abc

CONVENTIONS
- Structures simple spoken tex
- Uses everyday terms related
- Relies on simple sentences o
- Interprets and uses simple st

PROCESSES AND STRATEGI
- Talks about thinking with oth
- Uses a small range of proces
- Uses a small range of proces

ENVIRONMENT AND ATTITU
- Provide opportunities for rel
- Create a supportive environm
  home languages).
- Encourage students to see th

USE OF TEXTS
- Expose students to a range o
- Provide authentic opportuni
- Provide opportunities for stu
- Teach students to compose
  providing background informa
- Teach students to make con
- Teach students the metalang
  question, topic, message, St
  plan, memory.

CONTEXTUAL UNDERSTAN
- Discuss ways in which partic
  peers during outdoor play.
- Provide explicit feedback to
  small groups/to teachers.
- Help students recognise whe
- Provide support for students
- Provide opportunities for st
- Support students to recogni
  simile, rhyme, common sayinc

CONVENTIONS
- Provide opportunities for stu
- Model language structures
  on listener's understanding,
- Model the skills of conversa
- Teach speaking and listenin
  confirmation, providing suffic
- Model and discuss agreed v

PROCESSES AND STRATEG
- Model thinking aloud abou
- Encourage students to verb
- Provide opportunities for st
- Teach simple planning tools
- Teach simple planning tool
  for specific information.
- Model strategies to adjust c

se

in a range of contexts. They understand the
uence the interpretation of spoken texts. They
a range of purposes.

ns with a wide range of audiences.
ety of purposes.
spoken texts.

range of purposes and audiences.

s on complex themes and issues.
ge, persuade or influence an audience, e.g.

exts.
ive communication, e.g. intervenes sensitively,

oose complex speech.
e.g. monitors group to facilitate discussion.
omplex and challenging texts.

nication.
s' speaking and listening.
for community, school and family life.

d and planned speaking and listening.
ures and structures to suit a range of purposes.
peaking and listening.
and listening independently, analyse,
critique, values, intertextual.

r choices when speaking and listening.
ey interact with particular audiences.
ties.
s of social interest or concern.
of spoken language.

or speaking and listening devices.

eir vocabulary.
of audiences, e.g. formal presentations.
vey meaning and intentions with clarity.
ipulation of conventions, e.g. job interviews,

eeds of a variety of audiences, e.g. formal

jies to compose a variety of spoken texts.
riety of situations.
range of contexts.

TV, CD-ROM, PA system, telephone, etc.)

ation.

Steps Speaking and Listening Map of Development

Proficient Phase	Advanced Ph

ts' control of Standard English reflects their understanding of the way language
res are manipulated to achieve different purposes and effects. They evaluate the appropriateness and
en texts in relation to audience, purpose and context. They experiment with complex devices to
unication.

In this phase, students show a sophisticated control of Standard Englis
power and effect of spoken language, critically analysing factors that i
use complex devices to modify and manipulate their communication f

---

d information from a range of classroom texts dealing with challenging ideas and issues.
rs in structured situations to discuss familiar or accessible subjects.
of sustained spoken texts on challenging ideas and issues, noting key ideas and information in a

and structures for effect in unplanned and planned texts.
nglish in different contexts shows critical awareness of audience and purpose.

DERSTANDING
eness and effect of text form and register in relation to audience, purpose and context.
ts in speaking and listening to suit specific purposes and audiences.
and appropriate information to orientate their listeners, e.g. acknowledge differing opinions.
which spoken texts can include or exclude the values and beliefs of particular audiences.
signed to impact or influence a particular audience, e.g. irony, humour.

manipulates language structures and features in formal and informal situations, e.g. structures a
stains conversation with an unfamiliar adult.
some language structures and features that enable speakers to influence audiences
y to impact on target audience.
and listening behaviours appropriate to the purpose and situation when interacting, e.g. builds on
to achieve group goals, invites others to have a speaking turn.
lentifies and analyses structures and features that signal bias and points of view.

STRATEGIES
s appropriate strategies for monitoring and adjusting communication.
ects on spoken texts drawing on knowledge of differences in nonverbal behaviours, e.g. facial
ntact, proximity.
appropriate processes and strategies when speaking, e.g. uses anecdotes and data to influence an

appropriate processes and strategies when listening, e.g. records important data.
es to improve listening in challenging contexts, e.g. seeks clarification, confirms information.

USE OF TEXTS
- Makes sense of a range of spoken texts, including specialised topics.
- Offers advice, extends views and presents ideas effectively in discussi
- Uses a wide range of unplanned and planned texts that achieve a va
- Analyses sophisticated and challenging information in a wide range
- Uses Standard English in sophisticated ways.

CONTEXTUAL UNDERSTANDING
- Makes deliberate adjustments in speaking and listening to suit a wide
- Interacts inclusively with a wide audience.
- Can critically evaluate spoken texts that represent differing perspective
- Selects and manipulates devices designed to establish a rapport, enga
  anecdote, analogy, nominating others to hold the floor.

CONVENTIONS
- Draws upon a wide vocabulary to achieve planned effect.
- Controls and analyses language structures in formal and informal con
- Uses speaking and listening behaviours to facilitate and maintain effe
  redirects.
- Selects listening conventions to suit a range of purposes.

PROCESSES AND STRATEGIES
- Draws upon an extensive repertoire of strategies to interpret and com
- Adapts processes and strategies to interact responsively and critically,
- Adapts a range of processes and strategies to compose and improve

---

ND ATTITUDE
ities for relevant, challenging and purposeful communication.
e environment which values the diversity of students' speaking and listening development.
ts to see the value of effective listening and speaking for community, school and family life.

are a range of functional spoken texts.
ities for students to participate in authentic unplanned and planned speaking and listening.
ities for students to participate in extended talk for a range of purposes.
use effective text structures and features to suit a range of purposes.
extract and analyse complex and challenging information from spoken texts.
ts to use the metalanguage associated with speaking and listening independently, e.g. interaction,
rnative, style shifts, adjust, position, pace, convention, evaluate, reflection, rephrasing.

DERSTANDING
ities that challenge students to carefully consider their choices when speaking and listening.
reflect upon the way in which they interact with particular audiences.
consider the needs and background knowledge of their audience when selecting suitable content

r students to contribute to matters of social interest or concern.
extend their critical analysis to include complex themes and issues.
reflect upon the way in which they interact with their audience.
select and manipulate devices to suit a particular context.

to take responsibility for expanding, refining and using new vocabulary.
ities for students to compose complex spoken texts for known and unknown audiences.
d to sustain and facilitate communication in unplanned and planned situations, e.g. to interrupt,
redirect.
d to respond appropriately to the intellectual and emotional demands of different situations.

STRATEGIES
elect appropriate thinking strategies to explore complex concepts and ideas.
ities for students to engage in sustained conversations and discussions.
ities for students to adapt a range of processes and strategies to compose complex and challenging

ities for students to interact responsively in contexts where they are required to facilitate discussion.
ities for students to identify and use prompts that anticipate and manage likely disagreements.

ENVIRONMENT AND ATTITUDE
- Provide opportunities for relevant, challenging and purposeful commu
- Create a supportive environment which values the diversity of student
- Encourage students to see the value of effective listening and speaking

USE OF TEXTS
- Discuss and analyse a range of functional spoken texts.
- Provide opportunities for students to participate in authentic unplanne
- Support students to reflect upon and analyse their own use of text fea
- Support students to take responsibility for their own development in s
- Encourage students to use the metalanguage associated with speaking
  socio-cultural, ideology, world view, reiterating, deconstruct, regulate,

CONTEXTUAL UNDERSTANDING
- Provide opportunities that challenge students to carefully consider the
- Provide opportunities for students to reflect upon the way in which th
- Support students to design their own speaking and listening opportun
- Provide support for students to contribute to discussions about matter
- Support students to take responsibility for developing critical awaren
- Provide opportunities for students to analyse a range of spoken text:
- Provide opportunities for students to reflect upon and refine their use

CONVENTIONS
- Support students in taking responsibility for extending and developi
- Support students to compose spoken texts to meet the needs of a v
- Encourage students to select speaking and listening behaviours that v
- Involve students in a variety of situations that require sophisticated m
  giving impromptu speeches.

PROCESSES AND STRATEGIES
- Provide opportunities for students to compose spoken texts to meet the
  presentations.
- Encourage students to take responsibility for choosing processes and stra
- Support students in taking responsibility for interacting responsively in a v
- Support students in taking responsibility for adjusting communication in a

In this document:
Spoken texts include face-to-face, face-to-electronic/machine (film, radio, D
Spoken language refers to verbal and non-verbal communication.
Functional texts include everyday, literary and informational.
Context refers to a combination of factors including purpose, audience and

Early Phase

own variety of English language to communicate needs, express ideas and ask
ken language relating to personal and social interests and respond in their own way.
propriate ways of interacting in familiar situations.

with familiar others.
ed spoken texts independently.
me planned talk for school purposes.
nformation from spoken texts.

NG
and listening for familiar situations in a school context.
ckground between speaker and listener when speaking, e.g. may not give sufficient
tener.
ut their ideas.

s appropriately.
o their experiences and some subject-specific words.
uses simple connectives to link ideas.
tements, commands and questions.

S
ers, e.g. I think.
es and strategies when speaking, e.g. uses props to support speaking.
es and strategies when listening, e.g. asks questions to clarify.

DE
vant, challenging and purposeful communication.
ent which values the diversity of students' speaking and listening development (in their

e value of effective listening and speaking for community, school and family life.

f functional spoken texts composed in Standard English.
ies for students to participate in unplanned and planned speaking and listening.
dents to participate in extended talk.
poken texts using basic text structures e.g. using people's names in social situations and
ion in recounts, responding to questioning.
ections with their existing knowledge of common topics.
uage associated with speaking and listening and encourage its use, e.g. meaning,
ndard English, point of view, sharing, volume, expression, turn,

ING
lar spoken texts are suitable for different audiences, e.g. conversations with adults or

tudents who are adjusting their speaking and listening, e.g. when they are talking in

re background and supporting information are needed when speaking.
to recognise how they can contribute to discussions.
dents to analyse the meaning of spoken texts.
e how simple devices improve speaking and listening in different contexts, e.g. volume,

dents to develop and use new vocabulary.
nd features to suit the purpose, e.g. recount an experience using time order, checking
adding supporting detail, give explanations using conjunctions, e.g. if, then, and, because.
on.
behaviours that support meaning making, e.g. asking clarifying questions, seeking
nt detail.
ays to respond to spoken texts in school, e.g. when and how to take turns.

S
the selection of appropriate speaking and listening strategies.
ise own thinking.
dents to engage in conversations for specific purposes, e.g. to socialise, to get things done.
for speaking, e.g. plan recounts that orientate the listener, plan how …
to help students gain a listening focus, e.g. use drawings to respond to listening, listen

mmunication, e.g. self-correct to clarify meaning, rephrase if not understood.

Exploratory Phase

In this phase, students' use Standard English effectively within familiar contexts. Th
both structured and unstructured situations. They explore ways of using language
purposes.

USE OF TEXTS
◆ Listens effectively for a range of familiar purposes.
◆ Uses a range of unplanned spoken texts with connected ideas.
◆ Presents simple spoken texts using basic text structures in logical sequence, e.g.
◆ Obtains specific information from short informational and expressive spoken text

CONTEXTUAL UNDERSTANDING
◆ Tries different ways of adjusting speaking and listening, e.g. tone and pace.
◆ Provides some background information and supporting ideas for listener, e.g. fac
◆ Understands that people have different ideas.
◆ Talks about different audiences and purposes for own talk.
◆ Experiments with a small range of devices to enhance meaning of spoken texts,
  sayings.

CONVENTIONS
◆ Experimenting with vocabulary drawn from a variety of sources, e.g. literature, m
◆ Experiments with more complex structures and features to express spoken ideas
  supporting details.
◆ Responds to spoken language using common school conventions, e.g. takes turn
◆ Experiments with different speaking and listening behaviours, e.g. proximity, eye
  information when given instructions.

PROCESSES AND STRATEGIES
◆ Explores thinking strategies with others.
◆ Experiments with a small range of processes and strategies when speaking e.g. u
◆ Experiments with a small range of processes and strategies when listening e.g. d

ENVIRONMENT AND ATTITUDE
■ Provide opportunities for relevant, challenging and purposeful communication.
■ Create a supportive environment which values the diversity of students' speaking
  home languages).
■ Encourage students to see the value of effective listening and speaking for comm

USE OF TEXTS
■ Expose students to a range of functional spoken texts composed in Standard Eng
■ Provide opportunities for students to participate in authentic unplanned and plan
■ Provide opportunities for students to participate in extended talk.
■ Teach students to compose spoken texts using text features to enhance meaning
  and events in time order.
■ Teach students how to identify relevant information about new and familiar topi
■ Teach students the metalanguage associated with speaking and listening and en
  e.g. communicate, spoken text, audience, Standard English, verbal, non-verbal, menta

CONTEXTUAL UNDERSTANDING
■ Discuss ways in which speaking and listening can be adjusted for different purpo
  information in a classroom context, talking in the playground.
■ Continue to provide effective feedback to students who are adjusting their speak
  volume, amount of detail, code-switching/code-mixing.
■ Teach students to include relevant information to develop content and ideas wh
■ Provide support for students to contribute to discussions about matters that inter
■ Teach students to recognise different points of view when analysing different sp
■ Provide opportunities for students to express their opinions on a range of familia
■ Model and support students to use devices to enhance meaning, e.g. using appr
  appropriate level of detail.

CONVENTIONS
■ Provide opportunities for students to develop, refine and use new vocabulary.
■ Teach structures and features that help students extend and sustain communicat
  conjunctions to indicate cause and effect, maintaining the topic, taking turns.
■ Teach speaking and listening behaviours that support meaning making, e.g. body
  on others' ideas.
■ Teach conversational skills, e.g. turn taking, confirmation, clarification.
■ Teach skills of listening and responding in whole-class, partner and small-group
  agreeably.

PROCESSES AND STRATEGIES
■ Discuss and reflect on the use of thinking to make meaning in speaking and liste
■ Provide opportunities for students to engage in sustained conversations, e.g. wit
■ Teach a range of planning tools for speaking, e.g. how to share ideas.
■ Teach planning tools that focus listening before, during and after activities, e.g.
  graphic organiser.
■ Model responses to miscommunication, e.g. how to stop, rephrase and repeat, che

ment

<table>
<tr><td>

...ey communicate appropriately in
...or different speaking and listening

...description, instruction, recount.
...

...s and personal reasons.

...g. volume, simile, rhyme, common

...edia, learning area.
...nd information, e.g. provide some

...s in a conversation.
...ontact, volume, listens for specific

...es rehearsed phrases.
...aws a picture.

</td><td>

Consolidating Phase

In this phase, students use most language structures and features of Standard English appropriately when speaking in a range of contexts. They show increasing awareness of the needs of their audience. They experiment with ways to adjust listening and speaking to suit different purposes.

</td></tr>
</table>

USE OF TEXTS
- Listens effectively to obtain specific information from informational and expressive spoken texts.
- Composes spoken texts using most text structures and features appropriately in planned situations.
- Uses a range of unplanned spoken texts effectively as ideas are being developed.

CONTEXTUAL UNDERSTANDING
- Is aware that certain forms of spoken text are associated with particular contexts and purposes.
- Is aware that speaking and listening can be adjusted for different purposes, e.g. socialising, informing.
- Understands the need to provide background information to enhance meaning, e.g. give examples.
- Understands that people may represent their own points of view through spoken texts.
- Uses a small range of devices to enhance meaning, e.g. rephrasing, adjusting volume and speed of speech, negotiating meaning.

CONVENTIONS
- Varies vocabulary to add interest or to describe with greater accuracy.
- Uses most language structures and features appropriate to purpose, e.g. indicates cause and effect, adjusts level of formality according to context.
- Responds appropriately to spoken language in informal and some formal situations for different purposes, e.g. attends and contributes to small group discussions, by building on others' ideas, providing feedback.
- Selects listening and speaking behaviours to suit the purpose and audience in familiar situations, e.g. more formal with teachers than peers, adds more detail when listener is unfamiliar with context of speech, uses more comprehension checks when providing unfamiliar information.

PROCESSES AND STRATEGIES
- Reflects on speaking and listening activities and uses this knowledge in an attempt to improve communication.
- Uses a variety of processes and strategies when speaking, e.g. justifies and explains statements.
- Uses a variety of processes and strategies when listening, e.g. asks questions to seek confirmation.
- Selects and adjusts verbal and non-verbal behaviours for particular groups, e.g. younger children.

<table>
<tr><td>

...and listening development (in their

...unity, school and family life.

...lish.
...ned speaking and listening.

...e.g. recount includes introduction

...s.
...ourage its use,
...l picture.

...ses, e.g. socialising, providing

...ng and listening, e.g. changing

...n speaking.
...est or affect them.
...ken texts.
...r topics.
...priate expression, providing the

...on, e.g. using text connectives and

...language, facial expressions, building

...iscussions, e.g. how to disagree

...hing.
...peers, teachers and known adults.

...dentify key ideas, record ideas in a

...k comprehension.

</td><td>

ENVIRONMENT AND ATTITUDE
- Provide opportunities for relevant, challenging and purposeful communication.
- Create a supportive environment which values the diversity of students' speaking and listening development (in their home languages).
- Encourage students to see the value of effective listening and speaking for community, school and family life.

USE OF TEXTS
- Discuss and explore a range of functional spoken texts composed in Standard English.
- Provide opportunities for students to participate in authentic unplanned and planned speaking and listening.
- Provide opportunities for students to participate in extended talk.
- Teach students to extend ideas logically and coherently in spoken texts to suit a particular purpose.
- Teach students to locate and interpret complex information from spoken texts on new and familiar topics.
- Teach students the metalanguage associated with speaking and listening and encourage its use, e.g. orientation, conclusion, dialect, terms for forms of Australian English, e.g. slang, colloquial, negotiate, attend, facial expression, gesture, strategy, comparison, monitor.

CONTEXTUAL UNDERSTANDING
- Discuss ways in which spoken texts can be constructed and adjusted for different purposes, e.g. through register, dialect, vocabulary choices.
- Provide opportunities for students to reflect upon the way in which they interact with particular audiences, e.g. degree of formality, type of vocabulary, topics discussed, code-switching/code-mixing.
- Teach students to include relevant details and information of interest to their listeners when speaking.
- Teach students how to contribute to discussions of matters that interest or affect them.
- Provide opportunities for students to analyse the way people's beliefs and opinions influence the construction of spoken texts.
- Teach students to reflect upon the way in which they express their opinions.
- Teach the use of devices and discuss how they influence meaning, e.g. volume, tone, pace, emphasis, vocabulary choices, amount of detail, type of examples provided.

CONVENTIONS
- Provide opportunities for students to develop, refine and use new vocabulary.
- Teach structures and features that extend and elaborate communication in informal and formal contexts, e.g. how to state and justify an opinion.
- Continue to teach conversational skills, e.g. turn taking, negotiating meaning, managing topic changes.
- Teach students to recognise the different speaking and listening behaviours that are needed for different contexts.
- Teach students listening skills needed to respond appropriately in a variety of situations, e.g. how to offer alternate viewpoints sensitively, how to identify different points of view.

PROCESSES AND STRATEGIES
- Provide opportunities for students to reflect on thinking strategies used for speaking and listening, e.g. encourage students to set goals to improve speaking and listening, consider evidence to support an opinion, think through an issue before raising it with others.
- Provide opportunities for students to engage in sustained conversations and discussions, e.g. how to build on the ideas of others, paraphrasing, giving and seeking opinions.
- Teach students to select planning tools to help them speak effectively in a range of contexts, e.g. debates, in group contexts related to school contexts, with peers and unknown adults in social contexts.
- Teach students to use scaffolds to plan for listening, e.g. how to set goals for listening, how to make accurate notes, how to summarise key ideas from a spoken text.
- Teach strategies to repair miscommunication, e.g. by seeking feedback (confirmation check), clarifying message, rephrasing.

</td></tr>
</table>

Global Statement

Conventional Phase

In this phase, students recognise and control most language structures and features of Standard English when speaking for a range of purposes. They select and sustain language and style appropriate to audience and purpose. They are aware of the value of planning and reflecting to improve the effectiveness of communication.

Key Indicators

USE OF TEXTS
- Identifies main ideas and supporting details of a range of spoken informational and expressive texts.
- Develops and presents familiar ideas and information, and supports opinion with some detail, in a variety of classroom situations.
- Controls text features and structures effectively in planned and unplanned texts.
- Uses Standard English effectively in a range of contexts.

CONTEXTUAL UNDERSTANDING
- Considers the appropriateness of text form and register in relation to audience when speaking and listening in familiar situations.
- Adjusts speaking and listening appropriately for different familiar contexts.
- Includes information and text features to maintain audience interest, e.g. choice of vocabulary, appropriate level of detail.
- Understands that people's points of view and beliefs influence the construction of spoken texts.
- Uses a range of devices when attempting to influence a listener, e.g. tone, volume, expression, choice of style.

CONVENTIONS
- Selects vocabulary to enhance meaning and effect.
- Recognises and controls most language structures and features appropriate to the purpose in informal and some formal situations, e.g. can express and justify own opinion succinctly, can rephrase others' contributions to group discussions.
- Uses appropriate speaking and listening behaviours in informal and some formal situations, e.g. can style-shift when conversing with unfamiliar people, listens for general or specific information according to purpose.
- Is aware of the audience needs when responding, e.g. offers alternate viewpoints sensitively.

PROCESSES AND STRATEGIES
- Draws on a range of strategies and deliberately adjusts speaking and listening to meet the needs of the task.
- Adjusts information or adjusts tone of voice in response to a listener's reaction.
- Selects appropriate strategies when listening, e.g. asks questions to elicit additional information.
- Identifies a range of strategies used to enhance a talk.

Major Teaching Emphases

ENVIRONMENT AND ATTITUDE
- Provide opportunities for relevant, challenging and purposeful communication.
- Create a supportive environment which values the diversity of students' speaking and listening development (in their home languages).
- Encourage students to see the value of effective listening and speaking for community, school and family life.

USE OF TEXTS
- Discuss and compare a range of functional spoken texts.
- Provide opportunities for students to participate in authentic unplanned and planned speaking and listening.
- Provide opportunities for students to participate in extended talk.
- Teach students to incorporate text features and structures effectively in a range of spoken texts
- Teach students to recognise and evaluate complex and challenging information on familiar and unfamiliar topics.
- Teach students the metalanguage associated with speaking and listening and encourage its use, e.g. functional, literary, informational, multi-modal, recasting, contexts, style, pitch, active listening.

CONTEXTUAL UNDERSTANDING
- Teach students to make appropriate choices when speaking and listening to suit the context, e.g. style, content, dialect, text form.
- Teach students to reflect upon the way in which they interact with particular audiences.
- Teach students to consider the needs and background knowledge of their audience when selecting suitable content for spoken texts.
- Provide support for students to contribute to discussions about matters of personal and social interest.
- Teach students to analyse the different ways in which values and beliefs can be represented in spoken texts.
- Provide opportunities for students to justify their selection of spoken texts for different audiences.
- Teach students to select devices to influence a particular audience, e.g. irony, humour, counter-argue, rebuke and respond to others' comments.

CONVENTIONS
- Provide opportunities for students to develop, use and refine vocabulary.
- Teach structures and features to compose spoken texts for informal and formal contexts, e.g. how to greet unfamiliar adults, how to open and close a conversation, how to plan and present a formal speech.
- Teach speaking and listening behaviours that facilitate communication (in unplanned and planned situations), e.g. how to build on the ideas of others, effective use of body language.
- Continue to teach students the skills needed to communicate with others with critical awareness.

PROCESSES AND STRATEGIES
- Teach students to plan and monitor their use of thinking strategies when speaking and listening, e.g. determine importance, compare information.
- Provide opportunities for students to engage in sustained conversations and discussions.
- Provide opportunities for students to choose appropriate processes and strategies, e.g. analyse the requirements of the task.
- Teach students to select tools for listening, e.g. use graphic organisers to synthesise information from several texts.
- Teach students to anticipate and address possible points of miscommunication.

Speaking and Listening Map of Development

First Steps Second Edition was developed by the
Department of Education and Training (Western Australia).
It was written by:
Judy Brace
Vicki Brockhoff
Nicola Sparkes
Janene Tuckey

Second Edition

Authors' Acknowledgements

The *First Steps* writing team acknowledges all contributions to the development of this resource. We give our grateful thanks to the following people.

All teachers and students who were involved in the preparation of units of work, trialling the materials and offering feedback.

Those students and teachers who provided us with great work samples and transcripts to enhance the text. Special thanks to Vicki Brockhoff for her work in the creation and collection of many of these work samples.

The contribution made to the development of these materials by the research into oral language published by Professor Rhonda Oliver, Dr Yvonne Haig and Dr Judith Rochecouste.

The authors of the original *First Steps* Edition, developed by the Department of Education of Western Australia, and the efforts of the many individuals who contributed to that resource.

Contents

CHAPTER 1
About Speaking and Listening

This chapter focuses on what is important about the teaching and learning of speaking and listening. It outlines the basis of the *First Steps Speaking and Listening Map of Development* and the *First Steps Speaking and Listening Resource Book* (2nd Edition). The Speaking and Listening Map of Development (formerly known as the Oral Language Developmental Continuum) is designed to help teachers map their students' progress; it offers suggestions for teaching and learning experiences that will assist with further development in speaking and listening.

In the *First Steps* resource, each strand of Reading, Writing, Viewing and Speaking and Listening is broken down into smaller categories that are referred to throughout as aspects. The following table summarises how these aspects combine to capture the nature of speaking and listening.

Aspect	Speaking and Listening is...
Use of Texts: what students do with texts to convey and interpret meaning.	• composing and interpreting meaning from a wide range of everyday, literary, technical or mass media texts.
Contextual Understanding: • How the context affects the choice of language and the mode, medium and format used. • How the context affects the interpretation of text.	• a social practice used to accomplish a wide range of purposes across a wide range of cultural and situational contexts. • the awareness of a person's purposes, interests and biases when interpreting, responding to or composing spoken texts.
Conventions: structures and features of texts.	• the language patterns, vocabulary and behaviours that are chosen with understanding and critical awareness to compose and interpret spoken language.
Processes and Strategies: how students read, write, speak and listen and view.	• the thinking, planning and reflecting used to compose and interpret spoken texts.

Figure 1.1 The four aspects of speaking and listening

Understanding the Role of Speaking and Listening

Speaking and listening is central to the lives of all people. It is the means through which we communicate feelings, thoughts and experiences. It is also an integral part of thinking and learning.

Children learn the skills of speaking and listening as they participate as active members of a society through interactions with family members and members of the wider community. When children enter educational settings, their experiences of language will be diverse. Effective instruction recognises, accepts and values the existing language competence of students, including their use of non-standard forms of English. In all phases of development, students are encouraged to value and respect their home language while developing a critical understanding and effective use of the conventions of Standard English. The development of this knowledge enables students to choose appropriate language to function successfully in society in a variety of contexts.

About Speaking — Unplanned and Planned Speaking

Students speak to interact socially, to develop self-awareness and to explore ideas. Speaking underpins learning in all areas of the curriculum. Teachers can assist students to understand the way language works by developing the processes and strategies they need to successfully participate in a wide range of social interactions, classroom discussions and learning experiences.

Speaking is usually immediate and spontaneous yet speakers also think and reflect as they speak. The dynamic, interactive nature of unplanned spontaneous speaking is not only vital for the building of interpersonal relationships but also promotes inquiry and the exchange of ideas. Speaking that is more formal may be planned and deliberately constructed for different communicative situations. This type of speaking may be more reflective in nature, drawing together the ideas that have been previously developed. Teachers provide opportunities for both unplanned and planned speaking to support learning in a variety of situations.

Figure 1.2 outlines some of the differences between planned and unplanned speaking. Figure 1.3a and 1.3b are examples of planned and unplanned speaking. The transcripts are recorded conversations between an older child and a younger child who regularly visit each other's class as part of a buddy class arrangement.

Unplanned Speaking...	Planned Speaking...
– may be spontaneous and rapid as the speaker is thinking on the spot.	– is measured. Deliberate planning is done prior to speaking.
– can involve spontaneously using voice, pitch, rhythm, stress and body to assist communication as needed.	– uses previously chosen and rehearsed devices.
– can be hesitant, often punctuated with fillers such as *umm* and *er*.	– is concerned with precision. Words can be chosen for economy or can be elaborated on depending on the needs of the audience.
– may be repetitive.	– uses repetition deliberately to illustrate a point.
– is often disjointed and may contain false starts and incomplete sentences.	– aims for fluent speech using full sentences.
– contains the use of short, simple clauses often connected by the conjunctions *and* and *but*.	– is delivered using longer sentences with more complex and descriptive language.
– can be to an immediate audience who may interrupt, question, comment and overlap.	– can be presented with some distance between speaker and audience. Turn-taking is clear and questions are called for.
– is often interactive. The speaker judges an audience's reaction spontaneously and makes adjustments or decides whether to continue. Meaning is often jointly constructed.	– is researched or negotiated to determine what the audience needs to know prior to planning. The onus is on the speaker to clearly construct meaning.

Figure 1.2 Some of the differences between planned and unplanned speaking

Planned Speaking

(Elizabeth tells Joshua what she learnt about a guest visitor to her class from the post office. She has already rehearsed this recount earlier in the day with a classmate.)

Elizabeth:	Today, someone from the post office came in. Her name was Glenda. She was Miss Lyons' mum, and she, and she thought her job was good, she gets about ten thousand money in a day, in a day, and, and she had lots of things to show … her. We got two stamps, one is a phone stamp and the other stamp was a lick-on stamp, and when I licked it, when it went down, the lick taste went down my throat, it was very yucky. They had bags bigger than me and that's what I learned at, learned today. Miss Lyons even got a phone stamp and I was the only person who thought it was a phone. Thank you for listening.
Joshua:	What were some of the interesting things you saw?
Elizabeth:	We saw a Sir Donald, Sir Donald Bradman coin.
Joshua:	Yeah?
Elizabeth:	There's two types of Sir Donald's Bradman's ones. She didn't tell us about this one but we already know that, it's one we've got, you know that it's a twenty cent Sir Donald Bradman one, and so it is this one and this is what I'll describe. The Sir Donald Bradman one looks like the one in the thing… It had gold in the middle with Sir Donald Bradman on it, and silver round the outside that said twenty cents on it. And we saw nice shiny tiny two cents and one cents. There's two packets of those.

Figure 1.3a A transcript of planned speaking

Unplanned Speaking

(Overlapping is occurring.)

Elizabeth:	I wanna talk about frogs.
Joshua:	Why do you wanna talk about frogs?
Elizabeth:	You wanna talk about them, then?
Joshua:	I don't care.
Elizabeth:	Yeah, we'll talk about frogs. What do you know about frogs?
Joshua:	What?
Elizabeth:	What do you know about frogs?
Joshua:	That they're amphibians.
Elizabeth:	I know that they are frogs. I know they can breathe through their skin and lungs.
Joshua:	Can they? I didn't know that!
Elizabeth:	Yeah, that they are amphibians, that's all I know. Oh yeah, and that they jump for bugs and flies and stuff.
Joshua:	I know that they can be lots of colours and they can poison us.
Elizabeth:	And they can fly.
Joshua:	They can fly?
Elizabeth:	Some of them can fly.
Joshua:	Frogs can't fly.
Elizabeth:	They jump pretty high, but sometimes they jump, too, a bit too high so they fly.
Joshua:	Is the… That's because they're webbed, like their feet are webbed so they like kind of glide.

Figure 1.3b A transcript of unplanned speaking

About Listening

Listening is more than hearing; it is an interactive process obtaining information, for pleasure and for building relationships. Sensitive teachers will be aware of the differences that may exist across and within cultures. For example, in English-speaking societies, we depend on particular listening behaviours such as eye contact, nodding and saying '*Mmm*' to indicate that speech is understood. However, these behaviours may not be appropriate in other cultures and some students may feel uncomfortable or excluded when these behaviours are expected of them. Teachers can assist by explicitly teaching the processes and strategies needed to communicate effectively in a range of contexts.

Listening situations also vary as do the types of listening skills required as represented in Figure 1.4. (Nunan 1990, as quoted in Gibbons 2002). Listening occurs in four types of contexts.

Types of Listening

Two-way

Quadrant A	**Quadrant C**
Taking part in:	*Taking part in:*
– a conversation at a party	– a job interview
– a conversation at a bus stop about the weather	– a conversation involving the giving of directions or instructions
– a chatty phone call to a friend	– a phone inquiry about buying a computer
Quadrant B	**Quadrant D**
Listening to:	*Listening to:*
– someone recounting a personal anecdote	– the radio or TV news
– someone telling a story	– a lecture
– someone telling a joke	– phone information (e.g. a recorded timetable, or instructions for paying a bill)

interpersonal topics (left)   **information-based topics** (right)

One-way

Figure 1.4 Types of Listening (Nunan 1990, cited in Gibbons 2002)

These include situations where the listener is not required to respond verbally (such as listening to a performance or a radio program). Other situations may involve two or more people who take on roles as the speaker and listener in turn or in an overlapping style (such as in a conversation). Listening also varies in intensity. Some listening can be of a relatively superficial nature, as the listener attends only to the content (such as listening for entertainment). Other listening requires total attention (such as listening for key information, to critically analyse an argument or listening to identify emotions behind the words). These behaviours can be explicitly taught so that students are able to confidently recognise situations where their listening may need to be adjusted.

I don't wriggle about and I stay still at school, but I still wriggle about at home — I can still listen — 'cos my teacher says to stay still but you could still wriggle and listen. I can still hear when I wriggle but some people can't. They just find little bits of squiggly wire and play with it; it's strange!

(from a seven-year-old student)

Figure 1.5 A young student's interpretation of the differences between listening at home and listening at school

A Dynamic Interactive Model of Speaking and Listening

The *First Steps* Speaking and Listening model reflects the dynamic, interactive and complex nature of spoken language. At the centre of the model is speaking and listening. As speaking and listening is dependent on the context in which it is embedded, students need to be taught about situational and socio-cultural contexts. That is the purpose of the speaking and listening, the audience involved and the situation in which the speaking and listening is taking place.

The model should be seen as a dynamic process whereby speakers and listeners interact to make meaning. During this process, speakers and listeners make choices about how they will speak and listen to suit particular contexts. These choices are made from a developing repertoire of understandings and skills across the four aspects of Use of Texts, Contextual Understanding, Conventions and Processes and Strategies. While the elements of the model are described individually in this book, it is important that the four aspects are viewed as interactive and interconnected.

Context influences speaking and listening:
- Behaviours
- Content
- Text type
- Style

Students need to develop a repertoire of:
- Texts
- Understandings about context
- Conventions
- Processes and strategies to communicate effectively for a full range of functions in a range of contexts.

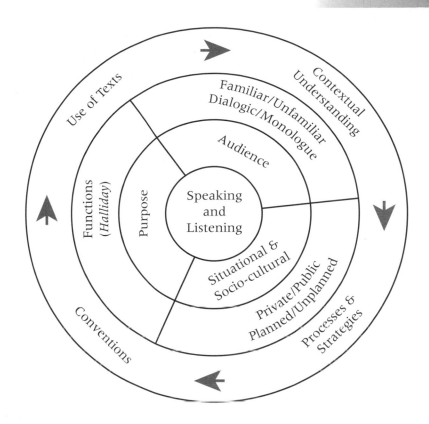

Figure 1.6 The Dynamic Interactive Model of Speaking and Listening

Context

In the Speaking and Listening model (see Figure 1.6), the context refers to the combination of factors that include audience, situation and purpose. These factors influence the level of formality, the text types used, the amount of detail included, the topic and the speaking and listening behaviours. As Green and Campbell point out:

> We need to think of language not as a set of cognitive skills that we either have or do not have, but as forms of behaviour that always take place in social and cultural contexts.
>
> *(Green and Campbell 2003)*

As so many factors influence context, students must learn to select and adjust their speaking and listening in response to the demands of different contexts. Each speaking and listening context is dynamic in the sense that it can alter as soon as one of the factors (audience, situation and purpose) changes. For example, a conversation about a family event between two friends is likely to change if another person joins the group. The relationships between the people will determine what happens to the original conversation after the initial greetings and the establishment of the new context.

Audience	Situation	Purpose
Who is in the interaction? • Familiar (known) to the unfamiliar (unknown) • Gender, age • Cultural groupings • Social groupings • Proximity of relationships, e.g. **close to distant**	Where and how does the interaction take place? • Physical (e.g. **indoors, outdoors, classroom, community**) • Proximity, e.g. **close to distant** • Cultural setting • Social setting	Why does the interaction take place? • Social • Learning • Functional • Cultural

Figure 1.7 Audience, Situation, Purpose

Audience

The type of audience also has an impact on the context of a speaking and listening situation. Factors to consider might be:

• Background knowledge of the audience: Is there a shared understanding of culture, topic and experience?

• The relationship between participants: Do the participants know each other? Is the relationship private or professional?

• Expectations of the audience: Is the audience a peer or a person in authority? Is the audience expected to respond and interact (dialogue) or are they expected to listen without interruption (monologue)?

• The emotional status of the participants: Do the participants share common interests? Are participants nervous, anxious or reluctant to contribute?

Audiences range from familiar (known) people to unfamiliar (unknown) people. Interactions also range from dialogic to monologic.

A dialogue is very interactive with participants having more or less equal input into the dialogue. Meaning in a dialogue is co-constructed as participants pass verbal and non-verbal messages to each other. Most of the spoken language in our lives is dialogic, where the audience plays a significant role in the construction of meaning.

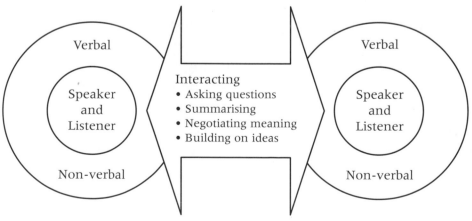

Figure 1.8 Dialogic spoken language

A monologue is less interactive as only one participant speaks while the other participant listens and constructs their own meaning. Monologues are rarely used in everyday lives and so require different planning and presentation.

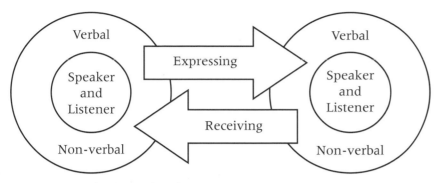

Fig 1.9 Monologic spoken language

Situational Context

Where and how a speaking and listening interaction takes place will influence what is communicated and its delivery. The formality of a situation will also depend on the purpose and the audience. Situations may be planned or unplanned. For example, small group work will involve unplanned speaking as students initially explore an idea or a problem. Later they may plan to present this information to another group. This sharing could be informal within the classroom, or formal if presented at an assembly. Speaking and listening could also change if a student was sharing the same information with a peer privately as opposed to sharing the information publicly.

Socio-cultural Context

Students need to understand how their speaking and listening is shaped by their socio-cultural background. Teachers will provide opportunities for students to analyse spoken texts to understand how particular word choices can position people in both positive and negative ways.

Purpose

The purpose of an interaction will influence what and how information is exchanged. The purpose relates to the intention of both the speaker and the listener. It can alter during an interaction so different language functions may be involved in one interaction. For example, during a social conversation, clarification about some content could be sought. The speaker could then provide the information required thus switching purposes from catching up with a friend to informing a friend.

The functions of language, as described in Figure 1.11 (Halliday), provide an effective framework for considering purpose in the classroom. Figure 1.11 provides some examples of what speakers and listeners learn to do for different purposes or functions.

The Four Aspects

The four aspects are represented in the outer circle of the model (see Figure 1.6). They all work together in an integrated way. Learning and teaching programs support students in developing a repertoire of skills and understandings across all four aspects so that they are able to make choices to communicate effectively in a range of contexts.

Supporting Speaking and Listening Development — Developing a Repertoire

The *First Steps* Speaking and Listening Map of Development supports teachers in ensuring that students develop the knowledge, skills and attitudes to communicate for a range of purposes in varied situations and with different audiences. It focuses on supporting students' development in Speaking and Listening through the four aspects of Use of Texts, Contextual Understanding, Conventions and Processes and Strategies.

This resource also draws on Halliday's model of the functions of language (1975). This model supports the development of a repertoire of speaking and listening skills to make meaning within a range of social and cultural contexts. Teachers may use the model in order to ascertain what students already know and which aspects need further development.

Teachable Moments

There are many teachable moments that occur within authentic spoken language situations within the school environment. Routine activities that occur on a daily basis require particular ways of speaking and listening that can be taught to students for example, when students in the classroom are packing away, they learn how to ask someone to help, or to inquire about the location of an object.

Collaborative situations also provide many teachable moments. For example, students learn how to negotiate when solving a problem by clarifying the problem, articulating alternative plans, telling others what they think and how they feel, asking questions and prioritising. These kinds of skills become part of the students' repertoire to be used to suit particular contexts. Students also need to participate in monologic, planned, formal speaking and listening opportunities.

The First Steps Speaking and Listening Map of Development suggests that teachers create conditions to observe and interact with students. These conditions will result in teachers being able to seize 'teachable moments' where new skills or understandings can be explained. The process for teaching new skills is influenced by the Gradual Release of Responsibility Model (Pearson and Gallagher 1983). This model guides teachers in modelling a new skill, involving students in sharing and guiding activities in preparation for the new skill to be applied independently.

In the following table, a teachable moment is demonstrated to show the way in which each Teaching and Learning Practice can be used for speaking and listening. In the example, students are expected to find their own groups for an informal discussion.

	Modelling	Sharing	Guiding	Applying
Role of the teacher	The teacher demonstrates the processes used by thinking aloud.	The teacher provides the direction and invites the students to contribute.	The teacher scaffolds help and provides support and corrective feedback.	The teacher offers support and encouragement as necessary.
Role of the students	*I'm having a bit of trouble joining in… I wonder what would happen if I just went and sat there. What would I do if someone just came and sat in my group without saying anything? I would feel a little uncomfortable I think. Perhaps I should say something I think I might say "Can I join your discussion group?" and see what happens.* Students participate by actively attending to the demonstrations.	*If I'm having a bit of trouble joining in…what should I say and do? Do you think I should ask or should I just go and sit there? How would I ask? Would I ask before I sat down in the group?* Students contribute ideas and information. Decision-making is negotiated between teacher and student.	*Has this happened to you before? Remember when we talked about ways to join a group. Which strategy are you going to try? Did that work last time for you?* Students do the speaking and listening with help from the teacher or other sources at predetermined points.	*Are you happy with the way you joined the group today? Why do you think it worked for you?* Students interact independently. They are in control of the conventions (e.g. **turn-taking**) and content.

Figure 1.10 An example of the teaching and learning process using the Gradual Release of Responsibility Model

A Functional Approach

The *First Steps Speaking and Listening Map of Development* is based on Halliday's functions of language to identify the different purposes of language use. It is important for students to have the opportunity to develop and use these functions at school. This will support further development of the repertoire of practices which students can draw upon in new contexts. Each function relates to the different ways language is used in different contexts in the community, school and home.

People communicate for...	Speakers learn to...		Listeners learn to...	
Getting things done (Instrumental)	Ask Refer Persuade	Request Facilitate Explain	Help Provide Do things asked	Find things Justify
Influencing the behaviour, feelings or attitudes of others (Regulatory)	Set tasks Help Instruct Direct	Manage Organise Negotiate Persuade	Follow instructions Follow rules Use facial expression Follow agreements	Extend interaction Ask questions Compliment
Getting along with others (Interactional)	Initiate Sympathise Argue Repair	Arbitrate Reconcile Direct	Analyse points of view Ask Repair/recast	Restate suggestions Empathise Encourage Accept
Expressing individuality and personal feelings (Personal)	State opinions Recount experiences State feelings	Express thoughts Confront Explain Predict	Hear points of view Redirect Judge Assess	Evaluate Reflect Recognise
Seeking and learning about the social and physical environment (Heuristic)	Interrogate Ask questions Prioritise	Discuss Clarify Investigate	Answer questions Summarise Remember/recognise	Apply knowledge Connect/relate
Creating stories, games, new worlds and new texts (Imaginative)	Tell stories Think of new ideas Imagine Experiment	Anticipate Predict Play	Respond Imagine Join in	Anticipate Predict
Communicating information (Representational)	Tell State facts Comment Inform	Impart knowledge Lecture Share skills Share history	Receive knowledge Ask Clarify Sort Refer	Relate Recognise Analyse Extract
Entertaining others (Diversionary)	Divert/initiate Perform Recite Seek attention	Play with words/ actions Make people laugh	Give attention Take turns Anticipate	Evaluate Consider feelings Use body language

Figure 1.11 Based on Halliday's 'Functions of Language', adapted from Anstey & Bull 2004

Teachers may use the list of functions in Figure 1.11 to assess the speaking and listening skills of students and ask questions such as:
- What can students already do? What functions can they use already?
- What speaking and listening skills do they have for? (e.g. **getting along with others**)
- What speaking and listening skills do they need for? (e.g. **persuading others**)

When planning to address identified needs, teachers will find support for suitable learning experiences in each phase chapter of this book.

Teachers may also find it useful to involve their students in investigating the different ways in which language is used in their local communities. Students could then identify areas of interest for further inquiry.

Considering Diversity

It is important that students' home language is recognised and valued. The spoken language that students use in their home environment is an essential part of their self-identity and it is important that students understand that the spoken language they learn at school is in addition to the speaking and listening behaviours and skills they already know. Students also need to develop their knowledge and competence in Standard English so they can speak and listen effectively in a range of contexts.

For further information on diversity, refer to Chapter 4 in *First Steps Linking Assessment, Teaching and Learning* book.

The Difference Between Spoken and Written Language

This *First Steps Speaking and Listening Map of Development* aims to support the development of students' communicative competence for academic and social purposes. It is important to acknowledge the complex nature of speaking and listening and the associated skills required. Students are often judged on their ability to prepare and perform planned speaking but this type of speech is not typically used in everyday social, academic and community life. When planning to provide support for students, it may be useful for teachers to consider the differences between written and spoken language.

Speakers ...	Writers ...
• point or refer to things in their environment.	• cannot assume a shared environment with their readers.
• expect encouragement and cooperation from listeners to produce conversation. Meaning is often co-constructed by the participants.	• have to create and sustain their own belief in what they are doing.
• use gestures, body language and facial expressions to assist meaning (kinaesthetic qualities).	• are removed from the time and place they are describing.
• use intonation, stress, volume and pace to help make their meaning clear (paralinguistic features).	• use graphic cues such as punctuation, paragraphing, bold print and diagrams to help make their meaning clear.
• rephrase or repeat when they think their message is not clear.	• take time to think and rethink as they write, often revising and editing their work.
• know their hesitations will be heard by, and are accepted by the listener.	• know that the reader will not see any rephrasing and alteration they make to the text in the process of writing.
• do not use sentence or word boundaries.	• organise language into words, sentences and paragraphs. These are not natural but are imposed by the written language system being used.
• know that the context of speech influences its flow, e.g. conversations with turn taking, interruption and feedback versus lecturing.	• organise language so it flows smoothly.
• use more imperatives, questions, exclamations, active rather than passive verbs.	• construct texts that are more dense by using more content words (nouns, verbs, adjectives and adverbs).

Figure 1.12 The differences between spoken and written language

CHAPTER 2
Understanding the Speaking and Listening Map of Development

The Speaking and Listening Map of Development contains behaviours, suggested teaching emphases, and a range of teaching and learning experiences for each phase of development. It validates what teachers know about their students. The organisation of the map assists teachers to link teaching and learning with assessment.

Although in practice, literacy integrates the four strands of Speaking and Listening, Writing, Reading, and Viewing, individual maps are necessary to represent the complexity of each strand. Breaking each strand into aspects provides further opportunity for more specialised analysis.

The organisation of the Speaking and Listening Map of Development into the four aspects of Use of Texts, Contextual Understanding, Conventions and Processes and Strategies provides a practical framework for looking at assessment, teaching and learning, and reflects current beliefs about how Speaking and Listening is defined. The features of the map help teachers to make informed, strategic decisions about how to support students' literacy development.

How the Map Is Organised

There are seven phases in the Speaking and Listening Map of Development:

- Beginning
- Early
- Exploratory
- Consolidating
- Conventional
- Proficient
- Advanced

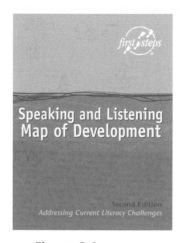

Figure 2.1

The same organisational framework is used for each phase.

PHASE NAME
The Phase Name is a description of a speaker and listener in that phase.

GLOBAL STATEMENT
The Global Statement:
- describes the typical structure of the language used by students in that phase.
- reflects students' awareness of audience.
- describes ways in which students improve, plan or refine their speaking and listening.

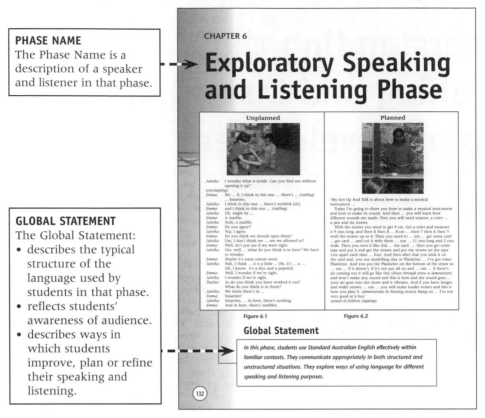

Figure 2.2 The Exploratory Phase Name and Global Statement

INDICATORS
Indicators:
- are organised under the aspect headings:
  – Use of Texts
  – Contextual Understanding
  – Conventions
  – Processes and Strategies
- describe speaking and listening behaviours.

Key Indicators:
- signify a conceptual leap in critical understandings.
- describe behaviours that are typical of a phase.

Other Indicators:
- describe behaviours that provide further details of the phase.

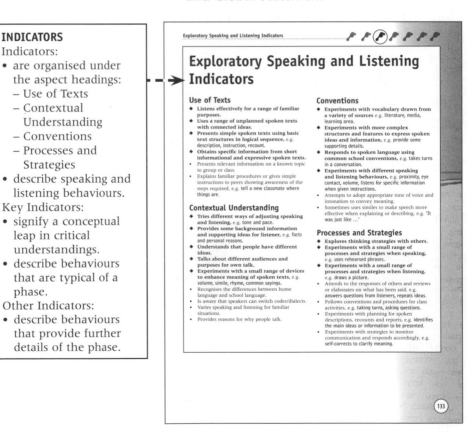

Figure 2.3 The Exploratory Speaking and Listening Indicators

MAJOR TEACHING EMPHASES (MTEs)

Major Teaching Emphases:

- are organised under the aspect headings:
  - Environment and Attitude
  - Use of Texts
  - Contextual Understanding
  - Conventions
  - Processes and Strategies
- are suggestions of appropriate priorities for teaching at each phase.
- are designed to help teachers support and challenge students' current understandings.

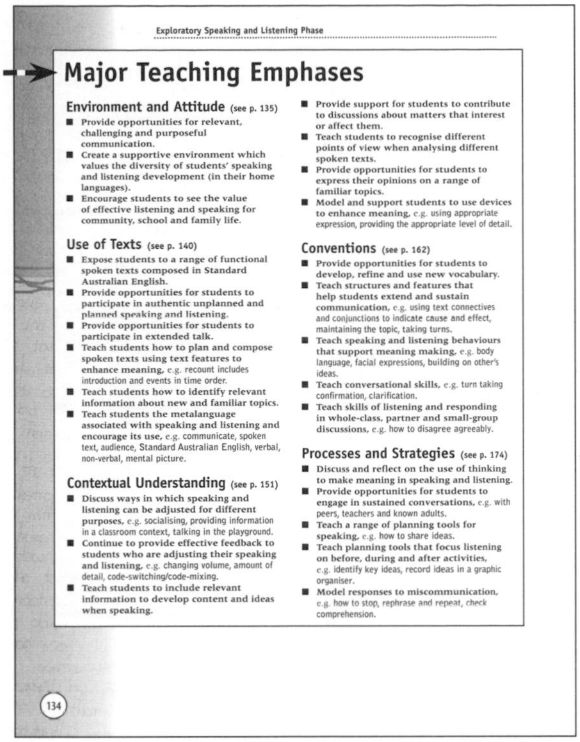

Exploratory Speaking and Listening Phase

Major Teaching Emphases

Environment and Attitude (see p. 135)
- Provide opportunities for relevant, challenging and purposeful communication.
- Create a supportive environment which values the diversity of students' speaking and listening development (in their home languages).
- Encourage students to see the value of effective listening and speaking for community, school and family life.
- Provide support for students to contribute to discussions about matters that interest or affect them.
- Teach students to recognise different points of view when analysing different spoken texts.
- Provide opportunities for students to express their opinions on a range of familiar topics.
- Model and support students to use devices to enhance meaning, e.g. using appropriate expression, providing the appropriate level of detail.

Use of Texts (see p. 140)
- Expose students to a range of functional spoken texts composed in Standard Australian English.
- Provide opportunities for students to participate in authentic unplanned and planned speaking and listening.
- Provide opportunities for students to participate in extended talk.
- Teach students how to plan and compose spoken texts using text features to enhance meaning, e.g. recount includes introduction and events in time order.
- Teach students how to identify relevant information about new and familiar topics.
- Teach students the metalanguage associated with speaking and listening and encourage its use, e.g. communicate, spoken text, audience, Standard Australian English, verbal, non-verbal, mental picture.

Contextual Understanding (see p. 151)
- Discuss ways in which speaking and listening can be adjusted for different purposes, e.g. socialising, providing information in a classroom context, talking in the playground.
- Continue to provide effective feedback to students who are adjusting their speaking and listening, e.g. changing volume, amount of detail, code-switching/code-mixing.
- Teach students to include relevant information to develop content and ideas when speaking.

Conventions (see p. 162)
- Provide opportunities for students to develop, refine and use new vocabulary.
- Teach structures and features that help students extend and sustain communication, e.g. using text connectives and conjunctions to indicate cause and effect, maintaining the topic, taking turns.
- Teach speaking and listening behaviours that support meaning making, e.g. body language, facial expressions, building on other's ideas.
- Teach conversational skills, e.g. turn taking confirmation, clarification.
- Teach skills of listening and responding in whole-class, partner and small-group discussions, e.g. how to disagree agreeably.

Processes and Strategies (see p. 174)
- Discuss and reflect on the use of thinking to make meaning in speaking and listening.
- Provide opportunities for students to engage in sustained conversations, e.g. with peers, teachers and known adults.
- Teach a range of planning tools for speaking, e.g. how to share ideas.
- Teach planning tools that focus listening on before, during and after activities, e.g. identify key ideas, record ideas in a graphic organiser.
- Model responses to miscommunication, e.g. how to stop, rephrase and repeat, check comprehension.

134

Figure 2.4 The Exploratory Speaking and Listening Major Teaching Emphasis

TEACHING AND LEARNING EXPERIENCES

- Teaching and Learning Experiences are organised under the following aspect headings:
  - Environment and Attitude
  - Use of Texts
  - Contextual Understanding
  - Conventions
  - Processes and Strategies
- Each aspect is divided into two sections: Teaching Notes and Involving Students.
  - Teaching Notes unpack the intent of the Major Teaching Emphases.
  - Involving Students contains a selection of developmentally appropriate activities that support the Major Teaching Emphases.

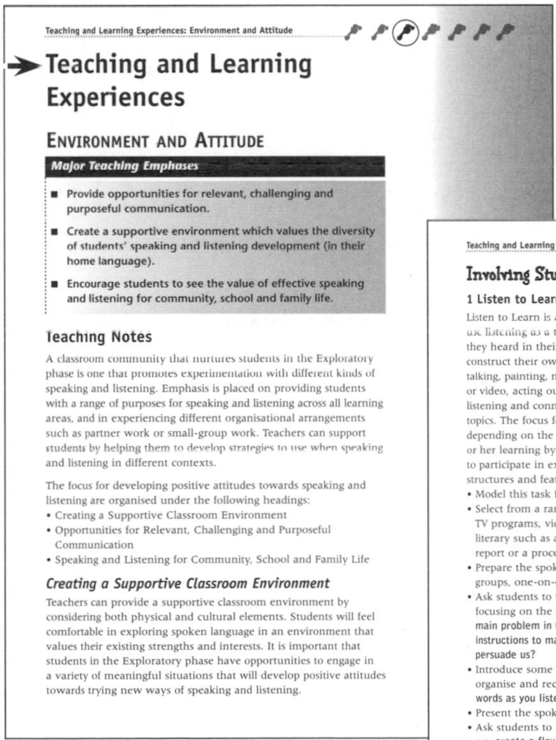

Teaching and Learning Experiences: Environment and Attitude

Teaching and Learning Experiences

Environment and Attitude

Major Teaching Emphases
- Provide opportunities for relevant, challenging and purposeful communication.
- Create a supportive environment which values the diversity of students' speaking and listening development (in their home language).
- Encourage students to see the value of effective speaking and listening for community, school and family life.

Teaching Notes

A classroom community that nurtures students in the Exploratory phase is one that promotes experimentation with different kinds of speaking and listening. Emphasis is placed on providing students with a range of purposes for speaking and listening across all learning areas, and in experiencing different organisational arrangements such as partner work or small-group work. Teachers can support students by helping them to develop strategies to use when speaking and listening in different contexts.

The focus for developing positive attitudes towards speaking and listening are organised under the following headings:
- Creating a Supportive Classroom Environment
- Opportunities for Relevant, Challenging and Purposeful Communication
- Speaking and Listening for Community, School and Family Life

Creating a Supportive Classroom Environment

Teachers can provide a supportive classroom environment by considering both physical and cultural elements. Students will feel comfortable in exploring spoken language in an environment that values their existing strengths and interests. It is important that students in the Exploratory phase have opportunities to engage in a variety of meaningful situations that will develop positive attitudes towards trying new ways of speaking and listening.

Figure 2.5 The Exploratory Speaking and Listening Teaching and Learning Experiences

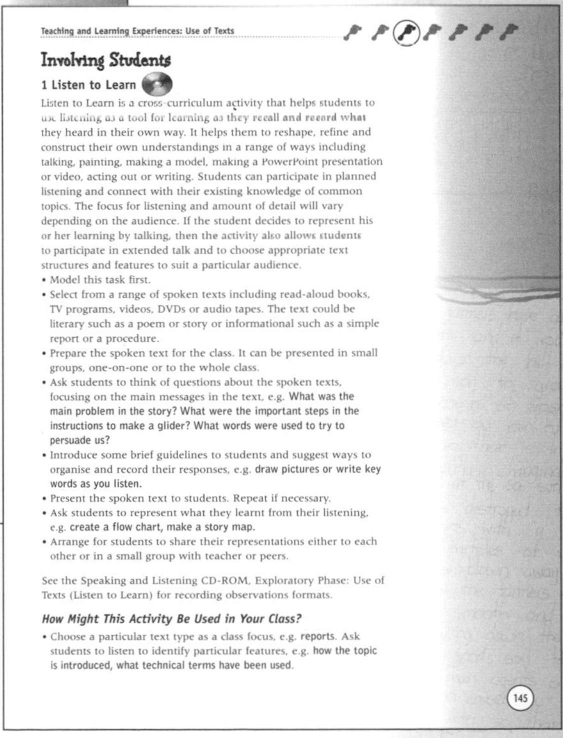

Teaching and Learning Experiences: Use of Texts

Involving Students

1 Listen to Learn

Listen to Learn is a cross-curriculum activity that helps students to use listening as a tool for learning as they recall and record what they heard in their own way. It helps them to reshape, refine and construct their own understandings in a range of ways including talking, painting, making a model, making a PowerPoint presentation or video, acting out or writing. Students can participate in planned listening and connect with their existing knowledge of common topics. The focus for listening and amount of detail will vary depending on the audience. If the student decides to represent his or her learning by talking, then the activity also allows students to participate in extended talk and to choose appropriate text structures and features to suit a particular audience.
- Model this task first.
- Select from a range of spoken texts including read-aloud books, TV programs, videos, DVDs or audio tapes. The text could be literary such as a poem or story or informational such as a simple report or a procedure.
- Prepare the spoken text for the class. It can be presented in small groups, one-on-one or to the whole class.
- Ask students to think of questions about the spoken texts, focusing on the main messages in the text, e.g. What was the main problem in the story? What were the important steps in the instructions to make a glider? What words were used to try to persuade us?
- Introduce some brief guidelines to students and suggest ways to organise and record their responses, e.g. draw pictures or write key words as you listen.
- Present the spoken text to students. Repeat if necessary.
- Ask students to represent what they learnt from their listening, e.g. create a flow chart, make a story map.
- Arrange for students to share their representations either to each other or in a small group with teacher or peers.

See the Speaking and Listening CD-ROM, Exploratory Phase: Use of Texts (Listen to Learn) for recording observations formats.

How Might This Activity Be Used in Your Class?
- Choose a particular text type as a class focus, e.g. reports. Ask students to listen to identify particular features, e.g. how the topic is introduced, what technical terms have been used.

145

Figure 2.6 Exploratory Speaking and Listening — Involving Students

SUPPORTING PARENTS PAGES

Supporting Parents pages:
- provide support for teachers in helping parents or caregivers assist their child's speaking and listening development at home.
- contain:
  - a general description of speakers and listeners in the phase.
  - the type of support that is important for speakers and listeners at this phase.
  - a list of activities appropriate for the home setting.

Each activity is available on the Speaking and Listening CD-ROM, and may be copied for distribution to parents.

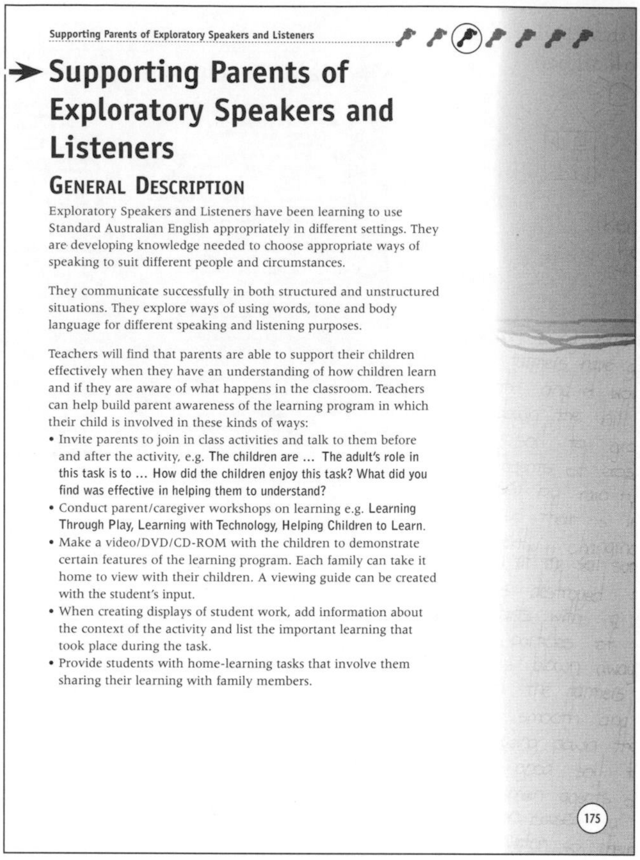

Supporting Parents of Exploratory Speakers and Listeners

Supporting Parents of Exploratory Speakers and Listeners

GENERAL DESCRIPTION

Exploratory Speakers and Listeners have been learning to use Standard Australian English appropriately in different settings. They are developing knowledge needed to choose appropriate ways of speaking to suit different people and circumstances.

They communicate successfully in both structured and unstructured situations. They explore ways of using words, tone and body language for different speaking and listening purposes.

Teachers will find that parents are able to support their children effectively when they have an understanding of how children learn and if they are aware of what happens in the classroom. Teachers can help build parent awareness of the learning program in which their child is involved in these kinds of ways:

- Invite parents to join in class activities and talk to them before and after the activity, e.g. The children are … The adult's role in this task is to … How did the children enjoy this task? What did you find was effective in helping them to understand?
- Conduct parent/caregiver workshops on learning e.g. Learning Through Play, Learning with Technology, Helping Children to Learn.
- Make a video/DVD/CD-ROM with the children to demonstrate certain features of the learning program. Each family can take it home to view with their children. A viewing guide can be created with the student's input.
- When creating displays of student work, add information about the context of the activity and list the important learning that took place during the task.
- Provide students with home-learning tasks that involve them sharing their learning with family members.

175

Figure 2.7 Providing parent support — Supporting Parent Pages

How to Use the Speaking and Listening Map of Development

The purpose in using the Speaking and Listening Map of Development is to link assessment, teaching and learning in a way that best addresses the strengths and needs of all students. The process used to achieve this may vary from teacher to teacher; it may be dependent on a teacher's familiarity with *First Steps*, the data already collected about students' speaking and listening development, the time of the school year, or the school's implementation plan.

This section outlines a possible process (see Figure 2.8). As teachers become more familiar with linking assessment to teaching and learning, strategic decisions about using the map can be made. Some may focus on using the map to profile students; for example, how many students and which ones, using which indicators, which recording sheets and over what period of time? Others may focus on the selection of Major Teaching Emphases (MTEs) and Teaching and Learning Experiences for individual, small-group and whole-class teaching.

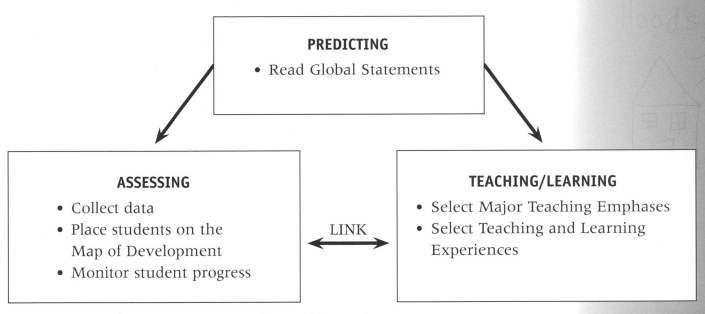

Figure 2.8 A possible process for using the Speaking and Listening Map of Development

Suggested Process for Using the Speaking and Listening Map of Development

Predict

Many teachers begin to use the Speaking and Listening Map of Development by making predictions about each student's phase of development. Predictions are made by reading through the Global Statements. Teachers are then able to use this information, together with their professional judgement, to make an educated guess in each case. The initial predictions, recorded on a class profile sheet, allow teachers to immediately begin linking assessment, teaching and learning.

These predictions can be used to begin selecting Major Teaching Emphases from appropriate phases for whole-class, small-group or individual teaching. The MTEs will then guide the selection of teaching and learning experiences to support students' development.

It is critical that teachers begin to collect data to confirm or amend their initial predictions.

Collect Data

The Indicators on the Speaking and Listening Map of Development provide a focus for data collection, which can be carried out on a continual basis using a range of tools in a variety of contexts. A balance of conversation, observation and analysis of products will ensure that information is gathered across all four aspects. Encouraging the involvement of students and parents or caregivers in the data collection will provide further information about students' speaking and listening development and interests (see Chapter 3).

First Steps Speaking and Listening Map of Development: Class Profile Sheet

Year Level: _____   Teacher: _____

	Beginning	Early	Exploratory	Consolidating	Conventional	Proficient	Advanced
1		Dixie	Ivy	William			
2		Gerard	Heather	Donna			
3		Thomas	Monique	Kerry			
4		Grant	Josh	Simone			
5		Stephen	Tim	Louise			
6		Annabelle	Michael	Jack			
7		Sui-Lee	Nikki				
8		Sian	Thi Chan				
9			Jayne				
10			Bradley				
11			Philip				
12			Jonathan				
13			Kris				
14			Ivan				
15			Tania				
16			Jacqui				
17							
18							
19							
20							
21							
22							
23							
24							
25							
26							
27							
28							
29							
30							

Major Teaching Emphases can be selected from a range of phases.
• Whole-class focus, e.g. Exploratory Phase
• Small-group focus, e.g. Early or Consolidating
• Individual student focus

Figure 2.9 Sample of a class profile

Profile Students on the Speaking and Listening Map of Development

The Speaking and Listening Map of Development can be used as a framework for recording a wide range of information gathered about students' speaking and listening behaviours. A number of recording formats have been designed, and have been successfully used by teachers. Samples of these are provided on the Speaking and Listening CD-ROM.

Information about the behaviours displayed can be recorded in a range of ways. The development of a system, such as highlighting or dating, is an individual or school preference. Marking the selected recording sheets in some way is referred to as 'profiling the student/s on the Map of Development'. There are a number of points that should be considered when placing students on the Map of Development.

- Indicators for each phase should be interpreted in conjunction with the Global Statement of the phase and with the indicators from the surrounding phases.
- With the exception of Beginning Speakers and Listeners, students are considered to be in the phase where they exhibit *all* Key Indicators.
- When students display *any* of the indicators of the Beginning Speaking and Listening phase, they are considered to be in that phase.
- For most students in the class, it will only be necessary to record information about the Key Indicators.
- It is important that any student behaviours (indicators) recorded have been displayed more than once, and in a variety of contexts.

First Steps: Second Edition — *Speaking and Listening Map of Development*

FIRST STEPS SPEAKING AND LISTENING MAP OF DEVELOPMENT: INDIVIDUAL STUDENT PROFILE SHEET — KEY INDICATORS ONLY

Student's Name: Sophia Browne

BEGINNING	EARLY	
USE OF TEXTS	USE OF TEXTS	
◆ Responds to spoken texts in own personal way.	✓ Makes sense of spoken texts with familiar others.	4/6
◆ Communicates in own personal way.	✓ Uses a range of brief unplanned spoken texts independently.	4/6
◆ Understands simple and familiar questions, e.g. *Are you hungry? Where would you like to play?*	✓ Participates with support in some planned talk for school purposes.	4/6
	✓ Recalls personally significant information from spoken texts.	4/6
CONTEXTUAL UNDERSTANDING	CONTEXTUAL UNDERSTANDING	
◆ Communicates to meet own needs.	✓ Beginning to adjust speaking and listening for familiar situations in a school context.	4/6
◆ Assumes a shared background between speaker and listener.	✓ Will often assume a shared background between speaker and listener when speaking, e.g. *may not give sufficient information to orientate the listener.*	
◆ Recognises meaning from familiar language, tone of voice and facial expression in familiar situations.	✓ Is aware that people talk about their ideas.	3/3
◆ Is understood by familiar adults in supportive or predictable situations.		
CONVENTIONS	CONVENTIONS	
◆ Uses a small range of vocabulary.	✓ Structures simple spoken texts appropriately.	4/6
◆ Responds to spoken language in ways appropriate to home language or culture.	✓ Uses everyday terms related to their experiences and some subject-specific words.	4/6
◆ Attends to spoken texts that are personally significant.	✓ Relies on simple sentences or uses simple connectives to link ideas.	4/6
◆ May ask many questions.	✓ Interprets and uses simple statements, commands and questions.	4/6
PROCESSES AND STRATEGIES	PROCESSES AND STRATEGIES	
◆ Relies on personal experience as a stimulus for speaking and listening.	✓ Talks about thinking with others, e.g. *I think.*	4/6
◆ Uses a limited range of processes and strategies when speaking, e.g. *uses repetition.*	✓ Uses a small range of processes and strategies when speaking, e.g. *uses props to support speaking.*	15/6
◆ Uses a small range of processes and strategies when listening.	✓ Uses a small range of processes and strategies when listening, e.g. *asks questions to clarify.*	15/6

Year: One Teacher: Ms Rose Year: ____ Teacher: ____ Year: ____ Teacher: ____

Figure 2.10 Sample of a student profile

Link Assessment, Teaching and Learning

Profiling students on the Speaking and Listening Map of Development is just the beginning of the assessment, teaching and learning cycle. It is crucial that teachers continue to analyse student profiles so they will be better able to plan appropriate teaching and learning experiences.

Once a student's phase of development has been determined, the Major Teaching Emphases provide the first step in linking assessment, teaching and learning. These are provided at each phase of development, and suggest appropriate priorities for students 'in that phase'.

Once Major Teaching Emphases (MTEs) have been selected for an individual, a small-group or a whole-class focus, appropriate Teaching and Learning Experiences can be chosen from the corresponding phase in the Speaking and Listening Map. The *Speaking and Listening Resource Book* and other teacher resource material can provide further support for the chosen MTEs.

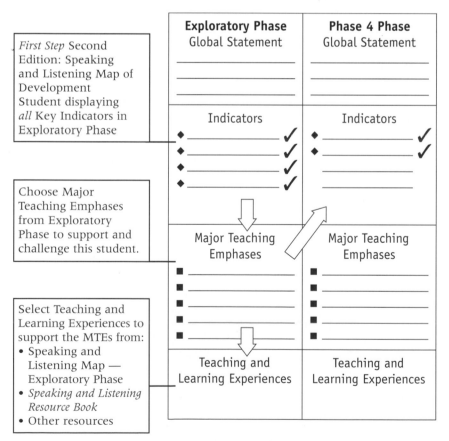

Figure 2.11 Choosing appropriate Major Teaching Emphases and Teaching and Learning Experiences

Monitor Student Progress

The Speaking and Listening Map of Development can be used to monitor students' progress over time. It is crucial that teachers update the profiles of each student often enough to direct teaching and learning in the classroom so that student needs are constantly being met. Decisions about the monitoring and updating process are a personal choice. Some teachers choose to focus on four or five students at a time; while others choose to focus on the indicators from a particular aspect, or on students from a particular phase. These options help to make the monitoring and updating process manageable.

Frequently Asked Questions

Can I start using the Major Teaching Emphases and the Teaching and Learning Experiences before I have profiled students on the Speaking and Listening Map of Development?

Yes. The best way to start is to predict the phase of development of each student based on the Global Statement. Once this has been completed, you are able to choose the Major Teaching Emphases from the predicted phase. You can then select appropriate Teaching and Learning Experiences and use these as a springboard for collecting data in an ongoing manner.

Does a student have to display all Key Indicators of a phase to be 'in that phase'?

Yes. The phase in which the student is displaying all the Key Indicators is considered to be the student's phase of development. There is, however, an exception to this when looking at students in the Beginning Speaking and Listening phase. When students display any of the indicators in the Beginning phase, they are considered to be in that phase.

Do I need to profile all students on the Map of Development?

It is important to be clear about your purpose for placing students on the Map of Development, and this will guide your decision about which students to choose. You may decide that for some students it is sufficient to predict using the Global Statement, and then use this information to select MTEs and Teaching and Learning Experiences. For others in the class you may gather information only about Key Indicators to create individual profiles. For a selected few, you may gather information about both Key Indicators and Other Indicators to create more detailed records of development.

How much evidence do I need to collect before an indicator can be marked or highlighted?

It is important to have sufficient evidence to determine whether a student consistently displays a particular behaviour. The most

23

effective way to do this is to see the behaviour displayed several times in a range of contexts. Your professional judgement will help you decide whether the evidence you have is strong enough to mark the indicator. When in doubt, leave it out and wait until you have confirmation that an indicator is being displayed.

When would I use other indicators?

The Other Indicators list additional behaviours you may notice some students displaying. You may choose to use them when you are looking for more detailed information about a student.

How long should a student be in a phase?

There is no definitive time span. Some students may progress quickly through a phase, while others remain in the same one for a length of time. Each student is unique, and no two developmental pathways will be the same. Providing developmentally appropriate teaching and learning experiences will assist students to move along the Speaking and Listening Map of Development.

How often do I need to update each student's progress on the Map of Development?

Data collection and analysis is an ongoing process, and the frequency of the collation of this information onto the map is your decision. However, it is crucial that you consider updating the profiles often enough to drive teaching and learning in the classroom so that student needs are constantly being met.

From which phase do I choose the Major Teaching Emphases?

Major Teaching Emphases are chosen from the phase where a student is displaying all Key Indicators; for example, if a student displays all of the key indicators in the Exploratory Phase, the MTEs will come from the Exploratory Phase. Major Teaching Emphases are designed to support students' current understandings and challenge them to begin displaying behaviours from the next phase.

Within a phase, which Major Teaching Emphases do I choose?

Any of the MTEs in the phase where students display all the Key Indicators will be appropriate. To select the most appropriate, you may take into consideration:
• the students' interests, strengths and needs
• any 'gaps' in previous teaching
• the grouping arrangements
• links to other literacy strands and what is being taught in other learning areas.

The Major Teaching Emphases are designed to be revisited many times in different contexts, using different texts. This selection and revisiting process continues until students consistently display all key indicators in the next phase.

How do I use the Student Self-Assessment pages?

The Student Self-Assessment pages are designed to be completed by the students. These pages can be completed over time either independently or with teacher support. This could happen during student conferences, reflection sessions or as part of an interview. These pages provide a springboard for individual goal setting. They can be found on the Speaking and Listening CD-ROM in Chapter 3 — Collecting Data to Assess Speaking and Listening Development.

Why are there no activities for students in the Processes and Strategies aspect in the Map of Development?

The activities for the Processes and Strategies aspect are in the *Speaking and Listening Resource Book*. The rationale for this is that all speakers and listeners make use of a range of processes and strategies that are not hierarchical, and are therefore not phase-specific. The activities in the *Speaking and Listening Resource Book* can be applied across a range of phases to develop efficient use of the processes and strategies being introduced or consolidated.

Can I use the Map of Development with students who have English as an Additional Language (EAL) or Students who have English as a Second Dialect (ESD)?

There are different considerations for EAL/ ESD students when using the map. Initially teachers should use ESL Bandscales (WA) until EAL students are demonstrating sufficient competence in English (about Level 7 or 8 Bandscales). The map can then be used to identify students' language strengths and needs. The behaviours exhibited could be across a number of phases; therefore, it may not be appropriate to identify an EAL/ESD student as being in one particular phase. In order to tailor instruction appropriately, you may need to select Major Teaching Emphases from more than one phase of the map (see *Linking Assessment Teaching and Learning*, Chapter 4, for further information about *First Steps* and Diversity).

Students who speak, read and write languages other than English may already be aware that each language is different. Some of these understandings can be transferred from one language to another; others cannot. This means that such students may have a well-developed understanding of language as a system, but not in those aspects of language that are peculiar to English.

CHAPTER 3

Collecting Data to Assess Speaking and Listening Development

Chapter 6 of *Linking Assessment, Teaching and Learning* provides detailed information about beliefs of assessment and evaluation that underpin the *First Steps* resource. The data-collection tools listed in that chapter are generic, and can be applied to all areas of literacy. The focus of this chapter is on how data-collection tools can be used specifically to make judgements about students' speaking and listening development. The ideas and suggestions provide support for teachers when constructing profiles of students, using the *First Steps* Speaking and Listening Map of Development.

Planning for success in speaking and listening requires teachers to find out what individual students know and can do. It is useful to ask the following questions.

- What abilities do I want to assess?
- What information is needed at an aspect level?
- What kinds of classroom contexts will provide this information?
- What are the most efficient and valid ways to collect the information, and who should collect it?
- How can the information be collected?
- How can the information be recorded?
- What can be done with the information?
- How can the information be shared with others?

To obtain a full picture of students' abilities in speaking and listening, it is essential that a student be observed over time, across learning areas and in different contexts. Traditionally, classroom assessment for speaking and listening has relied on evidence obtained from presentations and performances. However, presentation and performance tasks represent only a small component of the speaking and listening that students participate in. Consequently this type of evidence does not give a complete picture of students' abilities. It is necessary to provide students with the opportunities to participate in a variety of planned and unplanned talk, in both formal and informal contexts, and for a range of different purposes and audiences. Teachers need to build an understanding of the demands of different speaking and listening contexts that students will engage in as they interact in the classroom, school and the community. These contexts will be determined by the purpose of the speaking and listening, the situation in which it takes place and the audience that is involved. For example, a student needs to use different skills when giving a formal planned speech to the class compared to those skills a student will use when interacting with a peer in a cooperative learning context.

Teachers can then assess their students as they become involved in relevant learning interactions across different learning areas.

The challenge for teachers is to be able to build a realistic picture of how speaking and listening occurs in their classrooms. Building an overview of how students are experiencing speaking and listening in a class enables focused teaching, learning, and evaluation to take place. Figure 3.1 provides a framework for teachers to analyse their classroom programs in relation to speaking and listening. The framework in Figure 3.1 is adapted from the 1995 work of Comber and Cormack and the later 1999 work of Cormack.

This '8T's' framework invites reflection in the eight different aspects of the literacy curriculum relating to speaking and listening. Teachers can map the speaking and listening competencies in their program.

The audit sheet (see Figure 3.2) provides more details on how to provide a comprehensive speaking and listening focus. It lists a number of classroom interactions that provide the opportunity to observe the students' use of speaking and listening for a range of purposes. The list can be modified and extended according to the various phases of students' development.

Component	Question	Considerations
Topics	What issues or aspects of content are emphasised in your program?	Broad themes, units of work, texts issues as well as detail issues such as conversation about assignments, tasks, management and administration. Does the class program provide opportunities for the development of speaking and listening across the curriculum?
Techniques	What approaches to teaching, demonstrating, scaffolding, grouping and organising students do you employ?	How do you organise your class to teach? Do students experience speaking and listening in a range of different groupings: whole class, small group and individual? How do you instruct and what frameworks for learning do you establish?
Tasks	What do students have to do in your program that involves speaking and listening?	Assignments, how students demonstrate that they know, products, performances or conversations, e.g. the contexts for speaking and listening that you establish.
Talk	What sorts of speaking and listening occur in your classroom?	Purposes for speaking and listening, e.g. to demonstrate knowledge, thinking aloud, socialising, procedural talk, talk about texts, informal/formal and planned/unplanned speaking and listening.
Texts	What sorts of texts are available, in what quantities and when?	What texts are being discussed? What types of text are students experiencing? Do students have *access* to a range of different text types?
Tools	What do students use when doing tasks related to speaking and listening?	Basic technology such as pens, paper to computer technology.
Tests	What techniques do you use to make judgements about progress or ability or outcomes?	What kind of assessment are you using? Is there a mix of evidence from products, processes, performance and conversation? Is the data collected over time and across learning areas, in different contexts?
Territories	Where can students talk and listen?	What kind of speaking and listening can students do? Do factors such as volume levels, restriction on topics, available space, etc. influence the kind of speaking and listening that occurs? What arrangements have been made for students with special needs? What opportunities do non-English-speaking students have to talk in their home language? e.g. hearing impaired students.

Figure 3.1 The '8T's' in a Speaking and Listening program (adapted from Comber and Cormack 1995 and Cormack 1999)

Focus	What Are My Students Currently Doing?	What Students Learn to Do Next
Examples of Functional Spoken Texts Students Are Using	What text types are being experienced by students in my class?	What text type do I need to be explicitly teaching?
Everyday · **Literary** · **Informational** greeting · joke · recount conversation · narrative · description question · dramatisation · procedure message · poem · report instruction · chant · argument direction · song · explanation invitation · rap · debate apology · · anecdote request · · interview · · play	What are they competent in using? What other text types do my students need to be experiencing?	What sorts of experiences do I need to provide for students to become competent users of this text type?
Range of Contexts Students Are Experiencing	In what contexts are students competent in their speaking and listening?	What do I need to be explicitly teaching?
Possible Social Contexts formal/informal familiar/unfamiliar		
Possible Class/School Situations guided reading/writing · waiting time readers' theatre · class meetings literature circles · writers circle mat/sharing time · phys-ed time library/Art/Music time · play time drama/media class · assemblies whole class/small group · interviews class administration/management student-teacher conferences homework class	What sort of audiences do my students currently interact with?	What sorts of experiences do I need to provide for students to become competent speakers and listeners in differing contexts with a range of audiences?
Possible Audiences whole class · whole school partners · small group peer group · parents community · teachers administrators · assistants visitors/guests · family employers	How confident/competent are my students as they speak and listen with these audiences?	
Types of Behaviours Students Use to Communicate extending conversation · volume turn-taking · tone topic changes · pace proximity · gesture repair · using tact sustaining conversations repairing conversation breakdown	What behaviours can I see my students using in their speaking and listening? Are the behaviours they are using sufficient for the speaking and listening contexts and audiences they are engaging with?	What skills do I need to explicitly teach? What sort of opportunities can I provide for my students to develop the appropriate speaking and listening behaviours?

Figure 3.2 Speaking and listening audit sheet

Data Collection

Different data-collection tools will provide different perspectives on speaking and listening performance, so it is important to use a range. The type of data-collection tool selected will depend upon the aspect for which information is to be collected — Contextual Understanding, Use of Texts, Conventions, or Processes and Strategies. Decisions teachers make about which assessment tools to use, and how and when to use them, have an impact on the quality of the evidence gathered. These decisions can also have an impact on the messages given to students about 'what is valued' in speaking and listening. It is important to develop efficient and valid ways of assessing speaking and listening, and to involve students, parents or caregivers, and other teachers in the process of collecting and recording data.

What Are the Most Efficient and Valid Ways to Collect Speaking and Listening Information?

Data can be collected in several ways and can be grouped under the following broad headings.
- Focused Observation
- Product
- Conversations

Aspects of Speaking and Listening Assessment Tools	Use of Texts	Contextual Understanding	Conventions	Processes and Strategies
Focused Observation				
Informal	✓	✓	✓	✓
Formal	✓	✓	✓	✓
Speaking and Listening Products				
Self-assessment formats				✓
Personal goal-setting	✓	✓	✓	✓
Logs	✓			
Journals	✓	✓	✓	✓
Think-alouds		✓		✓
Work samples	✓	✓	✓	✓
Surveys and questionnaires		✓		
Tests			✓	
Spoken presentations	✓		✓	✓
Conversations				
Conferences	✓	✓	✓	✓
Interviews	✓	✓	✓	✓

Figure 3.3 Data–collection tools selected to make judgements about different aspects of speaking and listening

In any successful assessment regime, each tool is generally used in combination with another. For example, a teacher who has observed and made anecdotal notes about a learner's work (as part of focused observation) will then discuss these observations with the learner (as part of a conversation).

Focused Observation

Assessment takes place as an integral part of the teaching and learning cycle. It occurs as part of everyday teaching and learning when teachers are observing students at work in regular classroom activities. Teacher observation involves much more than simply watching or listening to students in the classroom; it involves systematic collection of observable data and analysis of that information. It allows teachers to assess specific strategies students use, or understandings they demonstrate, either during speaking and listening experiences, or in other learning areas.

Because of the dialogic nature of speaking and listening, much of the observation that occurs in the classroom will involve pairs or groups of children, e.g. **class groups, peer groups, family groups, sporting groups, etc.** The *First Steps Speaking and Listening Resource Book* provides detailed information on groups and group work for developing speaking and listening.

1 Informal Observations

Informal observations are unplanned. The teacher simply notes speaking and listening behaviours as they naturally happen. Because of the spontaneous nature of speaking and listening, rich data may be obtained from observing children in situations that are unplanned and occur naturally as a result of social interactions within particular contexts. For example, observing children as they interact during library time, while they are waiting before school starts, during play and peer group interaction.

Informal observations require teachers to watch and listen to students so they can form ideas about their development. As Goodman noted in her book *Kid Watching*, it is not simply enough to merely observe; the results of observation are not useful unless they are recorded and considered.

2 Formal Observations

Formal observations, sometimes called structured or systematic observations, are planned with a predetermined focus; this could be the speaking and listening behaviours to be targeted, or the students that will be observed. The teacher also decides when and how often formal observations will occur, and how they will be recorded.

Students may also be involved in observing their peers speaking and listening, using collaboratively developed checklists. An essential part of this process is the development of students' understanding of what each of the criteria in the checklist looks and sounds like.

What Information Can Be Collected?

Focused observations can provide teachers with information about student attitudes and student performance in all four of the aspects — Contextual Understanding, Use of Text, Conventions and Processes and Strategies. The following checklist may provide a focus for observation.

---

1 Know what outcome is being assessed.
2 Plan what will be seen as evidence.
3 Tell students what is expected of them.
4 Make sure any record keeping reflects the purpose.
5 Provide the students with feedback

Figure 3.4 Checklist to guide — a focus for observation

Speaking and Listening Products

The assessment of both process and product is important when gathering information about supporting students' speaking and listening development. Teachers will assess not only the final products that are a result of learning, but also products that have been created during the process of learning.

Observation and analysis of students' products such as self-assessment forms, think-alouds, work samples (including multi-media creations), surveys or questionnaires, all provide insight into speaking and listening development. The following products will support teachers in gathering information about students' speaking and listening development.

1 Student self-assessment products
2 Personal goal-setting
3 Logs
4 Journals
5 Think-alouds
6 Work samples
7 Surveys and questionnaires
8 Tests
9 Spoken presentations
10 Conversations

1 Student Self-Assessment Products

Self-assessment is a critical part of developing a student's responsibility for his or her own learning. Self-assessment can provide teachers with insights into speaking and listening development that otherwise might not be apparent. It is critical that formats are modelled and provided for students as a framework for recording information and their reflections. With teacher support and guidance, students can develop the skills necessary for them to assess their own and others' speaking and listening. A range of self-assessment formats, specifically designed for each phase, is provided on the Speaking and Listening CD-ROM. These formats are designed to:

• support teachers as they involve students in data collection
• support students to reflect on their own speaking and listening and to set goals for improvement
• reflect the indicators of each phase, but are written in student-friendly language
• be completed by the students.

Figure 3.5 Student self-assessment.
Students are filmed during a small-group task, then they review and reflect on how they took turns.

LISTENING SELF-ASSESSMENT

Name: Date:

Thinking About My Listening	Often	Sometimes	Not Yet
• I pay attention to the speaker.			
• I keep quiet when others speak.			
• I don't distract other listeners.			
• I show I am listening by using appropriate body language.			

I was good at: _____

I have difficulty with: _____

_____

I want to improve: _____

_____

Figure 3.6a Self-assessment sample

SPEAKING SELF-ASSESSMENT

Name: Date:

Thinking About My Speaking	Consistently	Sometimes	Not Yet
• I look at the audience.			
• I use a clear voice.			
• I have good volume control.			
• I speak at an appropriate pace: not too fast or slow.			
• I use expression in my voice.			
• I stay on the topic.			
• I can rephrase ideas when they are not understood.			
• I can answer questions.			

I was really good at: _____

I have difficulty with _____

_____

I want to improve _____

_____

Figure 3.6b Self-assessment sample

A student's ability to assess the learning of others — peer assessment — is just as powerful as self-assessment. Students are able to compare their knowledge, skills and understanding of other students and this helps to clarify their own understanding of the concept or task.

Two Stars and a Wish

Two Stars and a Wish provide students with a simple framework for reflecting on positive aspects of their work (the stars) as well as focusing on an area for improvement (the wish). It also provides a simple framework for peer assessment

What information can be collected?

Information for any of the four aspects of speaking and listening can be gathered using self-assessment formats.

---

first steps **First Steps:** Second Edition · Speaking & Listening Map of Development

Two Stars and a Wish

Two stars = things you can do or things you are good at
Wish = something for you to work on

Two Stars and a Wish for ___Brett___

☆ You tell great jokes. You can remember lots and make them up.

☆ You speak nicely and friendly when its recess time

I would like Could you let me talk take turns more at Think Pair Sheare?

from Joshua

© Western Australian Minister for Education 2006 · MAY BE COPIED FOR CLASSROOM USE ONLY

Figure 3.7 Two Stars and a Wish

---

2 Personal Goal-setting

Setting speaking and listening goals and assessing the achievement of these goals is another form of self-assessment suitable for all students. It can provide the teacher with valuable information about speaking and listening strategies, and can assist students to develop independence in speaking and listening.

Goals can be recorded in many ways. They may be written in students' speaking and listening journals or recorded on goal-setting sheets. Once a goal is recorded, the teacher and the student can work together to monitor its achievement. The cumulative record of goals can provide evidence of successful learning, showing both teacher and student the specific speaking and listening strategies and understandings that have been learnt. It also clearly demonstrates the progress that is being made towards improving speaking and listening. For students who are just beginning to set speaking and listening goals, goal-setting frameworks can provide support. A variety of goal-setting frameworks are provided on the Speaking and Listening CD-ROM.

What Information Can Be Collected

Reviewing students' speaking and listening goals will provide information about processes and strategies they are using to comprehend and compose spoken texts.

3 Logs

LEARNING LOGS

A speaking and listening log, in its simplest form, is a place to record the types of texts that have been spoken or listened to. Logs contain concise, objective information and are impersonal in tone. The purpose of the speaking and listening log — together with the age and experience of the student — will determine the way it is used and structured. Logs may be used to record the range of texts and contexts experienced by students (see Figure 3.8).

first steps *First Steps:* Second Edition				*Speaking and Listening Map of Development*	

Name: _____   Date: _____

Speaking and Listening Log

Date	Text Type	Purpose	Audience	Situation	Comments

© West Australian Minister of Education and Training: 2006   MAY BE COPIED FOR CLASSROOM USE ONLY

Figure 3.8 Sample speaking log

What Information Can Be Collected?

Speaking and listening logs provide teachers with information about a student's use of texts and give a valuable insight into a student's interests, preferences, attitudes or understandings.

4 Journals

Speaking and listening journals allow students to record their personal expectations, reactions and reflections, before during and after any speaking and listening event. Journals can be organised and used in many different ways depending on the purpose. The different kinds of speaking and listening journals include:
• Response journals
• Reflective journals
• Metacognitive journals
• Summative journals.

(Refer to *First Steps Learning Assessment, Teaching and Learning,* p. 99 for a more detailed explanation of the journals above.)

Speaking and listening journals provide a framework for students to:
• record responses to spoken text
• record topics for speaking
• reflect on their selection of text
• reflect on speaking and listening development
• record thought process when constructing texts
• reflect on the effectiveness of speaking and listening with a range of audiences and contexts
• reflect on past learning and consider it for future application to new learning
• clarify the thoughts about speakers' messages and purposes, and share their thoughts with other students.

What Information Can Be Collected?

Any type of journal entry provides a source of information about any of the four aspects of speaking and listening.

5 Think-alouds

Think-alouds are articulations of thoughts before, during and after communicative events. They may be spontaneous reactions to the text by students or may be responses encouraged or requested by the teacher. The analysis of think-alouds can provide a rich source of information about the processes and strategies being used by a student when both speaking and listening. Although think-alouds are not exact replications of a student's complete thinking, they do alert teachers to the hidden processes taking place in the student's mind.

What Information Can Be Collected?

When analysing a think-aloud, the teacher will be looking for patterns in the student's responses. These patterns will reveal the processes and strategies the student is using to comprehend and compose a range of texts.

6 Work Samples

A collection of samples gathered over time provides a clear picture of how a student has improved. Samples can be collected at any stage of the speaking and listening process, and should include both planned and spontaneous interactions in both formal and informal contexts. Samples may show work done independently or in a group. Work samples should be collected across all learning areas and may include transcripts of students' talks, recordings, videos, CDs, MP3, etc.

What information Can Be Collected?

Information for any of the four aspects can be gathered from students' speaking and listening. A range of samples across a period of time can clearly demonstrate the progress that a student has made.

7 Surveys and Questionnaires

Surveys and questionnaires about speaking and listening can take many forms and address a range of topics. They typically consist of a series of statements or questions about which the students or parents are asked to express agreement or disagreement (sometimes using a scale). The items to be included in the survey or questionnaire will be determined by the type of information required. The Speaking and Listening CD-ROM contains some sample surveys and questionnaires that can be used with either students or parents.

first steps **First Steps:** Second Edition   *Speaking and Listening Map of Development*

Name: _____   Date: _____

Parent/Caregiver Survey (Early)

Dear Parent/Caregiver,
You know your child better than anyone and I am interested in how your child learns at home. Your feedback will help me to plan to meet your child's needs. You can complete the following information and return it or you may like to make an appointment to discuss the points below.

What activities does your child enjoy?
_____
_____

What do you think about your child's problem-solving abilities?
_____
_____

What kinds of things does your child do for his or herself? How independent is your child?
_____
_____

What do you think about your child's speaking skills?
_____
_____

What do you think about your child's listening skills?
_____
_____

What are your child's interests?
_____
_____

© West Australian Minister of Education and Training: 2006   MAY BE COPIED FOR CLASSROOM USE ONLY

Figure 3.9 Parent survey

What Information Can Be Collected?

Surveys and questionnaires can be used to ascertain students' confidence and attitudes towards the various aspects of speaking and listening.

8 Tests

Testing is another way of gathering data about a student's speaking and listening development, and should be used in conjunction with other data collection tools. Using tests for speaking and listening needs careful consideration as speaking and listening is dynamic and varies much more than, for example, writing. Several types of tests are available, but generally they can be categorised under the following headings.

CRITERION-REFERENCED TESTS

Criterion-referenced tests are designed to measure how well students have learnt a specific body of knowledge or certain skills. Therefore they can provide information related to strengths and weaknesses.

NORM-REFERENCED TESTS

Norm-referenced tests are often referred to as Standardised Tests. They are the formalised tests in which scoring, norms and administration have been established as a result of each having been given to a large number of students. They are administered under specific conditions adhering to the directions set out in the examiner's manual. The performances of other students are presented as norms for the purpose of comparing achievement.

Standardised testing is useful in that it provides a generalised large-scale picture of the levels of achievement across a broad school, district, state or national context. However, often standardised testing does not provide teachers with the detailed specific information that they need to develop a cohesive classroom speaking and listening program that is responsive to students' needs.

TEACHER-MADE TESTS

Many teachers devise their own tests to measure student progress in speaking and listening. These are generally criterion-referenced, and measure the students' mastery of what has been taught. The advantage they have over other types is that they can be tailored to a specific group of students or to specific information the teacher is seeking.

What Information Can Be Collected?

Tests are context specific; they should not be the sole evidence of students' abilities in speaking and listening. Testing usually occurs in one day and relates to a specific context and set of skills. If a teacher wished to gain a comprehensive insight into the speaking and listening abilities of students (for example, to test their ability to listen for detail in a text; to deliver a formal speech to an unfamiliar audience), a more realistic picture of the students' abilities would emerge in evidence that had been collected over time and across different learning and subject areas in both formal and informal settings.

9 Spoken Presentations (Rehearsed and Unrehearsed)

Spoken presentations draw on the student's ability to convey meaning to an audience. By analysing students' spoken presentations, teachers can obtain a clear idea of the strategies that students are using successfully. It will also indicate those strategies that need more development. The types of spoken presentation will depend on the context of the lesson and the phase of development of the student, and may range from a simple recount to a structured debate. Spoken presentations can be either rehearsed or unrehearsed. Rehearsed presentations enable students to plan, refine, practise, and adjust their performance before presenting it 'in public'; the aim of a rehearsed presentation is to engage an audience through expression and fluency. Unrehearsed oral presentation usually involves spontaneous spoken presentation on a familiar or unfamiliar topic.

What Information Can Be Collected?

Spoken presentations are an opportunity to observe how students apply what they know about this type of speaking and listening — the formal monologue. It enables the teacher to collect information about the processes and strategies aspect, such as the ability to use planning. As the student speaks and responds to the audience, the teacher is able to determine and assess the processes and strategies the student is using and if any further development is required.

10 Conversations

As well as using focused observation and work samples, teachers can also consider what further information can be gathered through conversations. Both spontaneous and planned dialogue can provide valuable information and can be assessed to show the development of students' speaking and listening skills. Spontaneous dialogues are the speaking and listening interactions that happen during the course of any day — socialising, thinking aloud, demonstrating understanding and thinking. They may occur either with familiar audiences (for example, parents, adults that they know, peers) or with unfamiliar audiences (for example, other teachers, visitors to the classroom/school, students from lower/higher classes). Planned dialogues are those that are organised for a specific purpose and audience, for example interviews, debates, reporting to groups, etc.

Teachers who have conversations with individual students on a regular basis can gain a deeper understanding of their speaking and listening development. Conversations can be structured through conferences or interviews.

Conferences

There are a variety of ways to involve students in conferences. These include:

- one-on-one conferences — teacher and student
- peer conferences — student and student
- small-group conferences — students
- three-way conferences — student, teacher and parent/s.

Each of these types of conferences can provide a teacher with the opportunity to collect data. One-on-one conferences can also allow for individual instruction.

Effective one-on-one conferencing focuses on building relationships with individual students. For conferences to be successful, students need to know what is expected of them; for example, the conference structure, what their role will be, and the records that will be kept. Each student–teacher conference will be unique, but it can be helpful to have a planning framework, such as one shown below (see Figure 3.10).

The following charts indicate the role of the teacher and the student in a speaking and listening conference.

The role of the student in conferences
- Be prepared.
- Have current speaking and listening material and topics ready for discussion.
- Discuss any speaking and listening problems you have with the teacher.
- Review the speaking and listening goals you have set. Discuss problems or successes in achieving these goals.
- Be prepared to set a new speaking and listening goal or refocus the previous goal.

Figure 3.10

> **The role of the teacher**
> • Select a particular focus.
> • Encourage the student to talk.
> • Introduce new strategies and processes.
> • Provide feedback to students.
> • Review students' speaking and listening goals and assist them to set new ones.
> • Record information after each conference.
> • Use the information from conferences to plan future learning.

Figure 3.11

It is useful for teachers to use recording sheets before, during or after conferencing with students as these can provide a focus for conversations and for keeping records of shared information.

What Information Can Be Collected?

Conferences can be used to gain information in any of the four aspects, depending on the focus of the conference.

Interviews

Interviews are one-on-one, prepared question-and-answer conversations between a teacher and a student or between a teacher and a parent. Teacher–student interviews provide an opportunity for teachers to actively listen to students and encourage them to verbalise their thought processes. Teachers can design questions to focus on different aspects of speaking and listening, depending on the purpose and the desired outcomes of the interview. However, planning questions that elicit useful information and encourage students to do most of the talking is a challenge; effective questions should be focused, open and probing, and encourage answers of more than one word.

Further examples of speaking and listening interview questions can be found on the Speaking and Listening CD-ROM.

Interviews with parents or caregivers can also provide useful information about students' speaking and listening outside school. In all interviews, it is important to consider the following points.
• Explain the reasons for the interview and limit questions to those that will yield the most useful information.
• Let the parents know that you will be taking notes and the reasons for this.
• Be sensitive to parents' home and personal language usage as well as their levels of literacy.

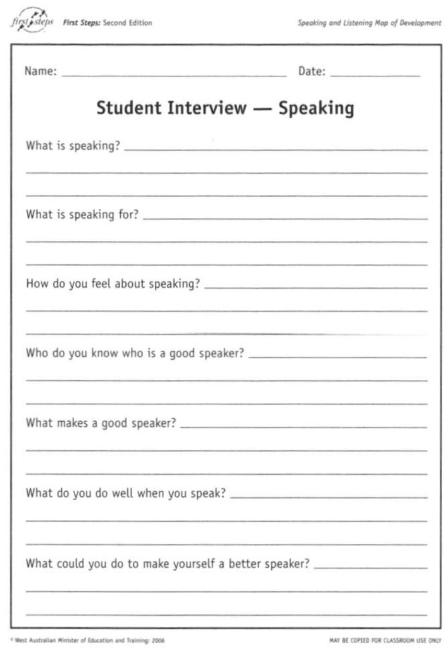
First Steps: Second Edition — Speaking and Listening Map of Development

Name: ______________________ Date: __________

Student Interview — Speaking

What is speaking? ______________________

What is speaking for? ______________________

How do you feel about speaking? ______________________

Who do you know who is a good speaker? ______________________

What makes a good speaker? ______________________

What do you do well when you speak? ______________________

What could you do to make yourself a better speaker? ______________________

© West Australian Minister of Education and Training: 2006 — MAY BE COPIED FOR CLASSROOM USE ONLY

Figure 3.12 Interview: Speaking

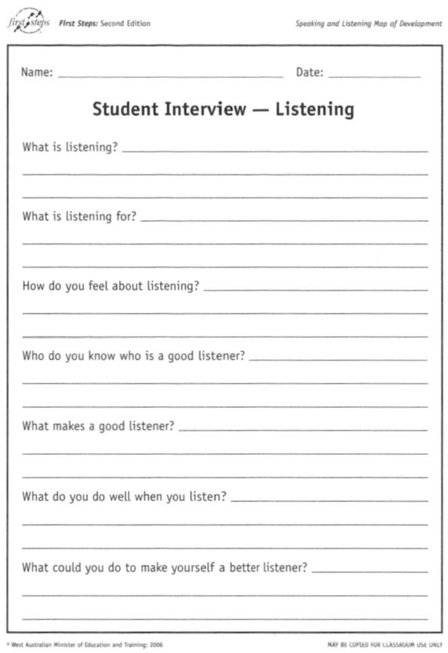
First Steps: Second Edition — Speaking and Listening Map of Development

Name: ______________________ Date: __________

Student Interview — Listening

What is listening? ______________________

What is listening for? ______________________

How do you feel about listening? ______________________

Who do you know who is a good listener? ______________________

What makes a good listener? ______________________

What do you do well when you listen? ______________________

What could you do to make yourself a better listener? ______________________

© West Australian Minister of Education and Training: 2006 — MAY BE COPIED FOR CLASSROOM USE ONLY

Figure 3.13 Interview: Listening

What Information Can Be Collected?

Interviews can provide information about any of the four aspects, depending on the questions being asked. The previous questions are suggested as a guide only, and can be modified to suit different students or teaching contexts.

How Can Information About Speaking and Listening Be Recorded?

Teachers use a range of ways to record the information they gather about students' speaking and listening development. The use of computers or Palm Pilots™ often helps streamline the time it takes to record information.

The following ways of recording information, on paper or electronically, are detailed.

1 Anecdotal notes
2 Checklists
3 Rubrics
4 Annotations
5 Audio and/or video recordings
6 *First Steps* Speaking and Listening Map of Development

1 Anecdotal Notes

Anecdotal notes are short, objective, factual descriptions of observations recorded at the time an event or activity occurs, or soon thereafter. Behaviours listed on the *First Steps* Speaking and

Listening Map of Development will provide a focus for observations.

- Making useful anecdotal notes takes time and practice. They should record an accurate description of the situation and information about students' strengths and weaknesses, and include comments and questions that may guide further observations.
- Notes should be written daily, and as soon as possible after an observation has been made. They can be written during a variety of speaking and listening contexts using a range of functional spoken texts, e.g. unplanned spontaneous conversations and guided speaking and listening sessions.
- The recording format should suit the teaching situation, the students and the teacher's personal style, e.g. grids, adhesive stick-on notes, *First Steps* Speaking and Listening Map of Development.

Speaking and Listening Teacher Observations			
Rachel listens actively to others and asks appropriate questions.	Rachel listens actively to others and makes appropriate comments about their contribution.	Rachel locates and obtains simple discreet information from informational and expressive texts.	Rachel observes conventions relating to turn-taking and interrupting.

Figure 3.14 Anecdotal notes

| Teacher: _____ Class: _____ |
| Date: _____ |
| Focus: _____ |

Name	Name	Name
Name	Name	Name

Figure 3.15 Observation grid

- The notes should be examined and analysed regularly to be sure that comments are being made for every student on a variety of speaking and listening behaviours in different contexts. They also need to be analysed to guide future teaching.

2 Checklists

A checklist is a list of skills or behaviours to be checked off as they are observed. However, it is critical to acknowledge that checklists, whether teacher-made or commercially produced, are static. Most may not be applicable to every student in one classroom at the same time.

3 Rubrics

Rubrics are recording frameworks that feature short, descriptive statements along a continuum of excellence. Teachers or students determine the quality of a performance against a set of predetermined criteria. For example, a retelling rubric may be helpful in assessing a student's performance using criteria such as selection and sequencing of ideas and events, introduction of the characters, and setting the scene. Rubrics can be marked using either a numerical system or descriptive words or phrases, such as 'well-developed', 'partially developed', or 'not developed'. Rubrics can be reused, adding levels of achievement as the skill level of students increases or by adding additional criteria for new concepts, skills or attitudes they display. There are many publications and websites that offer ready-made rubrics; however, many teachers may wish to create their own. Students also can be involved in the creation of rubrics, as ultimately it is their work that is being judged.

Creating a Rubric

- Deciding on the criteria.
  Students can be involved in brainstorming the criteria. If they have not had experience in generating criteria for evaluation, teachers may wish to show them some models of completed work. Characteristics of effective and not-so-effective samples can be listed and discussed for inclusion as criteria on the completed rubric.
- Articulating the qualities.
  It is often easier to decide on the two extremes first; that is, what makes 'best' performance and what makes 'worst' performance.
- Deciding on the number of gradations.
  It is a good idea to have an even number of gradations as this eliminates the tendency to rank in the middle.

- Deciding on the labelling.

  Labels to be used for the gradations need to be considered. Either a numerical value or a descriptive word can be used. Some teachers prefer to use 'neutral' words for the gradation labels; others prefer words that signal excellence, e.g. **Lead, Bronze, Silver and Gold rather than Unsatisfactory, Satisfactory, Competent and Excellent.**

Students may be involved in self- or peer-assessment, using the completed rubric, before work is formally submitted for teacher evaluation. Rubrics can be 'holistic' or 'analytic' in nature; holistic rubrics evaluate the task as a whole, while analytical rubrics evaluate each separate criterion.

Level of Achievement	Description
4	Discusses familiar ideas and information and supports opinions with some detail in a variety of classroom situations.
3	Interacts to express opinions and perceptions, participates in problem-solving discussions with peers.
2	Describes or recounts events in a logical sequence and sustains conversations on a familiar topic.
1	Discusses personal experiences; and conveys key information or ideas on a familiar topic.

Figure 3.16 Holistic rubric for discussion

Criteria	Quality			
Behaviours	4	3	2	1
Questioning and responding	Probing questions are asked of others.	Students ask for information and give responses that indicate attention to topic.	Responses given occasionally indicate attention to topic.	Students have difficulty giving appropriate responses.
Attending behaviours	Non-verbal cues are used to respond to, and sometimes shape, communication with others.	Non-verbal cues or body language are used for effect, e.g. **smile encouragingly, gesture for emphasis.**	Occasional gestures and body language are used for emphasis, to show support or to get attention e.g. **move into close proximity as group works.**	Eye contact is made with person speaking.
Active interest and involvement	Students paraphrase what others have said for clarification.	Students acknowledge and build on what has been said or done.	Acknowledgement is given to what has been said.	Students occasionally acknowledge what has been said.

Figure 3.17 Analytical rubric for small-group discussion

4 Annotations

Annotations are short descriptions of judgements made about a student's work, recorded directly onto the work sample. Annotations may be completed at the time of the event, but this can be done at a later time if the work sample, such as written work, is portable. Annotations need to be objective, factual comments, and should lead to the recognition and interpretation of individual patterns of learning over time.

5 Audio and/or Video Recordings

Audio and video recordings of students actively engaged in speaking and listening provide an excellent medium for capturing a student's progress over time and across contexts. Recordings can be completed at the time of the event, and then reviewed at a later time by the teacher, student, peers and others. When used as a source of assessment evidence, annotations, checklists or evaluations can be used throughout the recordings.

6 The First Steps Speaking and Listening Map of Development

The *First Steps* Speaking and Listening Map is an excellent framework for recording information about students' speaking and listening development. Some teachers choose to record their observations, the outcomes of conversations, or their analysis of products directly onto the Speaking and Listening Map; this can be done by writing comments on adhesive notes, highlighting the indicators the students are displaying or recording the date when behaviours were displayed. Other teachers prefer to use another recording method first — such as checklists, observations, audio recordings, analysis or rubrics — and then transfer the information onto the Speaking and Listening Map of Development.

The following recording formats can be found on the Speaking and Listening CD-ROM and may be photocopied for classroom use.

1 Class Profile Sheet
2 Individual Student Profile Sheet — Key Indicators only
3 Individual Student Profile Sheet — All indicators
4 Class Profile Sheets — Key Indicators only
5 Class Profile Sheets — All indicators
6 Speaking and Listening Map of Development—Parent version

CHAPTER 4

Beginning Speaking and Listening Phase

Unplanned	Planned

Unplanned

Teacher: Tell me about what you made, Ben.
Ben: A man.
Teacher: You're making a man?
Ben: I was angry.
Teacher: So what did you do when you were angry?
Ben: Told my mum ... I was angry.
Teacher: You told your mum you were angry?
(Ben pulls a scary face and makes growling sounds.)
Teacher: You sound angry!
Ben: Yeah ... man's not angry now.
Teacher: What is your man doing now?
Ben: I'm making it like that ... see?
(points to model)

Planned

Teacher: OK, Ben, could you show some other children how to play this matching game?
(Ben is silent.)
Teacher: Here are some pictures on wooden cards. Can you remember what we do with them?
Ben: Put it here? *(Ben picks one up and looks towards the teacher.)*
Teacher: Have a try.
Ben: Put that one there ...
Teacher: That's right, you do know what to do with them!
Ben: Find one of these ... this one goes... there.
Teacher: Why do we put that strawberry card in there?
Ben: It's the same one in there.
Teacher: It is, too. It matches! Now there are two strawberries!
Ben: So we put it there ... find this one ... put it there.
Teacher: That's right, you have to match the pictures.

Figure 4.1   **Figure 4.2**

Global Statement

In this phase, children use the language of the home and community to communicate with familiar others. They often rely on non-verbal cues to convey and comprehend spoken language. Their speech may be characterised by short utterances and they may require support in unfamiliar settings.

Beginning Speaking and Listening Indicators

Use of Texts

◆ Responds to spoken texts in own personal way.
◆ Communicates in own personal way.
◆ Understands simple and familiar questions, e.g. Are you hungry? Where would you like to play?
• Responds to messages conveyed through familiar technology, e.g. nods head when using the telephone, dances to familiar music from a television show.

Contextual Understanding

◆ Communicates to meet own needs.
◆ Assumes a shared background between speaker and listener.
◆ Recognises meaning from familiar language, tone of voice and facial expression in familiar situations.
◆ Is understood by familiar adults in supportive or predictable situations.

Conventions

◆ Uses a small range of vocabulary.
◆ Responds to spoken language in ways appropriate to home language or culture.
◆ Attends to spoken texts that are personally significant.
◆ May ask many questions.
• Overgeneralises some words, e.g. says 'bird' for seagull, magpie, finch.
• Uses some directional language, e.g. in, up, down, on, out.
• Begins to use words to describe characteristics, e.g. big truck.

Processes and Strategies

◆ Relies on personal experience as a stimulus for speaking and listening.
◆ Uses a limited range of processes and strategies when speaking, e.g. uses repetition.
◆ Uses a limited range of processes and strategies when listening.
• Relies on copying and approximating to compose spoken language.
• Requires some adult support to interpret spoken language.

Major Teaching Emphases

Environment and Attitude (see p. 51)

- Provide opportunities for relevant, challenging and purposeful communication.
- Create a supportive environment which values the diversity of students' speaking and listening development (in their home languages).
- Encourage students to see the value of effective listening and speaking for community, school and family life.

Use of Texts (see p. 56)

- Expose students to a range of functional spoken texts composed in Standard English.
- Provide authentic opportunities for students to participate in unplanned and planned speaking and listening.
- Provide opportunities for students to participate in extended talk.
- Teach students to share personal comments after listening.
- Build knowledge of common topics to which students can relate, e.g. toys, families, community.
- Teach students the metalanguage associated with speaking and listening and encourage its use, e.g. speak, listen, hear, speaker, listener, take turns, word, think.

Contextual Understanding (see p. 65)

- Discuss speaking and listening, referring to the audience and purpose.
- Provide effective feedback to students about their speaking and listening.
- Model and discuss how to include relevant information when speaking.
- Draw students' attention to the way ideas and feelings are communicated through speaking and listening.
- Encourage students to use verbal and non-verbal devices to create meaning.

Conventions (see p. 73)

- Develop and extend children's vocabulary for different purposes.
- Model speaking for different purposes, e.g. making requests, seeking information.
- Model speaking and listening behaviours, e.g. maintain a conversation.
- Model listening behaviours, e.g. responding to requests, questions, looking at the person.

Processes and Strategies (see p. 79)

- Model language to describe thinking.
- Involve children in conversations with family members and others.
- Model the language and behaviours of listening, e.g. Let's listen to the music. Would you like to hear this story?
- Model ways to improve communication, e.g. adjusting volume, respond to comprehension checks.

Teaching and Learning Experiences

ENVIRONMENT AND ATTITUDE

Major Teaching Emphases

■ Provide opportunities for relevant, challenging and purposeful communication.

■ Create a supportive classroom environment which values the diversity of students' speaking and listening development (in their home languages).

■ Encourage students to see the value of effective listening and speaking for community, school and family life.

Teaching Notes

A supportive and nurturing environment for students in the Beginning phase is one that accepts, values and accommodates a variety of communication styles. Students in this phase are involved in trying new ways of speaking and listening and will feel comfortable in 'having a go' when there is a relationship of trust and acceptance.

Students who are just starting school will have many experiences that can contribute to more formal learning environments. Teachers can gain insights into their students' worlds through different learning opportunities that reveal the students' background knowledge, vocabulary, concept development and thinking processes.

The focus for developing positive attitudes towards speaking and listening as well as creating a supportive environment is organised under the following headings:
• Creating a Supportive Classroom Environment
• Opportunities for Relevant, Challenging and Purposeful Communication
• Speaking and Listening for Community, School and Family Life

Creating a Supportive Classroom Environment

A supportive classroom environment is one in which both the physical aspects and the culture of the classroom are considered. Stimulating and innovative learning opportunities will draw on students' interests, knowledge and skills so that Beginning students will develop the confidence and enthusiasm to engage in these activities.

Physical Environment

The physical environment of the classroom will change according to the teaching and learning demands at any particular time. It is important to establish routines for forming groups, moving furniture and collecting and storing equipment. These routines also provide opportunities to identify speaking and listening needs and to negotiate and adopt classroom behaviours. The following list contains suggestions for creating an effective classroom environment.

- Space for small-group, whole-class interactions, e.g. class meetings, class games, partner work and small-group work.
- A table to display objects of personal interest, work samples or topic-related resources.
- Dress-up boxes as this allows students to engage in spontaneous role play, to re-live experiences and experiment with new ideas and vocabulary.
- A collection of puppets, both commercial and class-made, will encourage students to retell their favourite stories or engage in imaginative conversations.
- Telephones and message pads promote students to practise their conversational and inquiry skills.
- A listening post provides another opportunity for students to listen to a variety of audio recordings.
- A reading area that includes a variety of text types allows students to discuss stories and pictures.

Learning centres provide scope to explore a unit of work. Students can be involved with decisions on setting up areas to explore a particular question, topic or issue. Teachers may develop the ideas of an individual, a small group or the whole class. The following table shows an example of topics that could be explored. A planning guide is provided on the *First Steps* Speaking and Listening CD-ROM Beginning Phase (Creating a Learning Centre).

Unit of Work/Topic	Areas that Teachers/Students Might Create
Healthy food	grocery store, vegetable patch, kitchen or restaurant
Pets	veterinary surgery, pet shop
Australian animals	zoo, wildlife rescue, park ranger's office
Toys	toy shop, repair shop, toy factory
Transport	car yard, bus depot, garage, harbour, train station, airport
Leisure	fun park, bowling alley, cinema, park
Entertainment	theatre, circus, park, beach, river
Communities	hospital, library, doctor, dentist, hairdresser, fire station, agricultural show

Figure 4.3 Ideas for learning centres

Classroom Culture

A supportive classroom culture will help develop students' confidence to 'have a go' as they move from familiar to unfamiliar ways of speaking and listening. Learning opportunities can draw on students' interests, knowledge and skills. Students can also be encouraged to contribute to the decisions made in the classroom so that they develop a sense of belonging.

- Be sensitive to cultural differences (see Chapter 4 of the *Linking Learning, Teaching and Assessment* book for more information).
- Maintain an emphasis on enjoyment.
- Communicate your high expectations to the students.
- Value social talk and the use of home language.
- Provide opportunities for planned and unplanned speaking and listening.
- Build on students' prior learning and knowledge.
- Encourage all attempts at speaking and listening for new purposes.
- Ensure that students have a clear sense of what is expected of them.
- Provide opportunities so students can review their learning.
- Involve students in negotiating their learning.
- Take advantage of the interests that students display, e.g. **if a student brings tadpoles to school, utilise the opportunity to involve students in discussions to develop topic knowledge, explanations of life cycles, etc.**

Figure 4.4

Opportunities for Relevant, Challenging and Purposeful Communication

Students in the Beginning phase will benefit from a dynamic, interactive classroom where time is provided for them to speak and listen for a variety of purposes. Everyday occurrences that students experience will provide opportunities to observe their existing skills and determine which skills need to be taught. A planning guide can be found on the Speaking and Listening CD-ROM, Beginning Phase (Audit of Existing Classroom Contexts for Speaking and Listening).

Other ideas are listed below.
- Model the use of Standard English.
- Model attentive listening and paraphrasing to clarify meaning.
- Model the language to recall events or narrate stories.
- Involve students in inquiries and investigations with real problems to solve, e.g. deciding what to play and what equipment will be needed.
- Role play with students to model language used in different contexts, e.g. post office, restaurant, supermarket or hairdresser.
- Teach nursery rhymes, counting rhymes, songs and chants so that students hear and practise the sounds and structures of literary language.
- Read stories every day and invite older students, parents or community members to read to individuals or a class group.
- Read predictable stories that demonstrate the patterns and rhythms of the English language. Encourage students to join in and predict the next line or event.
- Provide puppets, felt boards, toys or magnetic pieces to retell favourite stories
- Invite guest storytellers to tell stories to the class.
- Model language to promote cooperative play and social skills, e.g. how to join a conversation or a game, how to ask for assistance, how to use verbal and non-verbal behaviours to share or to resolve a conflict.

Speaking and Listening for Community, School and Family Life

Students come to school speaking the language of their family and community. As the way we speak is very much a part of our identity, it is important to value and build on students' home language. However, the demands of interacting in school and in the broader community mean that students need to be taught different ways of speaking and listening for a variety of purposes. Students are supported in developing competence in all aspects of Standard English so that they can communicate effectively in a variety of situations and contexts.

Following are some suggestions to assist Beginning Speakers and Learners to adjust their speaking and listening behaviours both in and out of the school environments.

- Talk about personal experiences and offer opinions.
- Model group discussion behaviours, e.g. turn taking, look at your partner when you are speaking.
- Model and explicitly teach the body language associated with active listening in classrooms.
- Teach the skills of negotiation, e.g. help students to find the specific vocabulary to explain feelings and to clarify problems such as 'I would like a turn on the swing. Could I have a turn after you, please?'
- Teach ways of acknowledging a different point of view, e.g. James thinks it was OK for Goldilocks to go into the Bears' house but Sally says it wasn't.
- Model giving and following directions, e.g. Sometimes visitors come to our class because they don't know how to get to the office. How can we give them directions?
- Encourage students to ask different types of questions.
- Encourage students to suggest answers to questions.
- Teach appropriate ways to speak and listen in both informal and more formal situations, e.g. assembly, visiting performers.
- Model how to greet and farewell familiar and unfamiliar visitors, e.g. The school nurse is coming today to check everyone's eyes. You will need to say, 'Hello, Mrs ...'
- Teach how to join a conversation or a game, e.g. When you want to join in, you need to say the person's name and then say, 'Can I play, too?'
- Invite community members into the classroom so that students interact with visitors.
- Provide opportunities for speaking and listening outside the classroom, e.g. excursions such as to the post office provide opportunities to ask questions about sorting mail and parcels.

For further information about Environment and Attitude, see *Linking Teaching Assessment and Learning*, Chapter 5: Establishing a Positive Teaching and Learning Environment.

USE OF TEXTS

Major Teaching Emphases

- Expose students to a range of functional spoken texts composed in Standard English.

- Provide authentic opportunities for students to participate in unplanned and planned speaking and listening.

- Provide opportunities for students to participate in extended talk.

- Teach students to share personal comments after listening.

- Build knowledge of common topics to which students can **relate** e.g. toys, families, community.

- Teach students the metalanguage associated with speaking and listening and encourage its use, e.g. speak, listen, hear, speaker, listener, take turns, word, think.

Teaching Notes

The focus for supporting Beginning Speakers and Listeners in this aspect is organised under the following headings.
- Exposure to a Range of Spoken Texts
- Participation in Unplanned and Planned Spoken Texts
- Focusing on Text Structure
- Developing Topic Knowledge
- Developing Metalanguage

Exposure to a Range of Spoken Texts

Beginning Speakers and Listeners will benefit from ongoing opportunities to discuss and connect with a variety of functional spoken texts, which include everyday, literary and informational. Everyday spoken texts may include greetings, conversations, procedures and the exploratory talk associated with new learning. Literary and informational spoken texts may include poems, stories, recounts, songs, descriptions, procedures and reports. See *Linking Teaching Assessment and Learning*, Chapter 5: Establishing a Positive Teaching and Learning Environment.

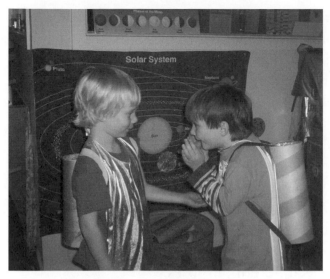

Figure 4.5

Participation in Unplanned and Planned Spoken Texts

Students' spoken language develops as they interact with others in a range of different situations and receive explicit supportive feedback. Beginning Speakers and Listeners need frequent opportunities to interact with each other in all learning activities throughout the day.

There are many authentic opportunities for Beginning Speakers and Listeners to participate in unplanned speaking and listening, such as the following, which occur naturally every day.

• Playing
• Lunch times
• Snack times
• Packing away
• Activity time, e.g. **construction, modelling, painting, water exploration, free writing**
• After reading together
• Collaborative tasks
• Planning activities with teacher or peers.

It is important to allow students to participate in extended talk in the above situations because this provides them with the opportunity to put their thoughts into words. Play and free choice time is vital to the development of speaking and listening as students also have the opportunity to practise some of the skills from structured Speaking and Listening sessions (see Figure 4.7).

Modelled, Shared and Guided Speaking and Listening sessions (see *Linking Teaching Assessment and Learning*, pages 126–129) provide ideal opportunities for Beginning Speakers and Listeners to participate in a range of unplanned and planned spoken texts. These sessions can be one-to-one, small group or whole class. They can be mini-lessons within another activity, part of the planned learning for the day, or occur incidentally as an opportunity arises. Some of the understandings about spoken texts that students will develop through Modelled, Shared and Guided Speaking and Listening sessions include:

- The connection between thinking, speaking and listening.
- Speakers and listeners use body language and different ways of producing sounds (tone, volume, pace) as well as words to make meaning.
- Speaking and listening achieves different purposes.
- Spoken texts are organised in particular ways to suit the context.
- Speakers and listeners take turns to speak (in dialogues).
- The relationship between spoken and written language is indirect.

Focusing on Text Structure

Discussions about spoken texts show students how to use a range of text forms for different purposes. Beginning Speakers and Listeners can also be supported using the Gradual Release of Responsibility Model (see Chapter One, Figure 1.10) to construct simple planned spoken texts in school contexts, using a basic text structure (see Figure 4.6).

Example of Typical Spoken Text in School Context	Example of Basic Text Structure
Meeting and greeting someone.	Say "hello" and the person's name.
Responding when someone gives you something.	Say "thank you" and take the item.
Asking a question to get something.	"Can you give/ May I have … please?"
Sharing own personal comments after listening.	I liked … My favourite …

Figure 4.6 Focusing on text structure

It is important that students realise that the spoken language is influenced by the context, with the audience and purpose determining the structure of a spoken text. The examples in Figure 4.6 provide a starting point to consider how to direct students' attention to text structures that suit particular purposes.

In the Beginning phase there is a focus on developing abilities to learn to use the full range of functions when speaking and listening (see Chapter 1, Figure 1.11). Teachers can provide valuable learning experiences so students can use functional spoken texts.

Beginning students communicate for …	Students in the Beginning phase speak and listen to …	Teachers can encourage students to share personal comments and do these things to draw students' attention to the different purposes of spoken texts:		
		Provide Direction	**Give a Comment**	**Ask a Question**
Getting things done	• role play with peers in the dress-up area. • find out if they can have/do things.	I can see you have opened up the shop. Perhaps you could find some customers.	You all look busy working in the shop together. I think I will go shopping too!	How did you work out which shopping jobs you needed to do?
Influencing the behaviour, feelings or attitudes of others	• convince a peer to let them use some equipment.	If you need that piece of Lego™, try telling Ben what you need it for.	You need to let Ben know why it is important for him to give you the Lego™ piece.	How will you let Ben know why it is important for you to have that piece of Lego™?
Getting along with others	• greet/depart. • join in a conversation.	You can say hello to your buddy from Room 7.	Your buddy from Room 7 will be happy if you say hello to him.	What do you need to say to your buddy when he comes over to see you?
Expressing individuality and personal feelings	• converse about a favourite toy. • share own experiences.	Tell me about your favourite toy.	It sounds like you play with your favourite toy a lot!	Why is that your favourite toy?
Seeking and learning about the social and physical environment	• find out what is going to happen next. • inquire about new items/new people/new ideas.	Ask Mrs Oliver about the blue box on the Curiosity Table.	When you need to find out something, you can ask someone.	Did you find out about the blue box when you asked Mrs Oliver?
Creating stories, games, new worlds and new texts	• create a story using the toy cars/puppets/painting.	You can tell me your story using the toy cars.	I enjoyed hearing the car story, especially the ending. I was surprised!	What have you been doing with your car?
Communicating information	• show someone how to do play with their electronic toy. • converse about own experiences.	Tell me what you did when you went to the shop.	You sounded busy; you did lots of things when you went to the shop yesterday.	What did you do yesterday?
Entertaining others	• share things enjoyed, sing a song, play.	Tell me what you like to talk about.	That sounds like fun!	What do you enjoy telling others? Why?

Figure 4.7 Examples for focusing on the functions of spoken texts

Developing Topic Knowledge

Students in the Beginning phase will have knowledge of topics relating to their immediate family and community experiences. Teachers can design learning experiences that begin with what students already know, moving on to developing new topic knowledge and understanding of new concepts. It is important that time is spent in discovering what students already know when introducing a new topic. This can be done through:
• Talking and listening to students in informal situations, e.g. snack time, in between activities, while waiting for parents or caregivers.

- Observing students as they engage in exploratory talk during free choice learning time, e.g. **What do they already know? What do they do with their information?**
- Observing students' representations and asking them to tell you about what they have represented, e.g. **paintings, models, drawings, role plays.**
- Interacting with students after their free time, e.g. **Why did you play in the blocks area today? What do you think you will do tomorrow? Why?**
- Conducting focused interviews with students individually or in small groups, e.g. **What do you think you could do with this equipment? Why would you do that? What did you learn when you looked in that book? Why did you choose that picture to talk to me about?**
- Negotiating familiar topics to study with the students, e.g. **What do you like to learn about? What do you know about …?**
- Talking with students' families and members of the community when determining a topic to study.

Developing Metalanguage

The language used to talk about language is known as metalanguage. Students need to be supported to build vocabulary they can use to discuss and describe their speaking and listening. When students are able to use metalanguage to talk competently about their own speaking and listening, it helps them understand how language functions. This knowledge also helps them understand the directions and feedback provided by teachers who use specific metalanguage in daily interactions.

It is important for teachers to use metalanguage as part of everyday teaching. This can be done across learning areas, as part of targeted discussions, during explicit demonstrations, during one-on-one conversations with students or as part of planned Modelled, Shared or Guided Speaking and Listening sessions.

Certain terms tend to be more prominent when focusing on different aspects of speaking and listening. For example, when working with Beginning Speakers and Listeners, consider the use of the following terms:

- Use of Texts: *speak, listen, hear*
- Contextual Understanding: *speaker, listener*
- Conventions: *take turns, word, eye contact*
- Processes and Strategies: *think, plan, reflect*

For further information about the Use of Texts aspect, see *Speaking and Listening Resource Book*, 2nd edition.
- Chapter 1: Use of Texts
- Chapter 4: Processes and Strategies.

Involving Students

1 What Shall I Do Today?

What Shall I Do Today? allows students to use extended talk and connect with their existing knowledge of common topics. A range of cross-curricula activities is set up so students use speaking and listening to make decisions such as who they will learn with and what activities they will do.

– Set out a range of collaborative and independent activities in areas around the room, e.g. construction, art/craft, dress-ups, story-making props, card games, reading area, writing area, listening area, computer area, blocks, etc. See the Speaking and Listening CD-ROM, Beginning Phase: Use of Texts, for sample planning formats (What Shall I do Today? Planning for Indoors, Planning for Outdoors, Records for Indoors and Records for Outdoors).

– Set up problem-solving situations as part of the activities, e.g. some activities may not have all of the materials, equipment will need to be shared, there is a task to design: What shall we make with these blocks?

– Explain the activities to students either in a large group or individually. Students can look around the classroom and encourage them to ask 'What shall I do today?'

– Students decide which activities they would like to do.

– Interact with students as they participate in the activities, supporting their selections and making suggestions where appropriate, e.g. What are you doing with the blocks? Have you had any problems today? How did you solve your problems?

– As students complete one activity, they can move on to the next activity.

– Students can help to pack away and ask relevant questions and give directions, e.g. Where shall we put these scraps of paper? Jamie knows where the glue goes; can you ask him to help you?

– Monitor students and redirect as appropriate, e.g. those students who tend to work on their own may need support to participate in an activity with others.

What Shall I Do Today? is also suitable for the Early and Exploratory phases.

How Might This Activity Be Used in Your Class?

• The activities might all relate to the class topic.
• Students can decide what kind of activities they would like at a class meeting.
• Explanations for the activities can be given to the whole class, to small groups or provided visually.
• Activities could be set up in the outside learning area.

61

2 Props with a Purpose

Props with a Purpose teaches students the structure of particular spoken texts for different contexts. Basic text features are modelled in a range of texts with props used as visual reminders. Students can learn to construct everyday, literary and informational spoken texts using this approach. This activity can be used with individuals, small groups or the whole class.

- Select a spoken text that will be relevant to students.
- With the students, select props to help construct the spoken text. Discuss with students the reasons for selecting particular props, e.g. peg puppets could be used for characters in a story; several pictures could be used for information about an animal; a picture of a face with a light bulb could be used to give an idea when trying to work out a social problem in a small group.
- Model the spoken text using the props, stopping at critical sections of the text to discuss the text with students, e.g. I'm going to tell you the problem in the story with this little shoe and these two characters. I have two pictures here to show what the butterfly can do. The light bulb means that I need to think of some ideas to solve the problem about who is going first and I need to say, "I think …"
- Direct students to find or make their own props for their own spoken text. Have a range of materials available, e.g. What will you need to find or make to remember what you want to say? What else do you need to include? What could you use for that?
- Invite students to compose their own spoken text with a partner or in small groups using their props.
- Ask questions and refer to the props and text structure as they construct their own spoken text, e.g. What happened after that? What is that prop for? What is the problem in your story? Where did it happen?
- Conclude the lesson by asking students to reflect and share their comments, e.g. What prop did you like using? Why? How did your props help you? What was the most interesting feature of the tiger?

Props for a Purpose is also suitable for the Early, Exploratory and Consolidating phases.

How Might This Activity Be Used in Your Class?

- Props can be available beforehand, rather than students creating them.
- A box of small toys would be an excellent support for storytelling.
- Collect props after a lesson and store them for students to use independently at another time.
- A letter could be sent out, inviting parents or caregivers to help in making the props.

3 Talk to Teach

Talk to Teach is an activity that provides an opportunity for students to explore the structures and features of informational texts. By using Talk to Teach, students are able to explore concepts and explain ideas. In this way, they refine their understanding of topics and text forms.

- Identify topics or skills that individual students show an interest in or perform well, e.g. a student may have an interest in a particular animal. Another student may have particular computer skills.
- Decide on an audience that would be interested in learning about a particular topic or skill, e.g. another student, a small group of students or an adult.
- Help students to plan what they would say by teaching appropriate vocabulary and organisation of key ideas.
- Provide time for students to rehearse what they will say.
- Provide time for students to teach another person.
- Involve students in reflecting on the way they used language to explain.

How Might This Activity Be Used in Your Class?

- When a new student arrives in your class you might have different students teaching the new student how to do things during the day.
- You might involve parents/caregivers and have the children 'teach' the class something with the support of their parent/caregiver. This works well when students can teach adult visitors something they can do at school.

4 Reflect and Respond

Reflect and Respond is an activity designed to provide an opportunity for students to discuss learning experiences. It enables students to use speaking and listening to review key understandings about topics and aspects of language used in learning and social interactions. In the Beginning phase this session will be facilitated by the teacher. The ultimate aim is for students to develop the necessary skills to engage in Reflect and Respond independently with a small group or a partner.

- Introduce Reflect and Respond by modelling the process with another adult, e.g the teacher may say, 'I enjoyed looking at tadpoles with the magnifying glass today. I learned something new when James told me about the noise the frogs were making in his backyard. His description helped me to find that type of frog in our books. What did you learn about today, Oliver?'
- When the students have had some experience with this pattern of reflecting and responding, invite one student at a time to respond. Support them by giving reminders of topics discussed during the day. Repeat and extend tentative answers.

- Aim to develop this pattern of speaking and listening until students are able to reflect and respond with a partner.

How Might This Activity Be Used in Your Class?

- You might focus on taking turns with a partner and use an object such as a cardboard microphone or magic talking stick for the person who is talking to hold.
- Try implementing this activity with different groupings, e.g. a small group after a structured activity in which they worked with a teacher or assistant.
- You might ask the students what they would like to discuss in Reflect and Respond time.
- Students might have a piece of work or an object to discuss in Reflect and Respond time.

5 Retell

Retell is an activity that provides an opportunity for students to practise the structures and features of different text forms. Students may retell stories that the teacher has read aloud or told. They may retell instructions, such as how to play a game, or procedures, such as how to make pancakes, after hearing them from a teacher or another student. Teachers could introduce the process of retell in some of the following ways:

- Take a favourite story and introduce puppets, magnetic shapes, felt pieces or toys. Model how to retell the story using the puppets (or other resources) to help sequence the events in the story. Students could try this activity in pairs. The teacher would need to support their attempts with reminders of the events and help with any difficult vocabulary.
- Take photographs of an activity that the students have been involved in such as making pancakes. Display the photographs in the correct sequence. Set up a table with containers, cooking equipment and playdough. Students could take turns to retell the procedure for making pancakes to another student or adult, using the photographs and the equipment to remind them of what to say.

How Might This Activity Be Used in Your Class?

- Use a set of sequence cards (these can be bought commercially). Ask a small group of students to take turns in a circle with the cards in the middle. Each person takes a card, in turn, and adds to the spoken text being reconstructed.
- After students have reconstructed the text orally, they may represent it visually by drawing, painting or making a model. This could be done independently, in a small group or whole class with teacher guidance.
- The reconstruction might be in the form of a whole-class dramatisation.

CONTEXTUAL UNDERSTANDING

Major Teaching Emphases

- Discuss speaking and listening, referring to the audience and purpose.

- Provide effective feedback to students about their speaking and listening.

- Model and discuss how to include relevant information when speaking.

- Draw students' attention to the way ideas and feelings are communicated through speaking and listening

- Encourage students to use verbal and non-verbal devices to create meaning.

Teaching Notes

The focus for supporting Beginning Speakers and Listeners in this aspect is organised under the following headings.
- Understandings About Context
- Providing Feedback
- Considering the Needs of the Audience
- Exploring the Way Ideas and Feelings Are Communicated
- Use of Devices

Understandings About Context

Students in the Beginning phase are mostly encountering formal schooling for the first time. When students enter a school setting, they will learn about new ways of using language. For example, they will learn how to take turns with a larger number of people; they will speak and listen to unfamiliar people (other students at school, other parents, teachers, the principal, etc.). They will learn about new topics and new ways to use language, for example, explaining new concepts or giving a reason for a particular point of view.

It is important that teachers create opportunities for students in the Beginning phase to speak for different purposes, with different audiences and in different situations. For example, students may have set up a science table to display a collection of different rocks. The teacher may provide books about rocks, pictures or videos that provide more information. Students may be asked to speak to different people, to describe locations, be involved in testing rocks for hardness or giving descriptions about different types of rocks.

Providing Feedback

Beginning Speakers and Listeners need to learn the language, vocabulary and text structures associated with different situations at school. It is important not to make assumptions about what a student knows, believes or understands about speaking and listening. The meaning students make from a spoken text is influenced by their life experiences, their knowledge of spoken language (the words and the behaviours) and the relationship with the speaker. Teachers may find it helpful to learn about the way a student's culture influences their speaking and listening. (See the Speaking and Listening CD-ROM, Exploratory phase: Contextual Understanding for parent/caregiver survey sheets.)

The feedback provided to students not only acknowledges and values the students' own language use but it also builds their confidence to communicate in different situations. Here are some suggestions for providing effective feedback.

- Focus on the message, not the way it has been conveyed.
- Acknowledge feelings, e.g. I can see that you are annoyed. You sound really happy about that.
- Wait before offering support. Students may be able to work out the meaning together and then positive comments can be given.
- Use positive statements when students adjust their speaking and listening, e.g. I noticed that you used a quiet voice in the library. I can see that you are facing me when I speak.
- Use reflective guidance when students are having difficulty making sense, e.g. I knew what you meant as soon as you pointed to the picture. You can point to the things you are talking about.

Considering the Needs of the Audience

Beginning Speakers and Listeners interact in ways that make sense to them. Modelled, Shared and Guided Speaking and Listening are ideal practices for teaching students to include relevant information for their audience. Encourage students by providing direction, responses and questions, and teaching them the appropriate verbal and non-verbal language, as shown:

- What do you think your mum would like to hear when she comes to collect you today?
- What will your dad need to know when you tell him how you made the boat?

- You told me your grandma came to see you. What did you talk about?
- What do you think the principal would like to hear about?
- I was interested when you told me about your hat. It reminded me of my hat.
- What story do you think your friend liked listening to?
- I can see what you're talking about because you are pointing to them.
- What do we need to do when someone is talking at group time?
- What are some things we can say when we meet people each day?
- How will make sure that our friends know that we want to listen to them?

By using the type of language exemplified above, students will learn that spoken language is adjusted according to the context, and language is influenced by the audience, purpose and situation.

Exploring the Way Ideas and Feelings Are Communicated

Beginning Speakers and Listeners will need support in developing understandings that ideas and feelings are communicated in different ways. Electronic spoken texts are valuable resources to use when discussing how ideas and feelings can be expressed in different ways. Teachers can support students by discussing some of the following questions.

- How did you feel as you listened to your friend?
- What did you say to make your friends laugh when you were playing in the sandpit?
- Did you like the way Mrs Oliver told the story? Why? Do you think everyone would like it?
- How do you let other people know that what they said makes you happy?
- What interesting words did you hear? Have you used those words?
- How did you know your friend was happy or annoyed?

Use of Devices

In the Beginning phase, teachers model and familiarise students with the way in which verbal and non-verbal devices are used to convey meaning. Devices are often used when trying to persuade others to accept a particular point of view or to convey emotion through descriptive terms and expressions. The teaching focus for Beginning Speaker and Listeners includes:

- Body position, e.g. facing the speaker.
- Affective displays, e.g. nodding to show they are listening.

- Eye contact, e.g. stopping an activity to look at the speaker.
- Greetings such as a handshake or waving.
- Adjusting volume, e.g. when to increase volume for emphasis, when telling an exciting part in a story.
- Questioning — When is it appropriate to ask questions and what to ask?
- Understanding that a rising intonation in the voice denotes that a question is being asked.

For further information about the Contextual Understanding aspect, see *Speaking and Listening Resource Book,* 2nd Edition, Chapter 2: Contextual Understanding. For further information on the teaching and learning practices referred to in this section see *Linking Assessment, Teaching and Learning,* Chapter 7: Effective Teaching and Learning Practices.

Involving Students

1 Talking About Speaking and Listening

Talking About Speaking and Listening is an activity designed to support younger students to analyse spoken texts. When students participate in this activity, they talk about how other people speak and listen in different contexts. They also learn about the way in which ideas and feelings are communicated through verbal and non-verbal devices used by the speakers and listeners.

- Select a spoken text such as a segment on a children's television show, audio tape of a conversation, audio tape of a story in which some characters are interacting.
- Listen to the spoken text.
- Ask students to listen for a specific focus, e.g. How did we know how she felt? What is the person talking about? What happened to her face? Or if it is a tape — What do you think her face looked like when she said how she felt? Why do you think that?
- Ask students to listen and discuss their own focus, e.g. What would you like to hear again? Why?
- Ask students to relate the main ideas to their own experiences or future speaking and listening, e.g. When might you need to let people know how you are feeling? Think of a time when you needed to let your family/teacher/friends know how you felt. What did you say? Did you have to change the way you said it for the different people?

It is useful to refer to points discovered in the session when appropriate in other contexts.

How Might This Activity Be Used in Your Class?

- You could include a session each week as part of your timetable.
- You might use this activity before and after the class visits another class in the school, using a relevant spoken text.

2 Personality Phones

This activity allows students to practise adjusting their speaking for different imaginary audiences. It also allows students to independently explore what they will say about matters of personal interest and to experiment with simple devices. One or several phones are set up with imaginary characters or personalities listed on a phone list. See the Speaking and Listening CD-ROM, Beginning and Early Phases: Contextual Understanding (Personality Phones) for sample phone lists.

Students can 'ring' and talk to the characters about topics, fears and celebrations, depending on the situation and personality of the character. The characters are to be designed to suit the students, e.g. if being positive is a class focus, one of the characters might be called Happy Henry who owns a smile factory. The phones become part of the classroom environment to be used by the students when they need or when they are asked to use them as part of the daily activities. Personality Phones can also be included in What Shall I Do Today? (see page 61).

- Show students a Personality Phone and the phone list.
- Tell students the phones are for everyone in the class to use when they need to talk to someone on their own. They might want to talk about feelings, ideas, problems, plans, celebrations, etc.
- Model using the phones for several different purposes. This may be done over several days, e.g. I'm finding it hard to work out what the problem is with one of my friends, so let's look down the list... Here's Penny Problem-Solver's number. Dial the number and have an imaginary conversation.
- Talk about how you feel after having a talk on the phone, e.g. I think I need to say sorry to my friend. I'll go and talk to him now.
- Show students where they can find the Personality Phones in the classroom.
- Negotiate and record some guidelines for using the phones with the students, e.g. When should we use them? How many people need to be near the phone? What are the phones for?

How Might This Activity Be Used in Your Class?

- The students might be involved in selecting the characters and their situation for using the phones.
- Assess the opportunities for linking this activity to writing.
- The personalities could be fluffy toys or puppets.

3 Class Meetings

Class meetings are held regularly for students to discuss and make decisions about matters that are important to the whole class. They provide opportunities for students to contribute personal ideas and feelings about a range of issues and topics. Students in the Beginning phase will need a simple introduction to class meetings. It may be useful to introduce the concept of a meeting when a decision that affects the students needs to be made. For example, students may need help with deciding how to share or store equipment, or how to modify behaviour in the classroom.

- Have students sit in a circle so that everyone can see each other.
- Introduce and explain the vocabulary that students will need, e.g. **meeting, taking turns, decisions, etc.**
- The teacher should 'chair' meetings in the Beginning phase.
- Discuss one item at a time. For the first meeting, one item will be adequate.
- Invite students to contribute their feelings and knowledge about the items or problem, e.g. **What do you think about this? How does it feel when this happens to you?** Use other adults in the classroom to model this process.
- Invite students to contribute ideas for a decision about the items, e.g. **What should we do?**
- Assist students to come to a class decision and record it.
- After the meeting, display the decisions and refer to them as appropriate, e.g. **We decided at our meeting that we would walk over to talk to a person instead of shouting across the room.**
  It is a good idea to read the decisions the next day and show students where you have displayed the decision. Visual as well as written recordings are useful.

How Might This Activity Be Used in Your Class?

- Keep a book to record the 'minutes'.
- Speakers may hold a 'microphone'.
- At certain times of the meeting, a round may be held so that each person has an opportunity to speak about in item. Students may say 'pass' in a round.
- Meetings should be held regularly in order to develop familiarity with the language needed in this context.

4 Act It Out

Act It Out is a small-group activity designed to give students time to imagine and practise what they will say and do in different situations. It provides them with the opportunity to discuss information that they may need to include and to try ways to improve the effectiveness of their speaking and listening. To prepare for this activity, teachers will need a set of cards with different scenarios to use as the starting points for the group to act it out. See the Speaking and Listening CD-ROM, Beginning Phase: Contextual Understanding for the sample set of scenario cards.

- Model the following process with another adult to introduce the activity.
- Pick a card and discuss these questions, e.g. **What is happening here? How do we know? What will we say and do so everyone understands what we mean? How could we say this so that it sounds like the talk we use at school? What will we do to show that we understand what has been said?**
- Decide who will act out the parts.
- Decide where the action will start — before, during or after the event on the card.
- Try acting it out.
- Students can reflect and discuss these questions, e.g. **What made sense? Why? Where else could we listen like this? Where else could we speak like this? What would we say differently next time? Why?**

How Might This Activity Be Used in Your Class?

- Base this activity around an identified need, e.g. **how to join a game.**
- Use some photographs of students in your class as a starting point, e.g. **students standing near the pile of blocks at packing away time.**
- Video-tape the students as they take part in the activity. They can then watch the tape for the reflection section of the activity.
- Students can tape the talk and then listen to it for the reflection section of the activity.
- Think of any possible props that the students could use.

5 People I Talk to, People I Listen to

This activity provides students with an opportunity to discuss different audiences and different purposes for speaking and listening. Teachers can draw on contexts both inside and outside the classroom. Introduce this activity by preparing photographs of people that students are likely to interact with at school, e.g. administration staff, school nurse, school dentist, gardener, canteen workers, other teachers and assistants, etc.

- Choose a photograph and discuss, e.g. When do we talk to ...?
  What do we talk about with ...? How do we speak when we talk
  to ...?
- Repeat with other photographs emphasising choices that are made
  according to topics that may be discussed or the purpose of the
  speaking.
- Students could draw pictures of the people they talk to at home or
  in the community, e.g. family members, people in the post office, the
  doctor, etc.

This activity is also suitable for the Early and Exploratory phases.

How Might This Activity Be Used in Your Class?

- Consider using photographs to create a display.
- Try giving the students a specific criterion first, e.g. draw some
  people you like talking to.
- Your class might draw the pictures and students can then sort
  them into their own criteria, e.g. people I like listening to and
  people I talk to every day.

CONVENTIONS

Major Teaching Emphases

■ **Develop and extend children's vocabulary for different purposes.**

■ **Model speaking for different purposes,** e.g. making requests, seeking information.

■ **Model speaking and listening behaviours,** e.g. maintain a conversation.

■ **Model listening, behaviours,** e.g. responding to requests, questions, looking at the person.

Teaching Notes

Teaching and learning experiences for children in the Beginning phase are organised under the following headings:
• Building Vocabulary
• Understanding the Conventions of Spoken Texts
• Understanding the Behaviours Associated with Speaking and Listening
• Understanding the Conventions of Listening

Building Vocabulary

Children's development in acquiring language skills is the result of cumulative experiences from birth onwards. Academic writers (Dickinson & Tabors 2003) describe three dimensions of children's experiences that are related to later literacy success as: exposure to varied vocabulary, opportunities to be part of conversations that use extended discourse, and home and classroom environments that are cognitively and linguistically stimulating.

Students can be supported to develop their vocabulary in the following ways:
• Encourage play and social interactions.
• Engage children in speaking and listening at every opportunity.
• Model choice of words for different purposes.
• Support children in providing names for new objects or experiences, giving explanations and elaborating on meaning, e.g. **toys, animals, food items when shopping.**
• Teach new words through encounters with new experiences, e.g. **visits to the zoo, the farm, a ferry ride.**

- Model the vocabulary needed for procedures, e.g. involve children with cooking, gardening, art/craft work.
- Model vocabulary needed in community settings, e.g. names and labels in post office, supermarket, etc.

 See the Speaking and Listening CD-ROM, Beginning Phase: Conventions (Plan: Developing Vocabulary — Excursion) for a guide to planning vocabulary related to an excursion.

Understanding the Conventions of Spoken Texts

The conventions of spoken texts relate to the choices that are made to ensure common understandings in a variety of contexts. These choices include vocabulary, tone and non-verbal behaviours. Conventions can be described in terms of the *structures* and *language features* of a spoken text. The *structure* of spoken text refers to the way ideas, feelings or communication are linked in the text. For example:

- turn-taking in a conversation
- making an apology
- introducing people.

The *language features* of a spoken text refer to the type of vocabulary, grammar, tone and pace chosen. For example:

- using colloquial words or sayings when conversing with friends
- using emotive language to persuade such as modelling language used in advertisements
- stressing certain words or altering volume to gain impact.

At all phases of development it is important that students are exposed to different models of speaking so that attention can be drawn to the conventions that suit particular purposes.

Students in the Beginning phase will develop understandings of the way language is structured through challenging, enjoyable experiences where they are able to explore and approximate language use.

- Encourage children to join in songs, chants and rhymes. This will help them to remember and use language patterns.
- Model Standard English where appropriate.
- Model the structures and features of the different functions of language:
  - request information
  - ask a question
  - relay a message
  - describe an object

– recount an experience
– greet or farewell a visitor
– tell a joke.
- Model the use of conjunctions when speaking, e.g. and, but, because
- Model the use of the correct tense.

Understanding the Behaviours Associated with Speaking and Listening

Students need to be aware of the behaviours associated with speaking and listening and how it affects meaningful communication in a variety of contexts. Teachers can involve students in choosing appropriate speaking and listening behaviours through modelling, explicit teaching and discussion. Jointly constructing Y charts or T charts will provide meaningful reminders. The following list of behaviours may provide some useful starting points.

- Discuss body language when speaking, e.g. appropriate eye contact, proximity of speaker and listener, use of gestures.
- Discuss body language when listening, e.g. nodding your head, proximity to the speaker.
- Discuss how an audience behaves, e.g. when listening to the teacher, when listening to another student, at assembly, at the theatre.
- Discuss how to take turns in a discussion.
- Discuss how to ensure everyone in a group has a turn.
- Discuss how to join or leave a game.
- Discuss how to express likes and dislikes sensitively.

Understanding the Conventions of Listening

Listening is an active, constructive process that involves making meaning from verbal and non-verbal cues. The way in which we listen is linked to the context of the communication. We listen differently during unplanned, spontaneous situations (such as in casual conversations) than we do when speaking and listening is planned and formal (such as in the classroom when instructions are being given). Teachers can assist students to become familiar with and use the conventions of listening in some of the following ways.

- Provide opportunities for students to listen to speech constructed for different purposes.
- Provide opportunities for students to respond to spoken texts, for example:
  – retelling a favourite part of a story
  – through drawing, painting, sculpting
  – by joining in and remembering songs, chants and poems
  – by responding to requests

– following directions
– responding to questions
– listening for key words and ideas
– commenting on another person's ideas
– joining in a game
– joining in a conversation.

Involving Students

1 Picture Talk

Picture Talk activities help to build vocabulary and provide opportunities for students to practise the structures and features of spoken language. They could be used to practise description, procedures, recounts or narratives.

Prepare pictures to suit your purpose. They could be from magazines, postcards, commercial posters or photographs taken in and around the school.

In the Beginning phase, the activity might focus on labelling by asking; **What can you see in the picture?** Extend the activity by asking questions, e.g. **What do you think will happen next? Have you been to a place like this?**

How Might This Activity Be Used in Your Class?

• Choose pictures to suit your purpose, e.g. student playing to highlight social skills.
• Select rural or urban scenes to practise vocabulary.
• Select works of art — discuss line, colour, pattern and shading.
• Refer to pictures from 'how-to' books to practise procedures.

2 Sorting and Classifying Activities

Sorting and Classifying activities help students to learn the features of descriptive language and develop the ability to structure their talk effectively by describing similarities and differences.

Introduce the activity by building on to everyday occurrences such as sorting blocks and other play equipment. Model the language of description by 'thinking out loud'. A simple sorting activity involves groups of items that belong in the same category but have some contrasting features. Try using marbles, pictures of food, buttons, shells, leaves. Provide children with containers to help with the sorting, e.g. marbles. **Let's sort out the marbles. We'll find all the small ones and put them in a bowl, and then we'll find all the big ones and put them in another bowl. Some marbles have one colour and some have more than one. Try finding all the marbles that have only one colour.**

This activity can also be adapted for the Early, Exploratory and Consolidating phases. (See Phase chapters for modified versions of this activity.)

How Might This Activity Be Used in Your Class?

This could be used in a maths lesson to sort and classify shapes or in a science class to sort and classify leaves.

3 What Can You Hear?

What Can You Hear? helps to develop listening skills by providing students with a focus question. It also develops vocabulary as students name things that they hear and listen to the responses of others.

Take the students for a walk to a local park. Make sure they are sitting comfortably and ask them to listen without speaking. Ask students to list the things they could hear. Elaborate on their responses by providing descriptive words and/or unknown vocabulary.

How Might This Activity Be Used in Your Class?

- Use as an introduction to a science topic on frogs, insects or birds or as an introduction to a Society and Environment topic on people-made, nature-made environments.
- Make charts of words when you return to the classroom; these words can be referred to and practised as your unit of work develops. Add digital photographs to act as a reminder of the experience.

4 Guessing Games

Guessing Games can develop vocabulary and the structures and features of description. They encourage students to use language accurately and provide an effective listening focus for other students in the group.

Prepare a 'feely bag' so students can put their hand inside to feel something that other students cannot see. Model the game until all students understand how it is played.

Link the game to a story or topic that the children have been immersed in, e.g. put a toy bear in the bag after reading *Goldilocks and the Three Bears*. Describe the features and invite the children to guess what is in the bag.

How Might This Activity Be Used in Your Class?

- Link the game to a Learning Area, e.g. attribute blocks for maths.
- Link the game to a topic about investigating toys or tools.

5 My Grandma Went Shopping

My Grandma Went Shopping develops vocabulary, memory and reinforces the behaviour of turn-taking. Students sit in a circle. (Keep numbers small for younger students.) One person starts by saying, 'My grandma went shopping and bought (e.g. apples).' The next person says, 'My grandma went shopping and bought apples and milk.' The game continues in a cumulative fashion with each person listing the previous items bought before adding one new item to the list.

How Might This Activity Be Used in Your Class?

- Provide concrete materials, e.g. have a basket containing plastic fruit and vegetables. Students choose an item from the basket and put it on the floor in front of them.
- Change the setting and the characters, e.g. choose things to take on a picnic, camping trip or going fishing. Prepare pictures of items needed to help with memory and to stimulate vocabulary.

6 Taking Turns

Taking Turns introduces the concept of taking turns to complete an activity in cooperation with others. It suits situations where turns can be taken in a random order. Emphasise the language of taking turns, e.g. 'It's your turn' and 'now it's Sam's turn.'

Write the names of the students in the group on cards. The cards are turned over so that the names cannot be seen. As the teacher needs a student to take a turn in the activity, a card is turned over and that student is chosen.

How Might This Activity Be Used in Your Class?

Link the shape of cards to a topic relevant to the class, e.g. regular two-dimensional shapes, Australian animals, articles of clothing hanging on a line or fruit shapes.

7 Generic Games

There are many common games that can be used to support understanding of the conventions of spoken language. See *First Steps Reading Map of Development*, 2nd Edition and *First Steps Writing Map of Development*, 2nd Edition for descriptions of games.

PROCESSES AND STRATEGIES

Major Teaching Emphases

■ **Model language to describe thinking.**

■ **Involve children in conversations with family members and others.**

■ **Model the language and behaviours of listening,** e.g. Let's listen to the music. Would you like to hear this story?

■ **Model ways to improve communication,** e.g. adjusting volume, respond to comprehension checks.

Organisation of the Processes and Strategies Aspect

There are several differences in the organisation of the Processes and Strategies aspect. Both the Teaching Notes and the Teaching and Learning Experiences (Involving Students) are in the *Speaking and Listening Resource Book*, 2nd Edition, Chapter 4: Processes and Strategies.

The rationale for this difference in organisation is that the processes and strategies of speaking and listening are not conceptually hierarchical and therefore not phase-specific. In all phases, a variety of speaking and listening processes and strategies need to be introduced, developed and consolidated. What varies from one phase to the next is the growth in:

• the number and integration of strategies used throughout the processes of speaking and listening
• the awareness and monitoring of speaking and listening processes
• the efficiency in the uses of the speaking and listening processes
• the ability to articulate the use of the strategies used in the process of speaking and listening
• the awareness of how the use of processes helps with composing and listening to texts.

Supporting Parents of Beginning Speakers and Listeners

GENERAL DESCRIPTION OF BEGINNING SPEAKERS AND LISTENERS

Beginning Speakers and Listeners imitate the sounds and patterns of language that they hear around them. They use words, body movements and sounds to express their feelings, their needs and to interact with others. Familiar adults and older children may help to work out their meaning by questioning and repeating what they have said.

Teachers will find that parents are able to support their children effectively when they have an understanding of how children learn and if they are aware of what happens in the classroom. Teachers can help build parent awareness of the learning program in which their child is involved in the following ways:

- Invite parents in to join in class activities and talk to them before and after the activity, e.g. **The children are … The adult's role in this activity is to … How did the children enjoy this activity? What did you find was effective in helping them to understand?**
- Conduct parent/caregiver workshops on learning, e.g. **Learning Through Play, Learning with Technology, Helping Children to Learn.**
- Make a video, DVD or a CD-ROM with the students to demonstrate certain features of the learning program. Each family can take it home to view with their children. A viewing guide can be created with the student's input.
- When creating displays of student work, add information about the context of the activity and list the important learning that took place during the activity.
- Provide students with home-learning activities that involve them sharing their learning with family members.

Supporting Beginning Speakers and Listeners in the Home

Beginning Speakers and Listeners will benefit from a range of experiences in the home setting. Ideas for providing appropriate experiences are available in the Parent Cards located on the *First Steps* Speaking and Listening CD-ROM. Teachers can select appropriate cards for each Beginning Speaker and Listener and copy them for parents to use at home.

Parent Cards

1 General Description of Beginning Speakers and Listeners

2 Developing an Understanding About Different Types of Speaking and Listening

3 Developing an Understanding About Contexts

4 Developing Vocabulary

5 Listening (Refer to the Early Phase Parent Cards.)

6 Family Meetings (Refer to the Early Phase Parent Cards.)

CHAPTER 5

Early Speaking and Listening Phase

Unplanned	Planned

Teacher: I wonder what is inside. Can you find out without opening it up?

Liam: (*lifting the container*) I think there'd be Smarties in there. What do you think there'll be in there, James?

James: Um... I think there'll be Smarties.

Liam: Aaar... I think there'd be a film in there and in that one I... think there would *beee*... um... maybe some... rocks, maybe? In there? What do you think'd be in that one or that one?

James: Camera.

Liam: Film?

James: Yeah, film (*overlapping and inaudible*)

Liam: Can we have a look?

Teacher: What do you think is in there?

Liam and James (together): Smarties, film and rocks.

Teacher: OK, which one is the Smarties?

Liam: This one. (*pointing*)

Teacher: Do you think so? Have a look!

Liam: Ooh! It buttons and ... bits of paper.

James: And a button!

Liam: First... um you get...

Teacher: Sorry, can I just stop you a minute, Liam. What are you going to tell us to make?

Liam: A money... a clay money box. First um... um... how to make a clay money box. First, you get a bit of clay and then you get a tin and then you get a bit of paper and then cut it... how much... how big the tin is and then wrap it around the tin, then stick the tin on and then get a bit of clay and wrap it around the tin and then make the bottom and then... um... do the um... do some pictures on it then make the top and cut a hole in it.

Teacher: And is that all, Liam?

Liam: Yep.

Teacher: OK, thanks Liam.

Figure 5.1   **Figure 5.2**

Global Statement

In this phase, students use their own variety of English language to communicate needs, express ideas and ask questions. They understand spoken language relating to personal and social interests and respond in their own way. They are becoming aware of appropriate ways of interacting in familiar situations.

Early Speaking and Listening Indicators

Use of Texts

◆ **Makes sense of spoken texts with familiar others.**
◆ **Uses a range of brief unplanned spoken texts independently.**
◆ **Participates with support in some planned talk for school purposes.**
◆ **Recalls personally significant information from spoken texts.**
• Asks and answers questions seeking information and clarification.
• Follows, one step at a time, short, simple instructions, e.g. for playing a game, completing a classroom task.
• Contributes personally significant knowledge, ideas and feelings to discussions.
• May use own variety of English to communicate in familiar contexts.

Contextual Understanding

◆ **Beginning to adjust speaking and listening for familiar situations in a school context.**
◆ **Will often assume a shared background between speaker and listener when speaking,** e.g. may not give sufficient information to orientate the listener.
◆ **Is aware that people talk about their ideas.**
• Often relies on gesture, intonation and repetition to convey meaning.
• Discusses appropriate ways to speak and listen in different situations.
• Recognises there are different spoken texts.
• Understands purpose and their roles in routine classroom activities involving speaking and listening.
• Can state purpose for own talk.

Conventions

◆ **Structures simple spoken texts appropriately.**
◆ **Uses everyday terms related to their experiences and some subject-specific words.**
◆ **Relies on simple sentences or uses simple connectives to link ideas.**
◆ **Interprets and uses simple statements, commands and questions.**
• Sequences speech in intelligible ways.
• Interprets and responds to non-verbal cues, e.g. facial expressions, gestures.

Processes and Strategies

◆ **Talks about thinking with others,** e.g. I think.
◆ **Uses a small range of processes and strategies when speaking,** e.g. uses props to support speaking.
◆ **Uses a small range of processes and strategies when listening,** e.g. asks questions to clarify.
• Shows understanding of spoken language in personal ways, e.g. responds with some relevant comments.
• Anticipates stages in familiar spoken texts, e.g. predicts next part of teacher's directions for an activity.
• Uses strategies to adjust speaking for different purposes, e.g. shares ideas and offers opinion in structured situations.
• Uses known familiar cues in order to clarify message, e.g. through body language, facial expression or simple response – What?

Major Teaching Emphases

Environment and Attitude (see p. 85)

- Provide opportunities for relevant, challenging and purposeful communication.
- Create a supportive environment which values the diversity of students' speaking and listening development (in their home languages).
- Encourage students to see the value of effective listening and speaking for community, school and family life.

Use of Texts (see p. 90)

- Expose students to a range of functional spoken texts composed in Standard English.
- Provide authentic opportunities for students to participate in unplanned and planned speaking and listening.
- Provide opportunities for students to participate in extended talk.
- Teach students to compose spoken texts using basic text structures e.g. using people's names in social situations and providing background information in recounts, responding to questioning.
- Teach students to make connections with their existing knowledge of common topics.
- Teach students the metalanguage associated with speaking and listening and encourage its use, e.g. meaning, question, topic, message, Standard English, point of view, sharing, volume, expression, turn, plan, memory.

Contextual Understanding (see p. 103)

- Discuss ways in which particular spoken texts are suitable for different audiences, e.g. conversations with adults or peers during outdoor play.
- Provide explicit feedback to students who are adjusting their speaking and listening, e.g. when they are talking in small groups/to teachers.
- Help students recognise where background and supporting information are needed when speaking.

- Provide support for students to recognise how they can contribute to discussions.
- Provide opportunities for students to analyse the meaning of spoken texts.
- Support students to recognise how simple devices improve speaking and listening in different contexts, e.g. volume, simile, rhyme, common sayings.

Conventions (see p. 113)

- Provide opportunities for students to develop and use new vocabulary.
- Model language structures and features to suit the purpose, e.g. recount an experience using time order, checking on listener's understanding, adding supporting detail, give explanations using conjunctions, e.g. if, then, and, because.
- Model the skills of conversation.
- Teach speaking and listening behaviours that support meaning making, e.g. asking clarifying questions, seeking confirmation, providing sufficient detail.
- Model and discuss agreed ways to respond to spoken texts in school, e.g. when and how to take turns.

Processes and Strategies (see p. 129)

- Model thinking aloud about the selection of appropriate speaking and listening strategies.
- Encourage students to verbalise own thinking.
- Provide opportunities for students to engage in conversations for specific purposes, e.g. to socialise, to get things done.
- Teach simple planning tools for speaking, e.g. plan recounts that orientate the listener, plan how …
- Teach simple planning tools to help students gain a listening focus, e.g. use drawings to respond to listening, listen for specific information.
- Model strategies to adjust communication, e.g. self-correct to clarify meaning, rephrase if not understood.

Teaching and Learning Experiences

ENVIRONMENT AND ATTITUDE

Major Teaching Emphases

- **Provide opportunities for relevant, challenging and purposeful communication.**

- **Create a supportive classroom environment which values the diversity of students' speaking and listening development (in their home languages).**

- **Encourage students to see the value of effective listening and speaking for community, school and family life.**

Teaching Notes

Students in the Early phase will need assistance to prepare them for the demands and challenges of formal learning. In the classroom, the purposes for speaking and listening place different demands on students to use spoken language in particular ways. Different audiences and situations will also be presented to students which will influence the types of speaking and listening they are required to do. Teachers can design teaching and learning activities that draw on students' interests, knowledge and skills. It is through these experiences that students develop the skills needed to interact with others in order to meet a variety of purposes.

The focus for developing positive attitudes towards speaking and listening as well as a supportive environment is organised under the following headings:
- Creating a Supportive Classroom Environment
- Opportunities for Relevant, Challenging and Purposeful Communication
- Speaking and Listening for Community, School and Family Life

Creating a Supportive Classroom Environment

A supportive classroom environment can be planned to include both the physical aspects and the culture of the classroom. Teachers can provide challenging teaching and learning experiences that enable students to improve their existing language strengths.

Physical Environment

The physical environment for Early phase students will need to be flexible to accommodate learning and structured play, both indoors and outdoors. Students will need to be taught routines such as moving in and out of groups, moving furniture, and collecting and storing equipment.

Figure 5.3

Other considerations for an effective physical environment are listed below.

- Teach students how to organise, use and store equipment.
- Include tables or pin-up boards to display students' items of interest, work samples or topic-related resources.
- Provide a selection of materials that will stimulate imaginative play, e.g. **cardboard boxes, old blankets, rope, steering wheels, blocks and items for students to 'dress-up'.**
- Provide a quiet, comfortable reading area that includes a variety of text types.
- Provide sets of telephones and message pads. Encourage students to ring each other, take messages and have conversations.
- Provide resources to assist with storytelling and imaginative conversations such as puppets, magnetic or felt characters.
- Provide tape recorders or listening posts with taped stories. Blank audio tapes should be available to record students' spoken language.
- Plan outdoor areas that will require students to interact, share equipment, experiment and investigate.
- Establish learning centres that will help students explore a topic or develop a unit of work. Students can contribute ideas and suggestions as to what equipment can be in a learning centre.

The table below shows examples of topics that could be explore in this way. Refer to the *First Steps* Speaking and Listening CD-ROM, Beginning Phase (Creating a Learning Centre and Audit of Existing Classroom Contexts for Speaking and Listening).

Unit of Work/Topic	Areas That Teachers/Students Might Create
Animals	veterinary surgery, zoo, pet shop
Food	restaurant (Chinese, Italian ...) kitchen, grocery store
Travel	travel agent, tourist information centre, airport (Choose a country to study.)
Toys	toy shop, repair shop, toy factory
Transport	car yard, bus depot, garage, harbour, train station, airport
Local community	hairdresser, petrol station, supermarket, swimming pool, video shop
Community services	first aid post, ambulance, fire station
Communities workers	doctor's surgery, dental surgery, library

Figure 5.4 Setting up learning areas

Classroom Culture

Students in the Early phase will need to feel supported as they interact in unfamiliar situations and with unfamiliar people. It is important to establish a classroom culture that accepts individual differences and encourages students to use speaking and listening to develop positive relationships with teachers and peers. It is also important to foster a sense of independence and confidence.

- Maintain sensitivity to cultural differences. (See *First Steps Linking Learning, Teaching and Assessment* for more information.)
- Teach students to think of others, e.g. to make space for others, to invite others to join in and to share equipment.
- Teach students how to take turns in a group, e.g. to speak, to decide who will go first when choosing equipment or playing a game.
- Teach students to ask for help when they are experiencing difficulty (help from teachers or peers).
- Teach students to discuss problems, e.g. teach words and phrases that will support students to describe their feelings.
- Provide positive feedback when students attempt to adopt new speaking and listening behaviours.
- Provide opportunities for students to choose their own activities.
- Teach students to share classroom responsibilities e.g. co-construct a chart of daily jobs, change the date on the calendar, set up the writing centre.

- Teach students the process of making decisions, e.g. to take a vote in a class meeting. Display the decisions made and refer to them when needed.
- Teach students the skills needed to act independently, e.g. to listen to instructions carefully, to ask questions when they are unsure (of teachers or peers), to watch what other students are doing to see if it helps them to understand a task.

> **How to Be Independent**
> 1 Listen carefully.
> 2 Look around at others.
> 3 Ask someone close to you.
> 4 Ask someone in your group.
> 5 Ask your teacher.

Figure 5.5

Opportunities for Relevant, Challenging and Purposeful Communication

Students in the Early phase use spoken language throughout the day as they explore relationships and gain an understanding of new topics and concepts. These everyday occurrences provide teachers with insight into the language functions that students control and those that need to be taught. A planning guide is located on the Speaking and Listening CD-ROM that will assist teachers to identify their students' range of functions.

Ongoing, Incidental Teaching

- Notice when students use home talk, e.g. when exploring a new idea, when role playing in the dress-up corner. Decide which aspects of Standard English will need to be taught.
- Teach students how to use Standard English for appropriate contexts, e.g. when talking to a visitor who may have a position of authority (police officer, a visiting teacher).
- Use shared experiences to model the language required to recount events in sequence.
- Teach attentive listening through modelling and paraphrasing.
- Teach students to resolve conflicts through language, e.g. next time you should say, 'I would like to use the scissors when you have finished, please.'
- Involve students in singing and chanting raps and rhymes every day. This will provide them with the practice needed to understand language structures and features.
- Read aloud every day. Invite other teachers and adults to read to students. Include some stories with predictable patterns or refrains so that students can join in. Read non-fiction topics that students have expressed an interest in.
- Tell stories and invite storytellers into the classroom.

Units of Work

Teachers can create relevant, challenging and purposeful speaking and listening experiences through planning units of work that integrate skills and knowledge needed to achieve educational outcomes across the curriculum. This can be done by developing units of work that provide meaningful contexts for learning. Some of the following questions, based on ideas from Murdoch (2004), may help to guide planning.

- How will the topic be chosen?
- Are there opportunities for choice or negotiation in this unit?
- How will this unit of work engage the students?
- What educational outcomes will be achieved?
- What are the vocabulary demands of the topic?
- How can we help students make connections between learning areas?
- How will students reflect on their learning?
- What assessment opportunities are occurring?

Design learning experiences that provide students with the opportunity to talk for a range of purposes.

Speaking and Listening for Community, School and Family Life

Students in the Early phase are becoming aware of different speaking and listening contexts and the need to adjust spoken language to suit different purposes and audiences. Teachers can assist students in the Early phase to develop awareness of different kinds of speaking and listening in the following ways:

- Talk about personal interests and experiences.
- Talk about behaviours that are appropriate inside the classroom, e.g quiet voices, words to be friendly and help with sharing.
- Talk about appropriate behaviours in the playground, e.g. choosing what games to play, making sure that everyone has a turn.
- Engage students in conversations with a variety of people including peers, teachers and visiting adults.
- Develop awareness of expected behaviours for more formal situations, e.g. assembly, a visiting performer.
- Model greeting and saying farewell to visitors to the classroom using words and phrases that have been previously taught.
- Engage students in role play, e.g. what is said when buying something at the shop, inviting a friend to a party.
- Invite guest speakers into the classroom, e.g. parents might talk about their jobs or hobbies, community workers might discuss matters of safety such as a fire-control officer talking about emergency procedures.

USE OF TEXTS

Major Teaching Emphases

- Expose students to a range of functional spoken texts composed in Standard English.

- Provide authentic opportunities for students to participate in unplanned and planned speaking and listening.

- Provide opportunities for students to participate in extended talk.

- Teach students to compose spoken texts using basic text structures, e.g. using people's names in social situations and providing background information in recounts, responding to questioning.

- Teach students to make connections with their existing knowledge of common topics.

- Teach students the metalanguage associated with speaking and listening and encourage its use e.g. meaning, question, topic, message, Standard English, point of view, sharing, volume, expression, turn, plan, memory.

Teaching Notes

The focus for supporting Early Speakers and Listeners in this aspect is organised under the following headings.
- Exposure to a Range of Spoken Texts
- Participation in Unplanned and Planned Spoken Texts
- Focusing on Text Structure
- Developing Topic Knowledge
- Developing Metalanguage

Exposure to a Range of Spoken Texts

Early Speakers and Listeners are developing an awareness that there are different types of spoken texts as they interact with others at school in their play, activity time and in conversations. Students in the Early phase need opportunities to engage with a variety of functional spoken texts, which include everyday, literary and informational.

Figure 5.6

Participation in Unplanned and Planned Spoken Texts

Students learn about language indirectly as they listen to others and observe the behaviours that accompany speech. They learn about language directly when teachers give explicit and supportive feedback.

There are many authentic opportunities for Early Speakers and Listeners to participate in unplanned and planned speaking and listening, such as the following, which occur naturally every day.

• Playing
• Lunch times
• Snack times
• Packing away
• Activity time, e.g. board games, sorting games, learning centre.
• Reading together
• Collaborative tasks.

It is important to allow students to participate in extended talk in the situations described above as it provides them with the opportunity to put their thoughts into words.

Planned, Modelled, Shared and Guided Speaking and Listening sessions (see *Linking Assessment, Teaching and Learning*, pp. 126–129) may provide ideal opportunities for Early Speakers and Listeners to compose a range of spoken texts.

Amy:	Hey Billie ... Oscar the shark.
Shae:	Amy, oh Rachel, I'll tell you a joke ... what's a ... don't tell her, OK? What's a dinosaur's worst enemy?
Matthew:	What's a tree's worst enemy?
Billy:	A T-rex.
Matthew:	... knock it down ...
Shae:	T-rex.
Billy:	I knew that.
Shae:	That's why I told *uuumm*
Unknown:	... said to Sophie.
Billy:	I knew that. I know tons about dinosaurs.
Matthew:	Don't you, babe.
Unknown:	Ooops!

Figure 5.8

Figure 5.7 Transcript of lunchtime talk

Some of the understandings about spoken texts that students will develop through planned and unplanned activities include:

- Speaking and listening is important for learning.
- Speaking and listening is important for developing and maintaining relationships.
- Speakers and listeners use body language and different ways of producing sounds (tone, volume, pace) as well as words to make meaning.
- Speaking and listening is used for different purposes.
- Texts are organised in particular ways according to the context.
- The relationship between spoken and written language is indirect.

Focusing on Text Structure

Students in the Early phase are building on their knowledge about the ways different spoken texts are structured. The focus for Early speakers and listeners is to learn about basic text structures of a small range of everyday, literary and functional spoken texts.

Early speakers and listeners can also be supported using the Gradual Release of Responsibility Model (see Chapter 1, Figure 1.10) to construct simple planned spoken texts in school contexts, using basic text structure as seen in the following chart.

Teachers can draw attention to basic text structures as students create texts independently for different purposes as shown in Figure 5.9. It is important that students realise that spoken language is influenced by the context. The examples in Figure 5.9 provide a starting point for teachers to consider how to demonstrate different text types.

Example of Typical Spoken Text in School Context	Example of Basic Text Structure
Using people's names in social situations	*Do you want to play, Chloe?* *Chloe, do you want to play?* • Say the name before or after. • Say what you want/need/think.

Recounts which provide background information	• Setting — who, where, when
	• Events in time order
	  – What happened first?
	  – What happened next?
	• Ending — personal comment, e.g. I liked ...

Procedures which include what is needed	• What is it? • What is needed? • How is it made? What do you do first? What do you do then? And then?
Replying to a question — when known and unknown	When unknown — • Say I don't know/ I'm not sure. • May shake your head / look puzzled. • Wait for some help from the speaker.
Making connections — what does that remind you of?	• Say *It reminded me of ...* or *I remember ...* • Say what you remember.

Figure 5.9

In the Early phase, it is important to provide experiences that address all language functions. (see Figure 1.11, Chapter 1) The following chart (see Figure 5.10) can be used as a planning and reflection tool to address different student needs.

Developing Topic Knowledge

Students in the Early phase will draw upon individual knowledge and experiences as they interact with others. As they listen, create and engage with spoken texts, students will connect and construct new knowledge and meanings for themselves. Over time, speakers and listeners will be exposed to a diverse range of topics. It is vital that they have the opportunity to share their knowledge and ask questions.

Before teachers determine a teaching focus they will gather information by:

- Talking and listening to students in informal situations, e.g. in the playground.
- Observing students as they engage in open-ended tasks — What do they already know? What do they do with their information?
- Observing students' representations and ask them to tell you about what they have represented, e.g. box construction, artwork.
- Interacting with students after their free time, e.g. What did you find out when you went to the science table?

Early students communicate for …	Students in the Early phase speak and listen to …	Teachers can do these things to draw students' attention to the different purposes and to basic text structures:		
		Provide Direction	**Give a Comment**	**Ask a Question**
Getting things done	• show someone how to play a game. • help others pack away. • make things. • instruct others.	Tell your dad how we pack away here at school and then he can join in with you.	I think you must have told your dad very well how we pack up, because he knew what to do!	What will you need to tell your dad so he knows how we pack up here at school?
Influencing the behaviour, feelings or attitudes of others.	• suggest a group activity, e.g. build a tower. • play a game.	Work out what you are going to build with the Lego™ together.	You sounded excited when you suggested you all build a tower together!	What did you say to your friends to make them want to build a tower, too?
Getting along with others	• greet/depart. • plan for play. • cooperate in a group.	Talk about something you both like to do together today.	It looked like you will have fun doing those things together today.	Did your partner have any different ideas? Maybe you could use them next time.
Expressing individuality and personal feelings	• share own experience. • discuss feelings.	Tell your Room 4 buddy about your classroom.	You talked about the furniture as well as the doors; they are important features of our room.	What features does our classroom have?
Seeking and learning about the social and physical environment	• raise questions about classroom routines. • inquire about new ideas/ information. • converse with an expert.	If you don't know what it means, say, 'What does that mean?'	I wonder if we can find out what that means.	What can you say if you don't understand something?
Creating stories, games, new worlds and new texts	• make up a new game with a friend. • roleplay in the dress-up area. • participate in music, movement, art.	You can pretend you are in the fire station in the dress-up area today.	I can see that the fire officers have been very busy. I heard someone say they were ready for a break.	What happened in the fire station today? What did the fire officer do?
Communicating information	• ask/answer questions. • inform parents/caregiver what they do during the day at school. • record ideas.	Tell your group what you have learnt today.	It's good to hear what you did and why you did it.	What did you learn today? What did you do to learn it?
Entertaining others	• retell and invent stories. • participate in drama, role play, music.	Talk about something your partner will enjoy listening to.	Your partner was enjoying that story and I think it was because it had an interesting problem.	Why do you like listening to your partner tell stories?

Figure 5.10 Suggestions for speaking and listening in all functions

- Conducting focused interviews with students individually or in small groups, e.g. **What can we use to find out more about ants?**
- Negotiating familiar topics to study with the students, e.g. **What do you like to learn about? What do you know about … ?**

Teachers can extend students' topic knowledge through learning that involves direct observation, language experience activities and discussion.

Direct Observation

Students observe things such as fish, snails or tadpoles in an aquarium. They may plant seeds and observe growth, or conduct simple science experiments. Students will be asked to describe their observations to others and explore possible causes and effects of observed events.

Language Experience Activities

Activities such as cooking, blowing bubbles or making clay models teach students to use language to describe and follow procedures. Students talk to make connections with previous experiences, make predictions and discuss observations.

Discussions

When students are involved in discussions about what they would like to learn, they are given opportunities to pose questions, e.g. **students may be involved in planning an excursion to learn more about community services such as the post office or fire control.** Students can brainstorm the types of questions that could be asked to gain information. They could role play questioning conventions in preparation for the excursion. Students can later discuss what they learned from asking questions.

These types of activities are what Jones (1996) describes as *language accompanying action* which helps students build first-hand knowledge of topics. These activities also reveal what students already know about topics and what they need to learn next. Teachers will also have the opportunity to observe the structures and features of students' spoken language to determine what needs to be taught, e.g. **technical vocabulary, organising key words and ideas in an explanation.**

Figure 5.11

Developing Metalanguage

Metalanguage is the language used to talk about language. It is important to teach students the words needed to discuss and describe their own speaking and listening and the processes and strategies that they use. Early Speakers and Listeners will become familiar with metalanguage when it is used as part of everyday teaching. This can be done across learning areas, as part of targeted discussions, during explicit demonstrations, during one-on-one conversations with students or as part of planned Modelled, Shared or Guided speaking and listening sessions.

Certain terms tend to be more prominent when focusing on different aspects of speaking and listening. For example, when working with Early Speakers and Listeners, consider the use of the following terms:

- Use of Texts: *meaning, question, topic*
- Contextual Understanding: *message, Standard English, point of view*
- Conventions: *sharing, volume, expression, turn*
- Processes and Strategies: *plan, memory*

For further information about the Use of Texts aspect, see *First Steps Speaking and Listening Resource Book*, 2nd Edition:
- Chapter 1: Use of Texts
- Chapter 4: Processes and Strategies.

Involving Students

1 What Comes Next?

What Comes Next? is an activity that helps students to understand the structure of different text types. They will listen to a chosen text several times so they are prepared when they reconstruct a part of a text.

Select a spoken text such as:
- an everyday spoken text, e.g. playing a game like I Spy, inviting someone to play.
- a literary spoken text, e.g. fairy tale.
- an informational spoken text, e.g. recount of recent excursion, making something.

Present the spoken text to be reconstructed. It can be repeated and presented in different ways, for example:
- Retell a story or event by using puppets or props.
- Read a story aloud, and then use the puppets to retell the story and show it on film.
- Read a recipe aloud. Use real ingredients and act out the instructions with toys from the dress-up area.
  - Ask the students to identify sections of the text, e.g. What do we need to include to retell this story? What do we need to remember to do in this recipe?
  - Record the basic structure of a text in a pictorial form. It can be recorded on large sheets of paper, a whiteboard or cards.
  - Make up sets of cards or charts for students to use as visual prompts when it is their turn to reconstruct the text. If students are working in small groups, the teacher will need to make cards or a chart for each group or have groups rotate to the single set of cards or chart. (See the Speaking and Listening CD-ROM, Early Phase: Use of Tests (What Comes Next?).

This activity is also suitable for the Beginning, Exploratory and Consolidating phases.

How Might This Activity Be Used in Your Class?

- Ask a small group of students to take turns in a circle with the cards stacked in the middle. Each person takes a card, in turn, and adds to the spoken text being reconstructed.
- Students may perform their spoken text to another group. Encourage the audience to ask questions or give comments.

- Small objects could be used instead of cards to remember sections of spoken texts, e.g. a story, recipe.
- After students have reconstructed the text orally, they may reconstruct it visually by drawing, painting or making a model. This could be done independently, in a small group or whole class.
- The reconstruction might be in the form of a whole-class dramatisation.

2 Props with a Purpose

Props with a Purpose is designed to teach students to construct their own spoken texts using basic text structures. Students learn to include text features in a range of texts, using props as visual reminders. This task can be performed by individuals, small groups or the whole class.

Figure 5.12

– Select an everyday, literary or informational spoken text that students need to learn more about.
– Model selecting props to help construct the spoken text and discussing with students the reasons for selecting particular items for props, e.g. a picture of a face with a light bulb could be used to give an idea when trying to work out a social problem in a small group; peg puppets for characters in a story; several pictures for information about an animal.
– Model the spoken text using the props. Stop at critical sections of the text to discuss the text structures with students, e.g.
  - The light bulb means that I need to think of some ideas to solve the problem about who is going first and I need to say, 'I think ...'
  - I'm going to tell you the problem in the story with this little shoe and these two characters ...
  - I have two pictures here to show what the butterfly can do ...

- Students can find or make their own props for their spoken text. Have a range of materials available to select from, e.g. **What will you need to find or make to remember what you want to say? What else do you need to include? What could you use that for?**
- Instruct students to construct their own spoken text with a partner or small group using their props.
- Ask questions and refer to the props and text structure as they construct their own spoken text, c.g. **What happened after that? What is that prop for? What is the problem in your story? Where did it happen?**
- Arrange an audience in the class to listen to literary and informational spoken texts.
- Ask students to reflect on the use of their props to remember the basic structures of their spoken text, e.g. **What prop did you like using? Why? How did your props help you? What was the most interesting feature of ... ? What other kinds of problems could you use the light bulb for?**
- Revise the basic text structures with students, e.g. **When you solve a problem with a friend, what do you need to say? What does a story need? How do you make it interesting for the listener? What did I include to help the listener to find out about the butterfly?**

How Might This Activity be Used in Your Class?

- Ensure props are available, rather than having students create them.
- Have a box or bag of small toys to make a story or to use for descriptions.
- Teach students to play games such as What Am I? and What Is Missing? using the props, particularly when focusing on descriptions.
- Place the props in a Mystery Bag. Students ask questions to find out what might be in the bag to describe, report, recount or retell.
- As you create a set of props for a particular spoken text, put them in a bag with a chart for independent use, e.g. **first you say how you feel, secondly, you say what would make it better for you and thirdly you think of ideas for next time.**
- Parents or caregivers may help to make props.

3 Listen to Learn

Listen to Learn is an activity designed to teach students how to listen in order to record and recall important information. It assists in building knowledge of the way spoken language is structured and introduces students to listening for main ideas and key words.

- Select a recorded spoken text that will support a current unit of work, e.g. a narrative, informational text or students speaking during a group activity.
- Decide on the particular structures that will be the focus of the lesson, e.g. the names of characters in a story, a fact about an animal, how someone shared material fairly.
- Decide how students will record the information they are listening for, e.g. draw a picture or write a word.
- Decide how students will share the information, e.g. talk to a partner, contribute to a whole-class discussion, contribute to a class chart.

This activity is suitable for all phases.

Figure 5.13 Journey of a letter — students watched and listened to this video

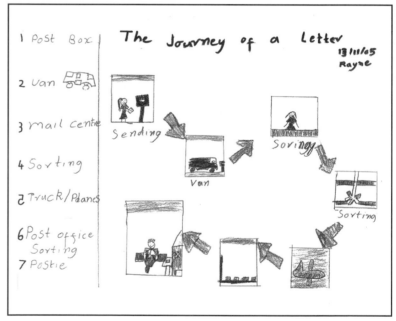

Figure 5.14

How Might This Activity Be Used in Your Class?

- The spoken text might relate to the students' unit of inquiry — the questions they have already asked.
- The activity might be set up in a reading or viewing area of the room for small groups to work in over several days.
- Students might have several spoken audio texts to select.
- The whole class might hear the same spoken text together and then work independently to represent their learning.

4 Talk to Teach

Talk to Teach is a cross-curricula activity that helps students to use speaking to inform, explain, instruct and narrate. It asks students to recall and represent what they know in their own way as it helps them reshape and refine their own understandings. Their task is to teach someone else what they know. The selection of the audience is important as there is no real purpose in teaching someone who already knows. Students are usually involved in deciding the audience and then inviting them to listen.

Teachers will need to model this activity first.

- Decide what students are able to share, e.g. information or skill. They could brainstorm things that they know/things they are good at. Teachers may observe particular strengths that a student can share.
- Decide on who will benefit from the information.
- Help students to plan what they will say and do. The planning may include discussions, a drawing, a flow chart or a collection of objects.
- Set a time for students to teach their audience.
- Provide guiding questions and comments for reflection.

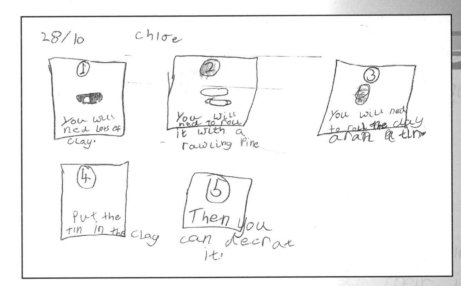

Figure 5.15

This activity is suitable for all phases.

How Might This Activity Be Used in Your Class?

- If a new student arrives in your class, have different students teach the new student how to do things during the day.
- Students can 'teach' the class something with the support of their parent/caregiver.
- Keep a list of 'experts' and draw upon it when needed, e.g. one student could teach another about using a computer program or how to use the new construction equipment.

5 What Shall I Do Today?

Refer to Chapter 4: Beginning Speaking and Listening phase, page 61. This activity is also suitable for the Exploratory phase.

How Might This Activity Be Used in Your Class?

- The activities might relate to the class topic.
- Students can explain what they need to do for some of the activities.
- Explanations for the activities can be given to the whole class or small group or the teacher may provide some pictorial instruments.
- The activity could take place in the outside learning area.
- This session could be called Free Time, Personal Learning Time, Independent Activity time, Play time or Activity time.

6 Reflect and Respond

Reflect and Respond is an activity that teaches students the language needed to review and reflect on learning. It can take place at the end of a lesson or the end of the day. Teachers will need to introduce the purpose for this activity through modelling and guiding questions with the whole class. The ultimate aim is for students to use the language of reflecting and responding in pairs or small groups.

Involve students in reflecting by asking questions or prompting, e.g. **What are the important things that we have learned in this lesson (this morning, today)? Tell me about an activity that was fun today. Tell me how you used words to sort out a problem today.**

Expand on answers that students give. Remind them of important points if they don't remember, e.g. **We found out something important about insects today. Can anyone remember? I noticed that James and Shelley had fun in the sandpit today. Tell us what happened? Zac was feeling sad when the other boys wouldn't share the blocks. Tell us what you said to solve your problem, Zac.**

This activity is suitable for all phases.

How Might This Activity Be Used in Your Class?

Encourage participation by sitting students in a circle. Provide a toy microphone or another object to hold. This will encourage students to take turns.

CONTEXTUAL UNDERSTANDING

Major Teaching Emphases

- **Discuss ways in which particular spoken texts are suitable for different audiences,** e.g. conversations with adults or with peers during outdoor play.

- **Provide explicit feedback to students who are adjusting their speaking and listening,** e.g. when they are talking in small groups/to teachers.

- **Help students recognise where background and supporting information are needed when speaking.**

- **Provide support for students to recognise how they can contribute to discussions.**

- **Provide opportunities for students to analyse the meaning of spoken texts.**

- **Support students to recognise how simple devices improve speaking and listening in different contexts,** e.g. volume, simile, rhyme, common sayings.

Teaching Notes

The focus for supporting Early Speakers and Listeners in this aspect is organised under the following headings:

- Understandings About Context
- Providing Feedback
- Considering the Needs of the Audience
- Contributing to Matters of Importance
- Exploring the Way Ideas and People Are Represented
- Use of Devices

Understandings About Context

In this phase, it is essential that students continue to develop their awareness of the way in which speaking and listening is influenced by the context — audience, purpose, situation and topic. Discussions in this phase focus on ways particular spoken texts are suitable for different audiences. Students learn about appropriate speaking and listening conventions for different contexts. Analysing and Reflecting are ideal teaching practices for teaching students to develop understandings about the way in which speaking and listening changes according to the purpose and the audience. In the Early phase, students will benefit from opportunities to make appropriate speaking and listening choices in Playing and Applying sessions. (See the *Linking Assessment, Teaching and Learning* book for Analysing p. 130, Reflecting p. 140, Playing p. 134, and Applying p. 132.)

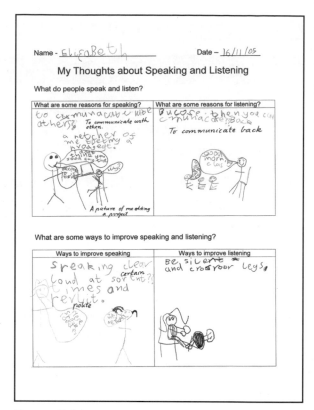

Figure 5.16

Providing Feedback

Teachers' knowledge and understanding of students' language development will develop over time, through ongoing interactions in a range of different situations.

Teachers may use focused observation schedules to guide their monitoring of individual students' language development (over time). This will ensure that information is gathered for each student in the class in a systematic way. See the Speaking and Listening CD-ROM, Early Phase: Contextual Understanding for the parent/caregiver survey sheets.

The feedback provided by teachers values and builds the students' own language use. As students will still be learning ways to adjust their speaking and listening for school purposes, teachers can provide feedback in the following ways:
• Focus on the message, not the way it has been conveyed.
• Use questions that show a genuine interest in what the student wants and needs to communicate.

- Acknowledge feelings, e.g. I can see that you are annoyed. You sound really happy about that.
- Use wait time before offering support, as students may be able to work out the meaning together. Give positive comments.
- Refer to class decisions about speaking and listening, e.g. We decided we would walk across to people when we needed to speak to them. Our class decided that we would have one person talking at a time in a group.
- Use positive statements when students alter their speaking and listening, e.g. I noticed that you changed your voice when you came to the group. I can see that you are facing me and nodding as you listen to me.

Considering the Needs of the Audience

Early Speakers and Listeners interact in ways that make sense to themselves and require guidance in considering the needs of their audience. Modelled, Shared and Guided Speaking and Listening are ideal practices for teaching students for doing this. Teachers can also provide direction, responses and questioning to support students, drawing their attention to appropriate verbal and non-verbal language, as shown below:

- Tell your partner something you think they will like to hear.
- What will your dad need to know when you tell him how you made the boat?
- What do you think the principal would like to hear about?
- What do you think your partner liked listening to?
- How will we show that we are interested in what our partner has to say?
- You pointed to the signs in the room so your mum knew what you were talking about.
- What do we need to do when someone is talking to the whole class?

Figure 5.17

Contributing to Matters of Importance

Early Speakers and Listeners need daily opportunities to contribute to matters that are of personal interest. When students are discussing topics that matter to them, their contributions will be meaningful and they are more likely to engage in extended conversations. These opportunities help students to develop their abilities to express ideas, opinions and feelings.

Explorative talk about frogs becoming extinct. Overlapping is occurring in some sections.

Elizabeth:	Frogs are going to get extinct, so I wanna walk to school.
Teacher:	Oh, I see.
Joshua:	It's too long to walk to school.
Elizabeth:	I know it's too long but … I still want to.
Joshua:	You'll be late.
Elizabeth:	Well, I'll go early.
Joshua:	What, what if stuff happens to you like … ?
Elizabeth:	My mum and dad will come to me and robbers don't usually come when adults are around.
Joshua:	Your mum and dad aren't gonna walk you there.
Elizabeth:	Well, they might, they might, Joshua, don't butt in, they might, they might, they really might do it. It's OK … If frogs were gonna get extinct before I'm big and leave my mum, well, I'm gonna be really sad because, I wanna be old enough to get a reptile licence …
Joshua:	Frogs aren't called reptiles.
Elizabeth:	Well, what are they?
Joshua:	Amphibians.
Elizabeth:	A-m-ph-i-b-i-a-n-s.

Figure 5.18 Transcript of two students discussing topic knowledge about frogs

Teachers can support students in the following ways:
- Negotiate with students and invite their ideas and opinions when planning, reviewing and organising tasks within the classroom.
- Have open-ended tasks which provide students with choices about topics and materials.
- Provide effective feedback when students do talk about matters of personal interest.
- Include sessions such as Class Meetings, What Shall I Do Today? and Time for Talk in daily timetables.
- Have displays which capture students' interest and invite discussion.
- Allow students to create and share their own displays. Make free time for students to play in the science, dress-up and the writing areas.

Exploring the Way Ideas and People Are Represented

Early Speakers and Listeners will need support in developing understandings that ideas and people can be represented in different ways in spoken texts. A range of electronic spoken texts are available to use for discussions of how people and ideas have been represented in particular ways. These include CD-ROMs, film, television and audio recordings of spoken texts such as stories, recounts, advertisements and reports. It is also possible to record some of the spoken texts within the school and classroom to use as a starting point for discussion. Students' discussions in this area in reading and writing will also support the development of this understanding. Early Speakers and Listeners will benefit from Analysing, Reflecting and Discussion sessions that focus on the following kinds of questions:

- Why do you think it was explained in that way? How would you explain it?
- How did it make you feel about the ideas or people as you listened? Who might like the way the ideas or people are shown in this? Why? Who might not?
- Do you think these things are true about the ideas or people? Why?
- Does that make sense?
- Does it sound right? Why?
- What interesting words have been used?
- What body language has been used? Did you see any body language that you use, too?
- What would be another way to say this about that idea or person?

Use of Devices

Early Speakers and Listeners benefit from ongoing discussions about how verbal and non-verbal behaviours convey meaning. Teachers explicitly model and guide students to recognise how simple devices improve speaking and listening in different contexts. The focus for Early Speakers and Listeners includes:

- Body position, e.g. proximity dependent on relationship between the people and the situation (social, personal, public).
- Affective displays, e.g. facial expression (showing pleasure, surprise, anger, pain, etc.)
- Eye contact, e.g. how the listener encourages the conversation or terminates it; how the speaker seeks feedback and reinforcement.
- Prosodic features, e.g. volume (pace and intonation of speech when reciting rhymes and poems) in contrast to the volume and articulation commonly used in the playground, classroom and school situations.

For further information about the Contextual Understanding aspect, see Chapter 2: Contextual Understanding, *Speaking and Listening Resource Book*, 2nd Edition. For further information on the teaching and learning practices referred to in this section, see Chapter 7: *Linking Assessment, Teaching and Learning*.

Involving Students

1 Act It Out

Act It Out is a small-group activity designed to give students time to imagine and practise what they will say and do in different situations. It allows them to discuss the information they need to include and to try ways to improve the effectiveness of their speaking and listening. It is usually initiated with adult support; however, once students become familiar with the routine, they may do it independently with a partner or in a small group. It could be included as part of What Shall I Do Today? (See Chapter 4: Beginning Speaking and Listening, p. 71.)

To perform the activity, a set of cards with different scenarios is required so each group can 'act out' a scenario. (See the Speaking and Listening CD-ROM, Beginning Phase: Contextual Understanding for a sample set of scenario cards.) Alternatively, teachers could design their own sets of cards. If the whole class is doing the activity at the same time, each group will need a set of cards as well as an adult to support the students with the guiding questions.

- Model the following process with a student as the other actor.
- Pick a card and discuss these questions:
  - What is happening here? How do we know?
  - What could have happened before this? Why do we think that?
  - What could happen after? Why do we think that?
  - What will we say and do so everyone understands what we mean?
  - How could we say this so it sounds like the talk we use at school?
  - What will we do to show we understand what has been said?
- Decide who will act out which parts.
- Decide where the action will start — before, during or after the event on the card.
- Try acting it out.
- Reflect and discuss these questions: What made sense? Why? Where else could we listen like this? Where else could we speak like this? What would we say differently next time? Why?

This activity is also suitable for all phases.

How Might This Activity Be Used in Your Class?

- Consider the focus areas in your class. The scenarios could come from your observations of the students or from issues that are raised at class meetings.
- Record some of the sentence starters that students use in other classroom sessions.
- Use some photographs of students in your class as starting points, e.g. **students standing near the pile of blocks at packing-away time.**
- Students could be filmed and then view the tape or their talk could be recorded and replayed to prompt their thinking in the reflection section of the activity.

2 Who Can I Talk to? Who Can I Listen to? How Do I Do It?

This activity helps students to reflect on the ways they speak and listen for different audiences. It asks them to think about the people they interact with and to think about why they choose particular topics for different audiences.

Students make pictures of the people they listen and talk to. They then sort the pictures according to a set criteria; cards that are similar in some way, e.g. **people who tell me what to do, people who listen to me when I am sad.**

Teachers can organise the criteria depending on their students' needs. The criteria are recorded on cards. This activity is led by the teacher and is best performed as a small-group activity but could be done by the whole class or individually.

- Model the following steps with the students first.
- Invite students to make pictures of the people they speak and listen to. Prompt them by asking questions such as: How many people could you think of? Have you thought of people in school and at home?
- Discuss the people using the following framework:
  When I talk to my mum, I… When I listen to my friend, I…
- Introduce the sorting criteria. Start with two phrases, e.g. **People who ask me questions. People who talk to me on the phone. People who talk to me when they see I am lonely. People who speak to me in another language. People who listen to my ideas for outside play. People I talk to about trucks/birds/home…** Write the phrases on cards and place them into hoops or onto a large chart.
- Have students sort the people into the criteria.
- Ask students to explain or give an example of the people they choose, e.g. **I talk to my grandma on the phone because she lives in**

109

another city. Sarah saw me when I was lonely and started talking to me.

– Store the pictures into an envelope or container to use later.

– Repeat the activity several weeks later. Ask questions, e.g. **Have you been talking and listening to anybody new? Have you been talking about or listening to any new topics?**

This activity is also suitable for the Exploratory Phase.

How Might This Activity Be Used in Your Class?

• Use photographs and create a display.
• Give the criteria to the students first.
• Your class might draw the pictures and sort them according to their own criteria, e.g. **People I like listening to and people I talk to every day.**

3 Personality Phones

Refer to Chapter 4: Beginning Speaking and Listening Phase, p. 69. See the Speaking and Listening CD-ROM, Early Phase: Contextual Understanding for a sample phone list.

Figure 5.19

How Might This Activity Be Used in Your Class?

• Students can select characters and situations.
• Consider how to link the activity to writing.
• The personalities could be fluffy toys or puppets.
• The frameworks developed for the What Comes Next? section in The Use of Texts activity could be left near the phones for students to use.

4 Exploring Speaking and Listening

Exploring Speaking and Listening is an activity designed to support students in recognising how speaking and listening needs to change to suit a particular context. Prepare a recording of a spoken text. This may be a segment from a children's television show, a video recording of assembly or an audio recording of students working in a group. Decide what the focus of the lesson will be. For example, students may listen to and discuss:

- the way a speaker adjusts their volume when indoors, outdoors, talking to one person or talking to a group.
- the type of listening that is occurring, e.g. **are people listening for information so they will know when to clap or ask a question?**
- when it is the right time to talk and the right time to be quiet.
- the types of words that people may use with friends or when talking to an adult.
- the words people are using to be friendly and to share fairly.

(See the Speaking and Listening CD-ROM, Early Phase: Contextual Understanding, Exploring Speaking and Listening framework.)

This activity is also suitable for the Exploratory phase.

How Might This Activity Be Used in Your Class?

- Include a session each week as part of your timetable.
- Use this activity prior to a visitor coming in to show something to the whole class.
- Introduce the activity before and after the class goes to the school assembly, using a spoken text from a previous assembly.
- Try doing sections of the activity as small groups, then sharing ideas as a class group to make a summary.
- Keep a chart or book called *Things We Know About Speaking and Listening* to record main ideas and summary statements.

Teacher:	Why do we listen?
Student:	'Cos if someone tried to tell you something, if they were doing something, they would need to explain.
Teacher:	Why do we talk?
Student:	So you can communicate.
Teacher:	What does that mean?
Student:	Um ... it's like when you're on the telephone, you speak to each other and hear each other, too.

Figure 5.20 Transcript of student discussing speaking and listening with a teacher

5 Class Meetings

Class Meetings help to develop language needed to express a point of view, negotiate and arrive at decisions. Students also develop understandings about taking turns. Meeting procedures will vary according to the needs of the class. However, there are some common features which include a person to 'chair' the meeting, time to review previous decisions and an agenda of new items to discuss. Suggested steps for meetings are as follows.

- Students sit in a circle so that everyone can be seen.
- The teacher takes on the role of 'chairperson' when first introducing the meeting procedure. Another adult may model the process of taking minutes.
- Discussions from previous meetings are reviewed.
- Agenda items are introduced. It is best to limit items for young students (two or three is enough).
- Discuss items.
- Record the decisions that are made on a class chart.
- Decide on a way to end the meeting, e.g. **by reviewing the decisions made, reinforcing appropriate meeting behaviours.**

To develop students' ability to participate in meetings, teachers will need to:
- Teach students how to express their points of view, supporting them with words and phrases that may be needed. Students should use neutral language, e.g. **I think that it is dangerous when other people don't stack the blocks carefully on the shelf.**
- Teach ways of making decisions, e.g. **take a vote or trial an idea.**

How Might This Activity Be Used in Your Class?

- Keep a book to record the 'minutes'.
- Speakers may hold a 'microphone'.
- At certain times of the meeting, hold a round so each person has an opportunity to speak about an item. Students may say 'pass' in a round.
- Think about when the class meetings will be held; once a week, once a fortnight, or as issues arise.
- Consider the assessments you could keep throughout the class meetings, e.g. **contribution of ideas, building on ideas, expressing opinions, raising issues/matters to discuss, etc.**

CONVENTIONS

Major Teaching Emphases

■ **Provide opportunities for students to develop and use new vocabulary.**

■ **Model language structures and features to suit the purpose,** e.g. recount an experience using time order, checking on listener's understanding, adding supporting detail, give explanations using conjunctions, if, then, and, because.

■ **Model the skills of conversation.**

■ **Teach speaking and listening behaviours that support meaning making,** e.g. asking clarifying questions, seeking confirmation, providing sufficient detail.

■ **Model and discuss agreed ways to respond to spoken texts in school,** e.g. when and how to take turns.

Teaching Notes

Teaching and Learning experiences for students in the Early phase are organised under the following headings:
• Building Vocabulary
• Understanding the Conventions of Spoken Texts
• Understanding Behaviours Associated with Speaking and Listening
• Understanding the Conventions of Listening

Building Vocabulary

Students in the Early phase develop vocabulary when they are involved in a range of learning experiences, discussions and conversations with adults and older students. It is important that teachers elaborate on conversations and explain new vocabulary. Students can be supported to develop their vocabulary in the following ways.
• Jointly construct charts of interesting words, unusual or favourite words. (These may come from stories, games, television, movies, songs, etc.)
• Value and build on student's home language.
• Model choice of words for different purposes
• Introduce subject-specific language and provide opportunities for students to explore and use new vocabulary. Add charts of words to learning centres or displays.

- Provide experiences through activities outside the classroom that will introduce new vocabulary for an authentic purpose, e.g. excursions.

Understanding the Conventions of Spoken Texts

The conventions of speaking refer to the language and behaviours that are expected in particular contexts. Conventions can be described in terms of the *structure* and the *language features* of a spoken text.

The *structure* of spoken text refers to the way ideas, feelings or communication are linked in the text. For example:
- turn-taking in a conversation
- making an apology
- introducing people.

The *language features* of a spoken text refer to the type of vocabulary, grammar, tone and pace chosen. For example:
- using colloquial words or sayings when conversing with friends
- using emotive language to persuade, such as referring to language used in an advertisement
- stressing certain words or altering volume to gain impact.

Teachers can involve students in a variety of experiences that will develop their understanding of the structure and features of spoken texts.
- Introduce chants and rhymes so students can explore the repetitive structures of these texts.
- Use audio or video tapes to focus on the structures and features of a spoken text.
- Model the use of conjunctions when speaking to include details, e.g. model a description of how something was made using the conjunctions because, and, if, etc.
- Model the use of the correct tense.
- Involve students in retelling stories or events to encourage sequencing, giving supportive details or by giving descriptions.
- Draw attention to the different structures and features of speech used for different purposes and for different audiences (see Figure 5.21).

Purpose	What Choices Do We Make?
Request information.	What tone of voice should be used, e.g. friendly, serious, polite?
Ask a question.	What words should be chosen?
Relay a message.	How loud should our voices be?
Describe an object.	How can we start off what we want to say?
Recount an experience.	How can we organise what we want to say in the best order?
Greet or farewell a visitor.	When should we slow down our speech?
Tell a joke.	
Ask someone to stop doing something.	

Figure 5.21

Conversations

Conversations are important in establishing and maintaining relationships through expressing feelings and sharing experiences. It is through conversations that we give and receive information and compare ideas. This type of unplanned speaking and listening not only develops self-awareness and interpersonal skills; it helps to build topic knowledge and develops processes for learning. Teachers can provide opportunities for students to engage in uninterrupted, sustained conversations by:

• modelling conversations.

• allowing students to converse about topics of personal interest.

• providing time each day to allow for conversations.

• encouraging conversations in response to books, movies, visitors or events.

• encouraging students to participate in conversations with students and adults from other areas of the school.

• teaching students ways to maintain and extend conversations, e.g. model ways to respond to questions by adding details.

• allowing students time to respond to a question or a conversational comment. This allows students to think through a response.

Understanding Behaviours Associated with Speaking and Listening

Students need to be aware of the behaviours associated with speaking and listening and how they affect meaningful communication in a variety of contexts. Teachers can involve students in choosing appropriate speaking and listening behaviours through modelling, explicit teaching and discussion. Joint construction of Y charts or T charts where students identify effective behaviours will provide meaningful reminders for them. Teachers

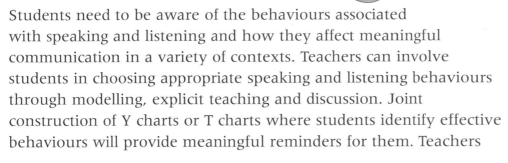

115

could involve students in reflecting on what they know about speaking and listening before commencing a series of teaching and learning activities. It is valuable to take time later to stop and ask students to record their reflections on what they have learned as a result of engaging in a series of activities. See the Speaking and Listening CD-ROM, Early Phase: Conventions, for an example of a Before and After recording sheet.

The following list may provide some useful suggestions for students when discussing effective behaviours.

- Speak clearly and with enough volume so that everyone in the audience can hear and understand.
- Use body language when speaking, e.g. appropriate eye contact, proximity of speaker and listener, facial expression, gestures.
- Behave appropriately when part of an audience, e.g. when listening to the teacher, when listening to another student, at assembly, at the theatre or a concert.
- Take turns in a discussion.
- Make sure everyone has a turn in a group.
- Include someone joining the group after a conversation has begun.
- Be aware of the language required when joining or leaving a game.
- Express likes and dislikes sensitively.
- Interrupt appropriately when adults are talking, peers are talking or when an urgent matter arises, e.g. wait for a pause in the conversation, then say, 'Excuse me. I'm sorry to interrupt, but ...'

Elizabeth:	I learned at post office today that, um... there, um... they had their own key to open the box, I thought that anyone could just open it by going 'ping'.
Oscar:	I learned that they have big boxes, small boxes, and medium-size boxes.
Elizabeth:	The person that was there was called Rad. Now it's your turn.
Oscar:	I had a lot of fun at the post office, and we got to put our stamps on our envelopes.
Elizabeth:	I felt happy because I got to send a letter to my grandma.
Danny:	Don't say anything else.
Oscar:	I was happy because I felt proud at myself and I felt really happy.
Elizabeth:	And just then, I didn't like it when Danny interrupted us.
Oscar:	I didn't like it then when Danny interrupted us.
Elizabeth:	We saw stamps with cockies on 'em, on them, and I had a yellow envelope.

Figure 5.22 Transcript of young students expressing their feelings about being interrupted

Understanding the Conventions of Listening

Listening is an active, constructive process concerned with making meaning from verbal and non-verbal cues. Effective listening depends on the expectations and predictions about content, language and genre that the listener brings to the text (Gibbons 2002). The way in which people listen is also linked to the context of the communication. People listen differently during unplanned, spontaneous situations, (for example, in casual conversations) than they do when speaking and listening is planned and formal, (for example, in the classroom when instructions are being given). Teachers can assist students to become familiar with and use the conventions of listening in some of the following ways:

- Model and discuss ways to respond to spoken texts in the classroom, e.g. taking turns during Think, Pair, Share; taking turns during a class discussion.
- Provide time for students to engage in conversations.
- Model active listening, e.g. repeat phrases in order to clarify meaning.
- Provide opportunities for students to listen to and discuss speech constructed for different purposes.
- Provide opportunities for students to respond to spoken texts, e.g.
  - retelling a favourite part of a story
  - through drawing, painting, sculpting
  - joining in and remembering songs, chants and poems
  - responding to requests
  - following directions
  - responding to questions
  - listening for key words and ideas
  - commenting on another person's ideas.

Involving Students

1 Picture Talk

Picture Talk activities help to build vocabulary and provide opportunities for students to practise the structures and features of spoken language. They could be used to practise description, procedures, recounts or narratives. Prepare pictures to suit your purpose. They could be from magazines, postcards, commercial posters or photographs taken in and around the school.

In the Early phase, the activity might focus on describing a scene, e.g. What can you see in the picture? Why have the people come to this place? What happened before? What will happen after? How are they feeling?

This activity is also suitable for the Beginning, Exploratory, Consolidating and Conventional phases.

How Might This Activity Be Used in Your Class?

- Choose pictures to help tell a narrative. Ask questions, e.g. What happened in the beginning? What happened in the middle? Was there some trouble? What happened in the end? Students could work in pairs or small groups to compose a narrative. This could then be shared with a larger group.

- Take photographs of students as they construct models, cook or create a work of art. They could then build a talk around the photograph, relating the procedure used to accomplish a activity. Model the process and allow students plenty of time to rehearse before sharing.

- Build subject-specific vocabulary related to Learning Areas by taking photographs, adding labels and encouraging students to use the words when explaining or describing. For example, take photographs during a maths or science lesson and make charts to emphasise.

2 Sorting and Classifying Activities

The Sorting and Classifying activities help to develop students' vocabulary to describe objects and their attributes. Students learn the features of descriptive language and develop the ability to structure their talk effectively by describing similarities and differences. A simple version of a Sorting Activity is described in the Beginning Phase (see p. 76).

Model the process of sorting objects into two groups. Emphasise the importance of precise descriptions and use of vocabulary. Model the process of naming the groups and justifying the classification.

Provide a selection of items and ask students to make two groups. Exclude those items that do not fit the selected criteria. Invite students to name the groups and explain 'the sorting rule', e.g. these are all the big shells; these are all the small shells; these materials are rough; these materials are smooth.

This activity is also suitable for the Early, Exploratory and Consolidating phases.

How Might This Activity Be Used in Your Class?

Use in a maths or science lesson to sort and classify shapes.

3 Guessing Games

Guessing Games develop vocabulary and the structures and features of description. They encourage students to use language accurately and provide an effective listening focus for other students in the group.

Prepare a 'feely bag' where students can put their hand inside to feel something that other students cannot see. Model the game until students understand how it is played.

Link the game to a story or topic that the students have been immersed in, e.g. **put a toy train in the bag after discussing the topic of transport.** Describe the features and invite the students to guess what is in the bag.

This activity is also suitable for the Exploratory phase.

How Might This Activity Be Used in Your Class?

Link the game to a Learning Area, e.g. **attribute blocks for maths** or a topic such as investigating toys or tools.

4 Comparison Activities

Comparison Activities develop vocabulary and promote the need to structure observations clearly and precisely. These activities can be done in pairs and can be linked to a unit of work being developed. A suggestion for a comparison activity is as follows. Students choose to draw a picture on the same topic, e.g. **a spaceship, their ideal bedroom, a monster.** The students create their drawings independently. The students then compare their drawings and discuss the similarities and differences, e.g. **Mine is the same as yours. Where? Mine is different to yours where you used… But I used…**

This activity is also suitable for the Exploratory Phase.

How Might This Activity Be Used in Your Class?

• Ask students to construct models from Lego™, blocks or other materials.
• Link this activity to a unit of work so that students can practise and develop new vocabulary.

Ask the partners to share their findings with a larger group or the whole class. In this way they have prepared a planned talk and have the opportunity to share with a different audience.

5 Telephone Talk

Telephone Talk develops understanding of the structures and features of telephone conversations. Organise an area where

119

students can use old phones and take messages.

Teachers model a situation that relates to a current unit of work, e.g. a restaurant may be set up in the classroom and students will role play ordering food or making a reservation. Teachers will model answering the phone, saying a greeting, repeating an order, ending a conversation and writing messages.

How Might This Activity Be Used in Your Class?

- Involve students in discussions about when, where and why people use the phone.
- Discuss the important nature of emergency calls. Teach students how to make an emergency call, giving essential details, e.g. name and address.

6 What Did You See? (Gibbons 2002)

What Did You See? is a memory game that enables students to practise their vocabulary. It could be played with a small group or the whole class. Place objects or pictures relating to a topic on a table. After students have looked at them for a few moments, cover the objects with a cloth and see how many objects the students can remember.

This activity is also suitable for the Exploratory and Consolidating phases.

How Might This Activity Be Used in Your Class?

- Relate this game to a science topic, e.g. equipment such as magnifying glass, thermometer, measuring jugs, scales, ruler, stopwatch, etc. This will help to reinforce vocabulary that may be needed for a unit of work.
- Extend this game by taking one object away when students are not looking. Ask students to name the missing item and ask them to explain how they knew it was missing.

7 My Grandma Went Shopping

Refer to Chapter 4: Beginning Speaking and Listening Phase, p. 78. This activity is also suitable for the Exploratory phase.

How Might This Activity Be Used in Your Class?

- Change the type of shop to support a unit of work, e.g. fruit and vegetable shop, post office, toy shop.
- Change the destination of the game, e.g. our family went camping and took …

8 Take a Turn

There are many activities that develop behaviours relating to taking turns. Knowing when to be quiet and listening to another person is a valuable social as well as learning skill. There are some students who tend to dominate the talk in a classroom and who need encouragement to include all members of the group. These activities also encourage reluctant or shy speakers as they participate in a supportive, non-threatening environment.

Conversation Web

Students sit in a circle. The teacher introduces a ball of string and a topic for discussion. The ball of string will be thrown about the circle as students indicate their willingness to take a turn to speak. At the end of the conversation, each student will be holding on to a piece of string and a web-like pattern will have been formed. Teachers could use the Conversation Web to discuss a class issue, to brainstorm ideas, to give opinions relating to literature or to share responses to a recent event.

This activity could be adapted at the beginning of the year to play a Getting to Know You game. The teacher throws the string to a student who says their name and something about themselves; they throw it to another student and so on until everyone has had a turn.

Use the activity to reinforce the use of eye contact. Before you throw the ball of string, say the person's name, make eye contact, and then throw the ball.

The Talking Stick

The Talking Stick could be any kind of prop — a toy microphone, a magic wand, a ball or a block. It allows only one person to speak at a time — the person holding the Talking Stick.

Teachers could use the talking stick as a way to include all students in a group. Debrief after the activity by asking, **Was it easier to talk when you knew that you would have a turn? Did you feel more confident knowing that everyone would be listening to you?**

Teachers could develop the concept of *building onto the ideas of others* by using the Talking Stick and modelling the language needed to acknowledge what another person has said and to build onto that.

The Magic Rock

The Magic Rock is an activity to help shy or reluctant speakers. Work with small groups of students of mixed abilities. Introduce the rock as having magical powers that help people say what is in their mind. Model the process. Support and encourage reluctant speakers, noticing the positive behaviours they display, e.g. **good volume, eye contact with other members of the group or interesting ideas.**

Inside/Outside Circle

This is a versatile activity that can be used from discussing issues to choosing partners for an activity. Form two circles, one within the other. The students in the inner circle turn and face the students in the outer circle. The numbers should be even. Nominate either the inside or the outside circle to do the moving, e.g. **students in the inside circle, raise your right arm. Now move to your right until you reach the third person. This person is your partner.**

Teachers then nominate students from one circle to be the speakers and the others to be the listeners. After a nominated time the roles will be swapped.

Use Inside/Outside Circle to recount a recent event or to explain a recent topic, e.g. **how the water cycle works, how you solved a maths problem, your opinion of the new school uniform.**

These activities are suitable for all phases in a modified version.

How Might These Activities Be Used in Your Class?

• What are the skills that you need to explicitly teach and model? Use these activities as opportunities to highlight certain skills and then to practise them.
• Jointly construct class charts to act as reminders. Engage the students in reflection time so that they can monitor their own progress and the progress of the group.

Figure 5.23

9 Generic Games

There are many common games that can be used to support an understanding of the conventions of spoken language. Refer to *First Steps Reading Map of Development*, 2nd Edition, and *First Steps Writing Map of Development*, 2nd Edition, for descriptions of games.

10 What Can You Hear?

Refer to Chapter 4: Beginning Speaking and Listening Phase, p. 77.

How Might This Activity Be Used in Your Class?

- Incorporate this activity when on a class excursion.
- Visit a local park and use as an introduction to a science topic on frogs, insects or birds.
- Use as an introduction to a Society and Environment topic on people-made, nature-made environments.
- Make charts of words when you return to the classroom; these can be referred to and practised as your unit of work develops. Add digital photographs as a reminder of the experience.
- Use this activity as a means to gather data when on an excursion to the shopping centre, post office, airport, etc.
- Ask students to reflect on this type of listening. How was this listening different? Was this listening difficult or easy? Why?

11 Barrier Games

Barrier Games are simple procedures based on giving and receiving instructions. They require students to interact and use language to complete an activity. Students develop a range of language skills depending on the complexity of the game. Speakers learn the importance of giving explicit and complete information to listeners. Listeners learn the importance of monitoring information and using questions to clarify or gain further information. Vocabulary related to the language of description is also developed; e.g. **students begin to use a variety of nouns, attributes and location words.**

Barrier games can be bought commercially or can be easily produced using a wide variety of formats and materials. The game is played in pairs and there is some type of 'barrier' so that the students cannot see what their partner is doing.

Introduce the game through modelling the type of language needed. To begin with, students could observe two adults playing or an adult and student playing. Teachers should 'catch' students who are using language effectively to model the game for other students.

Types of Barrier Games

Sequencing or Pattern Making

Describe successive items in an array or sequence such as bead threading, using attribute blocks or toys.

Matching Pairs

Students take turns to describe objects or pictures. One player describes an item until the other student locates and displays its matching pair. The process is repeated until all items are paired.

Assembly

Assemble pictures or objects from a choice of component parts, e.g. **use shapes to build a picture.** One player describes the picture and the other assembles the shapes to make the same picture.

Construction

One player describes the steps in building a particular construction, e.g. **using blocks.** The other player follows the steps and builds the same construction.

Location

Students choose and place items in relation to each other on a picture board. One player describes the location of the objects to be placed on the picture. The other player listens, follows the directions and places the objects in the same locations.

Grids

Students describe the position of marker objects on a grid, e.g. **one player places attribute blocks on a 3 x 3 grid and describes the position of each block.** The other player follows the directions and places the blocks in the same positions.

Mapping

One player describes how to get from one point on a map to a specified location. The listener draws the route on a corresponding map.

Spot the Difference

Give pairs of students several pictures that vary in small details. The students describe their pictures to each other and identify the differences. Students could create pictures or maps for 'spot the difference'. Photocopy a picture and alter some of the details.

12 Role Plays

Role plays provide students with opportunities to extend their language repertoire by providing opportunities to experience

various situations in a supportive environment. They are useful in exploring speaking situations where students may not be confident.

Discuss ways to include people and ways of politely refusing a request. Model the types of things that could be said. Discuss the tone of voice needed. Jointly construct charts to record prompts that students could use to initiate speaking. After brainstorming, assign roles and allow students to act out the scene. See Figure 5.24 for examples. Also refer to the Speaking and Listening CD-ROM, Exploratory Phase: Conventions, for scenario cards.

Scenario	Things to Say (Example)
Sam is eating lunch on his own because his best friend is away. He wants to join another group.	*'Hi (say names)'. 'Can I sit with you today?'* Use names, keep voice friendly.
John wants to join a game of handball with Emma and Ben. How should he ask? What should Emma and Ben say?	*'Hi Emma and Ben, could I play, too?'* *'We're just finishing this game, then you can play.'* *'John, we're playing the best out of three so we won't be finished for a while.'* Use names, keep voice friendly. Give short explanations.
Jan has arrived at school late and has missed the first part of a sharing circle. How can the other group members help her to feel included?	*'Hi everyone. Sorry I'm late.'* *'Hi Jan. Sally has just been telling us about her dancing class last night. They are going to put on a concert. You can have a turn after Dan.'* Jan joins the group quickly. The others tell her what is happening and how she can join in.

Figure 5.24 Role play scenarios

How Might This Activity Be Used in Your Class?

- Role plays can be related to the functions of spoken language (see Chapter 1).
- Use role plays to explore issues that students may experience in the playground or in the classroom.

13 Watch Your Tone

Watch Your Tone focuses on tone of voice and provides an opportunity for students to develop an understanding of tone and pitch variation. The teacher models the process by taking a phrase, saying it and then repeating it using a different tone of voice. For example try saying *'Come here, please'* as if you have a treat to give, and then try saying it in a frustrated tone of voice. Ask the students to suggest the meaning behind the words in each example. Students could record their responses through drawings, speech bubbles and captions. See the Speaking and Listening CD-ROM, Early Phase: Conventions (Watch Your Tone).

How Might This Activity Be Used in Your class?

- The use of tone may be interpreted differently due to social, cultural or individual differences. Discuss the use of tone sensitively to develop an understanding of the attitudes held by students.
- Ask students to repeat phrases using different tones of voice, e.g. **angry, surprised, curious, sad, happy,** etc. Try using whispers and loud voices.
- Invite students to reflect on the times they have noticed that the *tone* in someone's voice 'speaks louder' than the words.
- Ask students to reflect on how they can use tone to improve their communication.

14 Body Talk

Body Talk promotes the awareness of what attentive listening looks like and why it is important in particular contexts. It may provide a springboard into making class agreements on how students should behave when attentive listening is expected. Teachers could involve students in making charts as reminders.

Make a set of cards with words that describe behaviour, e.g. **fidgeting, looking around, mumbling to yourself, yawning and stretching, rocking back and forth,** etc. See the Speaking and Listening CD-ROM, Exploratory Phase: Conventions (Looking at Body Language, Investigating Body Language) for an example of cards.

Students work in pairs. The whole class could participate or a teacher may choose one pair to demonstrate the process for the rest of the class.

The speaker will be asked to talk about something familiar, e.g. **to describe a recent event.** The listener is given a card telling them how to behave.

Allow the activity to continue for about thirty seconds. Stop the class and debrief the activity by asking guiding questions, e.g. Speaker: How did you feel when... (listener) was fidgeting, looking around...

Listener: Were you able to understand... (speaker) when you were fidgeting, looking around...

Have students brainstorm behaviours that would assist communication. Discuss the contexts when attentive listening is expected. Ask them to role play these new behaviours and discuss the different effects. Students could record their findings in a journal.

How Might This Activity Be Used in Your Class?

Discuss different types of listening. When is it appropriate to be listening and doing something else at the same time?

15 Analyse a Video

Analyse a Video draws attention to body language and the way it assists communication.

Prepare a small segment of a video that students will be familiar with and that shows two or three people involved in a conversation. Ask the students to watch the video *without* any sound. Students can predict what the conversation might be about. Allow them time to think and discuss with a partner.

Share ideas with the whole class, highlighting the cues that were taken from the body language. Now watch the video with the sound on and compare it to the predictions made.

How close were the students in predicting content? Were they able to detect emotions? Was anyone correct with predicted words? Students could record their findings in a journal using drawings and labels.

This activity is also suitable for the Exploratory, Consolidating, Conventional and Proficient phases.

How Might This Activity Be Used in Your Class?

Appoint a student to observe body language in a group discussion. Ask: What body language could be seen? How did it help a person to make their message clear?

16 Zoom

Zoom allows students to develop an understanding of appropriate eye contact when speaking and listening in particular contexts, e.g. to show attention, to gain attention or to get a turn in a conversation. This game gives students an opportunity to practise the use of eye contact.

Students sit in a circle. One person starts and decides on a direction. The student says the word 'zoom' and the person in the nominated direction repeats the word. This continues until the word has travelled around the circle.

In the next round, eye contact and first names are used, e.g. Sally starts and says 'zoom Vicki', making eye contact. Vicki turns to the next person and says 'zoom John', and so on.

How Might This Activity Be Used in Your Class?

Any word or action can be used. Instead of a word, try a short clapping pattern.

Links to Other First Steps Materials

The following activities will also support the development of Early Speakers and Listeners:

Writing Map of Development, Personal Alphabet Chart, p. 78; Generic Games, p, 80.

Reading Map of Development, Word Walls, p. 125; Word Back Spied Her, p. 127; Word-Sorting Activities, p. 128; Innovation on Repetitive Sentence Patterns, p. 129; Share and Compare, p. 139.

PROCESSES AND STRATEGIES

Major Teaching Emphases

- **Model thinking aloud about the selection of appropriate speaking and listening strategies.**

- **Encourage students to verbalise own thinking.**

- **Provide opportunities for students to engage in conversations for specific purposes,** e.g. to socialise, to get things done.

- **Teach simple planing tools for speaking,** e.g. plan recounts that orientate the listener, plan how …

- **Teach simple planning tools to help students gain a listening focus,** e.g. use drawings to respond to listening, listen for specific information.

- **Model strategies to adjust communication,** e.g. self-correct to clarify meaning, rephrase if not understood.

Organisation of the Processes and Strategies Aspect

There are several differences in the organisation of the Processes and Strategies aspect. Both the Teaching Notes and the Teaching and Learning Experiences (Involving Students) are in the *Speaking and Listening Resource Book*, 2nd Edition, Chapter 4: Processes and Strategies.

The rationale for this difference in organisation is that the processes and strategies of speaking and listening are not conceptually hierarchical and therefore not phase-specific. In all phases, a variety of speaking and listening processes and strategies need to be introduced, developed and consolidated.

What varies from one phase to the next is the growth in:
- the number and integration of strategies used throughout the processes of speaking and listening
- the awareness and monitoring of speaking and listening processes
- the efficiency in the uses of the speaking and listening processes
- the ability to articulate the use of the strategies used in the process of speaking and listening
- the awareness of how the use of processes helps with composing and listening to texts.

Supporting Parents of Early Speakers and Listeners

GENERAL DESCRIPTION

Early Speakers and Listeners use their own version of the English language to talk to others, to socialise and to get what they need. They tell others about their ideas and ask questions. They understand when other people are talking about things in which they are personally interested and they respond in their own way. They are becoming aware of suitable ways of speaking and listening in familiar situations.

Teachers will find parents are able to support their children effectively when they have an understanding of how children learn and if they are aware of what happens in the classroom. Teachers can help build parent awareness of the learning program in which their child is involved in these kinds of ways:

- Invite parents in to join in class activities and talk to them before and after an activity, e.g. **The children are … The adult's role in this activity is to … How did the children enjoy this activity? What did you find was effective in helping them to understand?**

- Conduct parent/caregiver workshops on learning, e.g. **Learning Through Play, Learning with Technology, Helping Children to Learn.**

- Make a video, DVD or CD-ROM with students to demonstrate certain features of the learning program. Each family can take it home to view with their children. A viewing guide can be created with the students' input.

- When creating displays of student work, add information about the context of the activity and list the important learning that took place during the activity.

- Provide students with home-learning tasks that involve them sharing their learning with family members.

Supporting Early Speakers and Listeners in the Home

Early Speakers and Listeners will benefit from a range of experiences in the home setting. Ideas for providing appropriate experiences are available on Parent Cards located on the *First Steps* Speaking and Listening CD-ROM. Teachers can select appropriate cards for each Early Speaker and Listener and copy them for parent use.

Parent Cards

1 General Description of Early Speakers and Listeners

2 Developing an Understanding About Different Types of Speaking and Listening

3 Developing an Understanding About Contexts

4 Developing Vocabulary

5 Listening

6 Family Meetings

CHAPTER 6

Exploratory Speaking and Listening Phase

Unplanned

Jainika: I wonder what is inside. Can you find out without opening it up?
(overlapping)
Emma: We ... ll, I think in this one ... there's ... *(rattling)* ... Smarties.
Jainika: I think in this one ... there's nothink [*sic*].
Emma: and I think in this one ... *(rattling)*
Jainika: Oh, might be ...
Emma: A marble.
Jainika: Yeah, a marble.
Emma: Do you agree?
Jainika: Yep, I agree.
Emma: Do you think we should open them?
Jainika: Um, I don't think we ... are we allowed to?
Emma: Well, let's just see if we were right.
Jainika: Um, well ... what do you think is in here? We have to wonder.
Emma: Maybe it's some cotton wool.
Jainika: Nah, I think ... it is a little ... Oh, it's ... a ... Oh, I know, it's a dice and a popstick.
Emma: Well, I wonder if we're right.
Jainika: I wonder if we're right.
Teacher: So do you think you have worked it out? What do you think is in them?
Jainika: We think there's in ...
Emma: Smarties!
Jainika: Smarties, ... in here, there's nothing.
Emma: And in here, there's marbles.

Figure 6.1

Planned

'My Get Up And Talk is about how to make a musical instrument ...

Today I'm going to show you how to make a musical instrument and how to make its sound. And then ... you will learn how different sounds are made. First you will need scissors, a ruler ... a pen and six straws.

With the straws you need to get 9 cm. Get a ruler and measure it 9 cms long, and then 8 then 8 ... 8 cm ... then 7 then 6 then 5 with the straws up to 4. Then you need to ... um ... get some card ... get card ... and cut it with them ... um ... 11 cms long and 2 cms wide. Then you turn it like this ... the card ... then you get some tape and put it and get the straws and put the straws on the tape 1cm apart each time ... four. And then after that you stick it on the card and, you use modelling clay or Plasticine ... I've got some Plasticine. And you put the Plasticine on the bottom of the straw so ... um ... if it doesn't, if it's not put all on and ... um ... if there's air coming out it will go like this *(blows through straw to demonstrate)* and won't make any sound and this is how and the sound goes ... your air goes into the straw and it vibrates. And if you have longer and wider straws ... um ... you will make louder noises and this is how you play it. *(demonstrates by blowing straws)* Hang on ... I'm not very good at it but.'
(sound of children clapping)

Figure 6.2

Global Statement

In this phase, students use Standard English effectively within familiar contexts. They communicate appropriately in both structured and unstructured situations. They explore ways of using language for different speaking and listening purposes.

Exploratory Speaking and Listening Indicators

Use of Texts

◆ **Listens effectively for a range of familiar purposes.**
◆ **Uses a range of unplanned spoken texts with connected ideas.**
◆ **Presents simple spoken texts using basic text structures in logical sequence,** e.g. description, instruction, recount.
◆ **Obtains specific information from short informational and expressive spoken texts.**
• Presents relevant information on a known topic to group or class.
• Explains familiar procedures or gives simple instructions to peers showing awareness of the steps required, e.g. tells a new classmate where things are.

Contextual Understanding

◆ **Tries different ways of adjusting speaking and listening,** e.g. tone and pace.
◆ **Provides some background information and supporting ideas for listener,** e.g. facts and personal reasons.
◆ **Understands that people have different ideas.**
◆ **Talks about different audiences and purposes for own talk.**
◆ **Experiments with a small range of devices to enhance meaning of spoken texts,** e.g. volume, simile, rhyme, common sayings.
• Recognises the differences between home language and school language.
• Is aware that speakers can switch codes/dialects.
• Varies speaking and listening for familiar situations.
• Provides reasons for why people talk.

Conventions

◆ **Experiments with vocabulary drawn from a variety of sources** e.g. literature, media, learning area.
◆ **Experiments with more complex structures and features to express spoken ideas and information,** e.g. provides some supporting details.
◆ **Responds to spoken language using common school conventions,** e.g. takes turns in a conversation.
◆ **Experiments with different speaking and listening behaviours,** e.g. proximity, eye contact, volume, listens for specific information when given instructions.
• Attempts to adopt appropriate tone of voice and intonation to convey meaning.
• Sometimes uses similes to make speech more effective when explaining or describing, e.g. 'It was just like …'

Processes and Strategies

◆ **Explores thinking strategies with others.**
◆ **Experiments with a small range of processes and strategies when speaking,** e.g. uses rehearsed phrases.
◆ **Experiments with a small range of processes and strategies when listening,** e.g. draws a picture.
• Attends to the responses of others and reviews or elaborates on what has been said, e.g. answers questions from listeners, repeats ideas.
• Follows conventions and procedures for class activities, e.g. taking turns, asking questions.
• Experiments with planning for spoken descriptions, recounts and reports, e.g. identifies the main ideas or information to be presented.
• Experiments with strategies to monitor communication and responds accordingly, e.g. self-corrects to clarify meaning.

Major Teaching Emphases

Environment and Attitude (see p. 135)

- Provide opportunities for relevant, challenging and purposeful communication.
- Create a supportive environment which values the diversity of students' speaking and listening development (in their home languages).
- Encourage students to see the value of effective listening and speaking for community, school and family life.

Use of Texts (see p. 140)

- Expose students to a range of functional spoken texts composed in Standard English.
- Provide opportunities for students to participate in authentic unplanned and planned speaking and listening.
- Provide opportunities for students to participate in extended talk.
- Teach students how to plan and compose spoken texts using text features to enhance meaning, e.g. recount includes introduction and events in time order.
- Teach students how to identify relevant information about new and familiar topics.
- Teach students the metalanguage associated with speaking and listening and encourage its use, e.g. communicate, spoken text, audience, Standard English, verbal, non-verbal, mental picture.

Contextual Understanding (see p. 151)

- Discuss ways in which speaking and listening can be adjusted for different purposes, e.g. socialising, providing information in a classroom context, talking in the playground.
- Continue to provide effective feedback to students who are adjusting their speaking and listening, e.g. changing volume, amount of detail, code-switching/code-mixing.
- Teach students to include relevant information to develop content and ideas when speaking.

- Provide support for students to contribute to discussions about matters that interest or affect them.
- Teach students to recognise different points of view when analysing different spoken texts.
- Provide opportunities for students to express their opinions on a range of familiar topics.
- Model and support students to use devices to enhance meaning, e.g. using appropriate expression, providing the appropriate level of detail.

Conventions (see p. 162)

- Provide opportunities for students to develop, refine and use new vocabulary.
- Teach structures and features that help students extend and sustain communication, e.g. using text connectives and conjunctions to indicate cause and effect, maintaining the topic, taking turns.
- Teach speaking and listening behaviours that support meaning making, e.g. body language, facial expressions, building on others' ideas.
- Teach conversational skills, e.g. turn taking confirmation, clarification.
- Teach skills of listening and responding in whole-class, partner and small-group discussions, e.g. how to disagree agreeably.

Processes and Strategies (see p. 174)

- Discuss and reflect on the use of thinking to make meaning in speaking and listening.
- Provide opportunities for students to engage in sustained conversations, e.g. with peers, teachers and known adults.
- Teach a range of planning tools for speaking, e.g. how to share ideas.
- Teach planning tools that focus listening on before, during and after activities, e.g. identify key ideas, record ideas in a graphic organiser.
- Model responses to miscommunication, e.g. how to stop, rephrase and repeat, check comprehension.

Teaching and Learning Experiences

ENVIRONMENT AND ATTITUDE

Major Teaching Emphases

■ Provide opportunities for relevant, challenging and purposeful communication.

■ Create a supportive environment which values the diversity of students' speaking and listening development (in their home languages).

■ Encourage students to see the value of effective speaking and listening for community, school and family life.

Teaching Notes

A classroom community that nurtures students in the Exploratory phase is one that promotes experimentation with different kinds of speaking and listening. Emphasis is placed on providing students with a range of purposes for speaking and listening across all learning areas, and in experiencing different organisational arrangements such as partner work or small-group work. Teachers can support students by helping them to develop strategies to use when speaking and listening in different contexts.

The focus for developing positive attitudes towards speaking and listening are organised under the following headings:
• Creating a Supportive Classroom Environment
• Opportunities for Relevant, Challenging and Purposeful Communication
• Speaking and Listening for Community, School and Family Life

Creating a Supportive Classroom Environment

Teachers can provide a supportive classroom environment by considering both physical and cultural elements. Students will feel comfortable in exploring spoken language in an environment that values their existing strengths and interests. It is important that students in the Exploratory phase have opportunities to engage in a variety of meaningful situations that will develop positive attitudes towards trying new ways of speaking and listening.

Physical Environment

Opportunities to develop skills in speaking and listening occur throughout the day in all learning areas, in routine organisation and in social interactions. The organisation of the physical environment of the classroom will therefore change according to the teaching and learning demands at any particular time. It is important to establish routines for moving in and out of groups, moving furniture and collecting and storing equipment. These routines provide opportunities to identify speaking and listening needs and to negotiate and adopt appropriate classroom behaviours. Other considerations for an effective physical environment are listed below.

- Provide space for small-group, whole-class interactions, e.g.
  - class meetings
  - class games
  - partner work
  - small-group work.
- Make the behaviours for arranging furniture and resources explicit through role play, class charts and modelling.
- Provide a table for students to display objects of personal interest, work samples or topic related resources.
- Set up learning centres of independent activities to stimulate conversation and discussion. Encourage students to be responsible for the care and storage of materials and equipment.
- Set up a Listening Post with a variety of books and audio tapes to encourage students to listen for pleasure. Students can also engage in repeated listening experiences to practise listening skills, as an aid to memory or as a springboard for discussion.
- Use hand-held dictaphones to enable students to record speaking to share with others. The recordings could also help in reflecting on performance and in goal setting.
- Display songs, poems and chants that have been taught in class. Encourage students to recite them for other people, practising the patterns and rhythms of language.

Classroom Culture

It is important to develop a culture of acceptance so students in the Exploratory phase feel they can confidently explore new ways of interacting with others. The following ideas will help to develop positive relationships.

Figure 6.3 Class goal

- Remain sensitive to cultural differences.
- Maintain an emphasis on enjoyment.
- Communicate high expectations to students.
- Provide opportunities for social talk and encourage students to speak the language used in their homes.
- Continue to build on students' prior knowledge and learning.
- Provide authentic purposes for speaking and listening.
- Ensure that students have a clear sense of what is expected of them.
- Support students in preparing for new speaking and listening contexts by discussing the demands of a new context, e.g. What is needed to allocate tasks in a small group? What is needed when explaining the rules of a game?
- Provide multiple opportunities to practise and refine new knowledge and skills.
- Teach problem-solving procedures that relate to speaking and listening, e.g. how to decide who will go first, how to take turns in a small group, how to reach a compromise when someone does not agree.
- Encourage students to speak to all members of the class.
- Provide opportunities to reflect on learning, e.g. students record ways in which speaking or listening helped their learning.
- Provide choices and support decision making, e.g. involve students in negotiating units of work.

See the *First Steps* Speaking and Listening CD-ROM, Exploratory Phase for a planning guide to assist with negotiation and inquiry.

Figure 6.4 A chart about speaking and listening by students

• Develop independence, e.g. students take responsibility for daily organisation and equipment.

Opportunities for Relevant, Challenging and Purposeful Communication

Students in the Exploratory phase will benefit from a dynamic, interactive classroom where time is provided for them to speak and listen every day for a variety of purposes. Examples that can be incorporated into classroom routines are listed as follows.

• Model language to promote effective social interactions e.g. how to join a conversation or a game, how to ask for assistance, how to share or resolve a conflict.
• Model attentive listening and paraphrasing to clarify meaning.
• Read a variety of fiction and non-fiction texts every day.
• Read or recite poetry to students every day.
• Read predictable stories that demonstrate the patterns and rhythms of literary language. Encourage students to join in and predict the next line or event.
• Tell stories and invite guest storytellers.
• Involve students in talk for exploring ideas in all learning areas, e.g. explain the findings of a science investigation to the class.
• Develop units of work that engage students to use spoken language to inquire about problems or issues that affect them (see *First Steps* Speaking and Listening Resource book, Chapter 1, Small Group Inquiry).

Speaking and Listening for Community, School and Family Life

Students in the Exploratory phase are beginning to encounter speaking and listening contexts that require them to develop new skills. These contexts may involve situations such as answering the telephone at home; taking part in planned speaking events at school such as school assembly; giving a talk; or expressing an opinion in a writer's circle. Students will also need to know which contexts demand the use of Standard English and which behaviours are most appropriate.

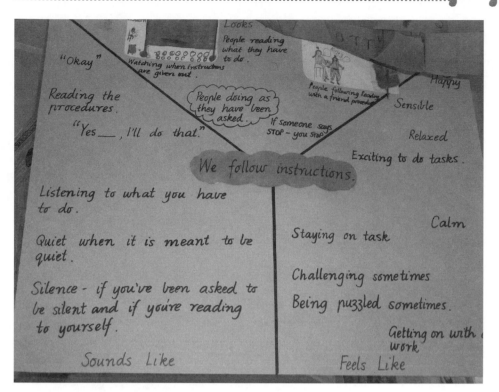

Figure 6.5 A class Y chart

Teachers can assist students in the Exploratory phase to value speaking and listening for classroom learning, interacting socially and developing self-awareness. With appropriate support through modelling, investigating and analysing speaking and listening contexts, students can develop the knowledge, skills and attitudes to:

• talk about their personal experiences.
• offer opinions.
• refer to their personal experiences as a way of connecting with the experiences of others as they listen, read texts, view films, DVDs, etc.
• investigate and discuss the ways speaking and listening are used outside of school.
• make links between skills learned at school, in the family and community to better understand the speaking and listening choices they need to make.
• use group discussion behaviours, e.g. turn taking, Think-Pair-Share.
• use skills of negotiation for group discussions, class meetings or social conversations.
• explore appropriate ways to request something of peers and adults.
• explore ways of acknowledging another point of view.
• develop competence in giving and following directions.
• ask different types of questions.
• suggest answers to different types of questions.
• organise and present information.

USE OF TEXTS

Major Teaching Emphases

■ **Expose students to a range of functional spoken texts composed in Standard English.**

■ **Provide opportunities for students to participate in authentic unplanned and planned speaking and listening.**

■ **Provide opportunities for students to participate in extended talk.**

■ **Teach students how to plan and compose spoken texts using text features to enhance meaning,** e.g. recount includes introduction and events in time order.

■ **Teach students how to identify relevant information about new and familiar topics.**

■ **Teach students the metalanguage associated with speaking and listening and encourage its use,** e.g. communicate, spoken text, audience, Standard English, verbal, non-verbal, mental picture.

Teaching Notes

The focus for supporting Exploratory Speakers and Listeners in this aspect is organised under the following headings.
• Exposure to a Range of Spoken Texts
• Participation in Unplanned and Planned Spoken Texts
• Focusing on Text Structure
• Developing Topic Knowledge
• Developing Metalanguage

Exposure to a Range of Spoken Texts

Students in the Exploratory phase are exploring ways of using language for different purposes and require more specific feedback about the ways to structure their spoken texts. Familiarising, Modelling and Discussing continue to be important teaching and learning practices to support students' development in using a range of spoken texts. (See Chapter 7 in the *First Steps Linking Assessment, Teaching and Learning* book.)

Students in this phase will benefit from daily opportunities to discuss and connect with a variety of functional spoken texts, which include everyday, literary and informational. For the purposes of this resource, everyday spoken texts include greetings, conversations, directions and talking to explore new concepts and knowledge.

Literary and informational spoken texts may include poems, jokes, stories, recounts, songs, descriptions, instructions and reports. Teachers use and select texts that are composed in Standard English to provide a model of the language students need to develop. Texts chosen could be face-to-face or multi-modal including film, DVD, CD-ROM, PA system or telephone. They may be planned and performed for a young audience or unplanned and delivered spontaneously.

Participation in Unplanned and Planned Spoken Texts

Exploratory Speakers and Listeners need frequent opportunities to speak for a range of purposes as they work throughout the day. Teachers encourage students to use their speaking and listening skills to assist learning in situations such as using construction equipment to create models, explaining a procedure in a learning centre or asking for help when undertaking a personal project.

Modelled, Shared and Guided Speaking and Listening sessions provide ideal opportunities for Exploratory Speakers and Listeners to compose a range of unplanned and planned spoken texts.

It is essential that students know that:
• Speaking and listening is important for learning.
• Speaking and listening is important for developing and maintaining relationships.
• Speakers and listeners use spoken texts that are organised in particular ways for particular purposes.
• Texts can be planned for different audiences and purposes.
• Planning can improve the meaning of spoken texts.
• The different ways of speaking and listening depend on the situation.

Focusing on Text Structure

Many everyday interactions are formulaic and follow common structures (see the Conventions Chapter in *Speaking and Listening Resource Book*). Students in the Exploratory phase will need explicit instruction on when and how to use Standard English. They will also need instruction on how to communicate effectively in more formal academic contexts such as reporting on a group investigation.

Discussions about spoken texts will show students how to become

141

successful speakers and listeners. There is a continued focus in the Exploratory phase on the use of a range of text forms for different purposes. Teachers may utilise everyday interactions to explicitly teach text structures by implementing some of the ideas in the following table.

Example of Typical Spoken Text in School Context	Example of Basic Text Structure with Added Features to Enhance Meaning
Meeting and greeting familiar adult or student visitor to the classroom	• Say the greeting, e.g. Good morning. Hello. • Say the person's name. • Give a welcoming comment or ask a question, e.g. Welcome to our class. How can we help you? • Directing the person to the teacher, e.g. Mrs Smith is over in the Mathematics area.
Sharing and taking turns during group work	• Someone gives direction for the discussion, e.g. What shall we do now? What ideas do we have about … ? Who will do the group roles today? • Say what you want. Wait for others to say what they want. • If someone has not said anything, ask for their ideas. • Someone gives a closing/resolution. • Give your agreement, e.g. OK, thanks, that's great. • Someone gives new directions, e.g. Let's get on with the task now.
Introducing a planned report on their group's progress	• What is the report about? • Who is doing what? • What tasks have been set? • Is there any help needed? • Which tasks have been completed?
Inviting others to join their activity or game	• Say what it is. • Give a list of what and how much is needed. • Describe how you use the items step by step. • Give a statement of result. • Say what the activity/game is, e.g. We're playing… • Invite someone, e.g. Would you like to… ? Can you come and… ? • Say the person's name. • Give some details to encourage them, e.g. It's a lot of fun.

Figure 6.6 Focusing on text structure

As students compose spoken texts, teachers can draw their attention to the different text structures and features used for a range of speaking purposes in different contexts.

Exploratory students communicate for …	Students in the Exploratory phase speak and listen to …	Teachers can do these things to draw students' attention to the different purposes and to basic text structures.		
		Provide Direction	**Give a Comment**	**Ask a Question**
Getting things done	• organise an activity. • get the things they need. • let a new class member know how to use the school's canteen.	Tell Group 2 how to do the science experiment so they can do it, too. Include how many items are needed.	Group 2 had the right amount of water for that experiment and they poured it just as you told them to.	What will you need to tell Group 2 to collect to do this experiment? What do they need to do with the materials?
Influencing the behaviour, feelings or attitudes of others.	• persuade a peer to read a favourite text. • convince a teacher to change a class routine.	Plan what you will say to encourage a friend to read your favourite book.	I think I would like to read that book, too!	What did you say to your friend to make them want to read your favourite book?
Getting along with others	• greet others. • join in a conversation. • make plans for play.	After you greet your partner, ask them what mathematics game they would like to play with you today?	It feels good when people ask what you would like to do.	How did it feel when your partner asked you what mathematics game you would like to play today?
Expressing individuality and personal feelings	• recount own experiences. • retell a favourite activity. • let others know how they feel.	Talk about how you felt when you worked in your group today.	You had a few different feelings today. Your group must have worked through some problems.	How did you feel in your group today? When did you feel like that? Why?
Seeking and learning about the social and physical environment	• gain further information from an expert. • form own questions for a project.	After the talk from our visitor, there will be some time for your questions.	I was wondering what that meant, too. I've never heard that word before.	What else would you like to know about frogs before our guest speaker leaves?
Creating stories, games, new worlds and new texts	• give ideas for a collaborative story using Lego™ models. • design a game to play.	Listen to each other's ideas for the story and then try them out.	Your story has used both of your ideas.	How did you decide which ideas to use to create your story? Why did you choose that idea?
Communicating information	• inform the class about the life cycle of a butterfly. • let others know how to complete a science experiment.	Introduce your animal, talk to your group and explain its life cycle.	We knew what you were talking about because you introduced it and you used words that helped us understand the life cycle.	How will you introduce your animal talk? What words will be important to use when you explain the life cycle?
Entertaining others	• discuss humorous topics. • retell simple stories. • retell jokes and riddles.	For free talk today you need to choose a text to entertain your group.	Your group enjoyed your jokes and you kept them entertained.	What kind of texts can entertain your classmates?

Figure 6.7 Examples for focusing on the functions of spoken texts

Developing Topic Knowledge

Exploratory Speakers and Listeners will require support as they learn about topics that are beyond their immediate experience. It is important that they learn about a range of topics in order to discuss learning in all subject areas.

Teachers can accumulate information about students' current knowledge and interests in a range of ways:

- Talking and listening to students in informal situations, e.g. in between tasks, at recess and lunch times, while waiting for parents/caregivers.
- Observe students as they engage in open-ended tasks during free choice learning time, e.g. What do they already know? What do they do with their information?
- Observe students' representations and listen to them as they tell you about what they have represented, e.g. painting, model, drawing, role play.
- Interact with students after their free time, e.g. Could you show me how you inserted a picture into your document on the computer? How would you explain the steps?
- Conduct focused interviews with students individually or in small groups, e.g. What are some different uses for this equipment? Why would you do that? How can we find more? Why did you choose to begin your research here?
- Negotiate topics to study with students. Ask: What do you like to learn about? What do you know about?

Developing Metalanguage

The language used to talk about language is known as metalanguage. When students can use metalanguage to talk about their own speaking and listening, it helps them understand how language operates. It is essential to use metalanguage as part of everyday teaching in all learning areas.

Exploratory speakers and listeners will become familiar with the following terms:

- Use of Texts: *meaning, communicate, spoken text, media.*
- Contextual Understanding: *audience, Standard English, point of view.*
- Conventions: *verbal, non-verbal, volume, vocabulary.*
- Processes and Strategies: *reflect, interrupt, negotiate, mental picture.*

For further information about Use of Texts, see *Speaking and Listening Resource Book*, 2nd Edition:
- Chapter 1: Use of Texts
- Chapter 4: Processes and Strategies.

Involving Students

1 Listen to Learn

Listen to Learn is a cross-curriculum activity that helps students to use listening as a tool for learning as they recall and record what they heard in their own way. It helps them to reshape, refine and construct their own understandings in a range of ways including talking, painting, making a model, making a PowerPoint presentation or video, acting out or writing. Students can participate in planned listening and connect with their existing knowledge of common topics. The focus for listening and amount of detail will vary depending on the audience. If the student decides to represent his or her learning by talking, then the activity also allows students to participate in extended talk and to choose appropriate text structures and features to suit a particular audience.

- Model this task first.
- Select from a range of spoken texts including read-aloud books, TV programs, videos, DVDs or audio tapes. The text could be literary such as a poem or story or informational such as a simple report or a procedure.
- Prepare the spoken text for the class. It can be presented in small groups, one-on-one or to the whole class.
- Ask students to think of questions about the spoken texts, focusing on the main messages in the text, e.g. **What was the main problem in the story? What were the important steps in the instructions to make a glider? What words were used to try to persuade us?**
- Introduce some brief guidelines to students and suggest ways to organise and record their responses, e.g. **draw pictures or write key words as you listen.**
- Present the spoken text to students. Repeat if necessary.
- Ask students to represent what they learnt from their listening, e.g. **create a flow chart, make a story map.**
- Arrange for students to share their representations either to each other or in a small group with teacher or peers.

See the Speaking and Listening CD-ROM, Exploratory Phase: Use of Texts (Listen to Learn) for recording observations formats.

How Might This Activity Be Used in Your Class?

- Choose a particular text type as a class focus, e.g. **reports.** Ask students to listen to identify particular features, e.g. **how the topic is introduced, what technical terms have been used.**

- Choose spoken texts that will help students identify relevant information, e.g. **when listening to a report.** This could be recorded through drawings or writing in preparation for a discussion.
- When introducing a new topic, ask students to list what they know and what they would like to find out. Ask students to list ways of obtaining the information through listening, e.g. **to find out more about snakes, invite a guest speaker from the local office for conservation and land management, listen to an audio or video recording.**
- Suggest that students record notes and make drawings while listening.

2 Talk to Teach

Talk to Teach is an activity that can be used in all areas of the curriculum. It is an effective means of students reproducing what they have learned, thus adding depth to their understanding of a topic or a concept. Talk to Teach is explained in detail in Chapter 5 and can be adapted for Exploratory students by using some of the following ideas. See the Speaking and Listening CD-ROM, Exploratory Phase: Use of Texts for planning guides.

- Ask students to think of a skill they have that others may not have, e.g. **how to make a table on the computer, make an origami model, play a skipping game.**
- Make a list of people who would be interested in learning the skill.
- Help students to plan what they will say and do. This planning may include discussions, drawings, flow charts, written notes or collections of artefacts or objects.
- Provide visual, spoken and brief written prompts for the text types selected by the students.
- Organise a time for the activity to take place.

Amy:	I'm going to teach you how to do a cartwheel. First you have to start in an X shape with your arms and your legs, then you'll look like a wonky K then you'll um … turn over and your arms will be on the ground and your feet will be in the air, and your arms have to be very strong. Then you'll come down sort of roley poley shape then um, you'll get back up into the shape that you're already in.
Teacher:	So standing back up tall.
Amy:	*(repeats)* Standing back up tall.

Figure 6.8 A transcript of a student telling someone how to do a cartwheel

Figure 6.9 Sample of student planning

3 To Summarise

To Summarise is an activity that provides students with practise in listening for key words and ideas. It helps them to recall and explain important information. Students can work with a partner.

- Have students listen to information text. This could be from an audio or video recording.
- Ask them to record key words as they listen. (Choose a graphic organiser — see Chapter 4, *Speaking and Listening Resource Book.*)
- After listening, students should work with a partner to write three or four summary statements about what they have learned.
- Combine pairs of students into groups of four. Students report what they learned to others.

How Might This Activity Be Used in Your Class?

- Combine pairs into groups of six. Ask students to write questions based on the important information they listened to. Use the questions to hold a class quiz.
- Role play an interview. Ask one student to interview another student by asking questions based on the information they listened to.
- Ask students to work with a partner and compose statements based on the information they listened to. They should make three statements that are true and three that are false. Combine pairs into groups of four or six. One person reads the statement and the other students have to consider whether it is true or false and give a reason for their answer.

4 Reflect and Respond

Reflect and Respond is a cross-curricula activity that can become a regular part of the class timetable. It allows students to spend some time thinking and reflecting about what they did or said throughout the day. It can be performed in pairs, small groups, as a class or with familiar visitors such as older students (class buddies) or parents/caregivers. This activity works best if it takes place at the end of a task, a session or the day.

- Model the task for students with another student or teacher.
- Discuss with students where and how they need to sit, e.g. face-to-face, in a circle, etc.
- Tell students what they are expected to say in their reflection and their response, e.g. What kinds of listening did you do today? What is something interesting you did today or yesterday? Ask your partner a question.
- Provide the necessary amount of time for students to reflect.

Use A Thinking Framework if necessary. See the Speaking and Listening CD-ROM, Exploratory Phase: Use of Texts (Listen to Learn).

- Conduct a whole-class discussion, prompting students to discuss the main ideas or points that they have learnt to conclude the session, e.g. What different kinds of listening did our class do? What kinds of questions did our partners ask about our recounts?
- Main ideas can be recorded individually in journals, or as a class summary.
- Ask questions that focus on identifying new and relevant information, e.g. What new information did you hear today? What made it easy to understand? How did you learn it? Ask your partner a question about that topic. How could you make your recount more interesting?

5 What Comes Next?

What Comes Next? is an activity that encourages students to retell a particular spoken text. It enables students to practise the structures and features of particular types of spoken texts. What Comes Next? is explained in detail in Chapter 5. It can be adapted for students in the Exploratory phase by increasing the amount of text to be retold as well as the complexity of a text to be listened to. Teachers could choose from some of the following ideas.

Decide on a spoken text that can be listened to and then retold such as:
- a narrative.
- a report, e.g. an animal report that may have featured on a children's television program.
- an interview, e.g. choose a suitable interview shown on the TV news. Students choose a role and re-enact the interview.

How Might This Activity Be Used in Your Class?

- Ask students to listen carefully to descriptive words, technical terms, where the speaker paused, how the speaker introduced important information. Ask students to record the selected features to encourage their use.
- When reflecting, focus on the structure and the added features of their spoken text, e.g. Did you remember to include information about ... ? Did you include the step? Where ... ? How did people know what you were talking about?
- Invite an audience to ask questions afterwards.
- Students could use props to assist the retelling, e.g. toys, magnetic

characters or felt pieces to retell a story, pictures of an animal and its habitat to retell a report.
- Students can reconstruct an oral text visually, in a written form or as a play.

6 Props with a Purpose
Refer to Chapter 5, Early Speaking and Listening Phase, p. 98.

7 Time for Talk

Time for Talk is a partner activity that encourages students to make choices regarding text form, topic and audience that can be performed on a daily basis. It allows students to practise organising their speaking and listening to suit the needs of the listener. The aim is for students to choose topics independently; however, teachers will need to nominate a topic to begin with, e.g. **Tomorrow, we will all talk about our favourite TV show.** Teachers may also support reluctant speakers by displaying suggested topics along with phrases that will encourage them to introduce an idea, e.g. **talk about your pets, 'Today I am going to tell you about my pets ...'**

Introduce Time for Talk as time to:
- speak and listen to a partner.
- talk with different class members. (The aim should be for a student to speak with every member of the class.)
- choose a topic.
- choose a text form, e.g. **recount, explanation, narrative, description.**
- speak for a certain amount of time. (Suggest two minutes to begin with and extend.)
- listen and encourage the speaker. (Teach students to use encouraging body language, questions to probe for more information and questions to seek clarification.)

Students can reflect on Time for Talk by:
- recording the topic, text form and name of their partner every day. See the Speaking and Listening CD-ROM, Exploratory Phase: Use of Texts (Time for Talk student records).
- keeping a journal. This may occur once a week. Students could refer to the notes that were kept daily and reflect on the different people they spoke to or listened to, note any speaking or listening goals or make note of future ideas for talks. Teachers may use guiding questions, e.g. **What topics are being discussed? What were some of the interesting and challenging ideas being discussed this week? How can you explain difficult ideas or procedures so that others understand what you are trying to say? What text types have been**

used this week? Who have you found to be a particularly interesting speaker and why?

• involving students in self- and peer-assessment.

Figure 6.10 Student viewing own talk with peer

How Might This Activity Be Used in Your Class?

• Have the class keep a record of their daily Time for Talk sessions over a set period of time. Students can review their choices of text types, audience and topic and set goals for themselves.

• Collate records of text types and topics in the class and these could appear in a graph and be analysed, e.g. What is the most popular text type used by students in our class?

• Use Time for Talk to assess students' skills using a particular text type, e.g. tell students that they must tell a story this week and that you and a small group of students will be their audience.

CONTEXTUAL UNDERSTANDING

Major Teaching Emphases

- Discuss ways in which speaking and listening can be adjusted for different purposes, e.g. socialising, providing information in a classroom context, talking in the playground.

- Continue to provide effective feedback to students who are adjusting their speaking and listening, e.g. changing volume, amount of detail, code-switching/code-mixing.

- Teach students to include relevant information to develop content and ideas when speaking.

- Provide support for students to contribute to discussions about matters that interest or affect them.

- Teach students to recognise different points of view when analysing different spoken texts.

- Provide opportunities for students to express their opinions on a range of familiar topics.

- Model and support students to use devices to enhance meaning, e.g. using appropriate expression, providing the appropriate level of detail.

Teaching Notes

The focus for supporting Exploratory Speakers and Listeners in this aspect is organised under the following headings.
- Understandings About Context
- Providing Feedback
- Considering the Needs of the Audience
- Contributing to Matters of Importance
- Exploring the Way Ideas and People Are Represented
- Use of Devices

Understandings About Context

In the Exploratory phase, students try different ways of adjusting their speaking and listening and are aware of the way in which speaking and listening is influenced by the context — audience, purpose, situation and topic. Students study the behaviours and processes involved in speaking and listening when teachers use Analysing and Reflecting teaching practices. In these sessions, students are familiar with the way speaking and listening changes in different school contexts including the playground, assemblies, and a range of whole-class and small-group activities.

Teacher:	How can you improve listening?
Elizabeth:	Speak louder.
(Teacher raises eyebrows and gave an expression for more information.)	
Elizabeth:	If you don't hear, say, 'Can you say that again because I didn't really hear it?' Or you could say 'Can you explain it in a better…no another way?'

Figure 6.11 A transcript of student discussing speaking and listening

Teachers can discuss with Exploratory Speakers and Listeners the way particular spoken texts are suitable for different audiences and purposes. This can occur before, during and after students participate in unplanned and planned speaking and listening. For example, before a visit from another class of younger students, teachers can prepare students by asking the following questions, e.g. **'Room 3 children have not been into our room before, what might we need to tell them when we meet them?'** During the visit, the teacher can instruct students, **'With your partner, find an activity to do. How will you do this together?'** After the class has left, teachers can ask, **'How did you include your younger partner in the decision about which activity to do? Did you have to change the way you talk? Was that because the children were younger or because you did not know them?'**

Providing Feedback

Exploratory Speakers and Listeners are now familiar with most school routines but may still need to be supported in new situations and in developing relationships with others. It is crucial that teachers do not make assumptions about what a student knows, believes or understands about speaking and listening. Speaking and listening involves the interaction of personal, cultural and interpersonal processes. The meaning students make from a spoken text is influenced by their life experiences, their knowledge of spoken language (the words and the behaviours) and the relationship they have with the speaker. Teachers may find it helpful to learn about how the student's culture influences their speaking and listening and interactions with parents/caregivers are a valuable source of discovering more about your students. (See the Speaking and Listening CD-ROM, Exploratory Phase for parent/caregiver interview-survey sheets.)

Figure 6.12 Student's informal unplanned interaction with teacher

Figure 6.13 Student's formal planned talk with teacher

Teachers can provide valuable feedback in the following ways:

- Focus on the message, not the way it has been conveyed.
- Pose questions that show a genuine interest in what the student wants and needs to communicate.
- Acknowledge student's feelings, e.g. I can see that you are annoyed. You sound really happy about that.
- Refer to class decisions about speaking and listening, e.g. We decided we would get people's attention by facing them and using their name. We were going to say 'excuse me' when we need to talk to someone during an activity.
- Use positive statements when students alter their speaking and listening, e.g. I noticed that you added some more information when your group did not understand you. I saw that you moved closer; the story became exciting, didn't it?
- Use guiding questions to assist students to reflect on their speaking and listening in unfamiliar contexts, e.g. We know that didn't work this time. What could you do differently if something like this happened again?

Considering the Needs of the Audience

Exploratory Speakers and Listeners are more confident when speaking with familiar audiences but may still need support to include relevant information, express their opinions and make appropriate choices. Teachers will use Modelled, Shared and Guided teaching practices to develop an awareness of the needs of different audiences. The following guiding questions may help to develop relevant discussions.

– What will the class need to know when you tell them how you do that experiment?

– What do you need to include in your recount so that we have a good mental picture of what you did and where you were?

– What do you think the principal would like to hear about when she visits our class?

– What do you think your partner liked listening to? How do you know?

– How will we show that we are interested at the assembly?

– What do we need to do when someone is talking to the whole class?

– What are some different ways we can start our talk about our project?

– How will we make sure that our visitors know that we want to listen to them?

Mikayla:	Yes sometimes 'cos you can sometimes interrupt but politely.
Teacher:	OK, so where would you be able to interrupt politely?
Mikayla:	If somebody said, 'Oh well, I went to AFL to see something' and somebody could say 'I went there as well.'
Teacher:	Mmm, so you would do that when you're sitting in a small group but you wouldn't do it if they were having a get up and talk. Yeah.
Mikayla:	'Cos you have to listen to them 'cos they're the one that is talking and they don't, um, they're not that, um, there's a big group. You can't just interrupt in the big group.

Figure 6.14 A transcript about interrupting in different contexts

Figure 6.15 Think, Pair, Share

Contributing to Matters of Importance

Exploratory Speakers and Listeners need daily opportunities to discuss matters of interest or those matters that affect them. They soon realise that speaking and listening helps to raise awareness and that action can be taken to solve problems. Through these opportunities, students also develop their abilities to express ideas, opinions and feelings. Teachers can support students in the following ways:

- Invite students to share their ideas and opinions when planning, reviewing and organising activities.
- Have open-ended activities with a range of topics and materials.
- Provide effective feedback when students raise matters or issues.
- Construct interesting displays that promote discussion.
- Motivate students to create and share their own displays in areas such as science, drama or writing.

Exploring the Way Ideas and People Are Represented

Exploratory Speakers and Listeners continue to require support in understanding the different ways ideas and people can be represented in spoken texts. A range of electronic spoken texts are available that explore a wide range of different points of view and representations of ideas and people. CD-ROMs, films, television programs and audio tapes are valuable resources for listening to stories, recounts, advertisements and reports. It is also possible to record some of the spoken texts from the school and classroom that could be a starting point for discussion. Consider the following kinds of questions:

- How did it make you feel about the ideas or people as you listened?
- Who might like the way the idea or people are portrayed in this text? Why? Who might not?
- Do you think these things are true about the ideas or people? Why?
- When you were listening, what were you thinking?
- Why do you think the people or ideas were explained in that particular way?
- What do you think is the main message about the people or ideas? Why?
- What would be another way to say this about that idea or person?
- Does it sound right? Why?
- What interesting words were used? Would you use those words? When?
- What body language was used? Do you use that, too?
- Does the text make sense?

Use of Devices

Exploratory Speakers and Listeners begin to experiment with verbal and non-verbal behaviours to convey meaning. Teachers explicitly guide students to reflect on how they as speakers and listeners adjust their spoken language and non-verbal language to enhance meaning. The focus for Exploratory Speakers and Listeners includes:

- Body position, e.g. proximity to indicate closeness or distance in relationships and to show or acknowledge power.
- How verbal and non-verbal devices are often combined to convey meaning, e.g. if a person says 'I disagree' and shakes his/her head, changes their facial expression and perhaps step back or changes the pitch in their tone.
- How to use non-verbal language to show they believe or disbelieve a speaker (facial expressions, body position, posture, eye contact, gestures and movement).
- How to use verbal language (such as pace, volume, intonation) to inform, to entertain, to indicate an opinion, to agree or disagree with the listener.
- How to use expression when giving a planned talk, e.g. to emphasise certain words and to vary the pace of speaking to add interest to a recount.

For further information about the Contextual Understanding aspect, see Chapter 2: Contextual Understanding, *Speaking and Listening Resource Book*.

For further information on the teaching and learning practices, see Chapter 7: *Linking Assessment, Teaching and Learning*.

Involving Students

1 Communicating in the Community

This activity involves students researching speaking and listening in the school and wider community. It is adapted from *Tackling Talk* (Haig, Oliver, and Rochestouste).

Teachers and students decide on an area of focus and design a research project. Students can work in small groups or individually. The research could be conducted by the whole class or small groups. Students record their observations and present them to the class. The findings are discussed, sorted and summarised.

- Decide whether the students will work as a whole class or as a small group.

- Decide on an area of focus. This might be related to a local event, an identified need or from a list of communication settings that has been developed with the students.
- Discuss and record student responses to: *What do we already know? What questions do we have?*
- Plan the action research with the students. (See the Speaking and Listening CD-ROM, Exploratory Phase for the Planning Sheet.)
- Support students to carry out their research. This might involve going on an excursion or include some home-learning observations. Parent support may be needed.
- Provide time for students to plan the way in which they will present their findings.
- Support students to discuss, compare and sort the findings. This will need to be organised if more than one group presents their research.
- Record any summary statements.
- Reflect and discuss — Is there anyone else who might be interested in our findings? How can we let them know? Are we able to communicate in that setting? Why?

Action–Research Ideas for Early and Exploratory Speakers and Listeners

- Who asks and answers the questions in our class/school office/home?
- What are the reasons for talking and listening in our class and at home?
- What instructions are given in our class and homes?
- What words do you need to participate in assembly at school?
- What words do you need to participate at a friend's party?

2 Class Meetings

Class meetings are explained in Chapter 5 (see p. 112) and can be easily adapted for students in the Exploratory phase. Students in this phase will be ready to take more responsibility for running a meeting and will be able to cope with more agenda items. They will be able to assume a greater control of the roles required to run a class meeting, such as taking the role of chairperson, secretary, timekeeper, etc. (See Chapter 1 in the *Speaking and Listening Resource Book* for more information about class meetings.)

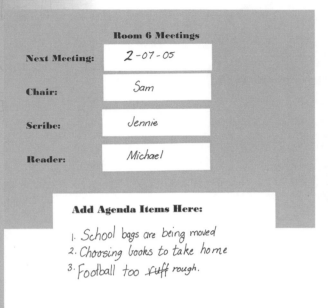

Figure 6.16 A chart showing decisions made in meetings

Figure 6.17 A class chart of a meeting agenda

How Might This Activity Be Used in Your Class?

- Keep a book to record the 'minutes'.
- Have a new agenda in place, ready for students to record new items.
- Speakers hold a token or item to indicate who is speaking.
- A round may be held so that each person has an opportunity to speak about an item. Students not wishing to speak may say 'pass'.
- Discuss some of the agenda items in small groups.
- Students can take turns to be the chairperson, reader, time-keeper, scribe and any other role.
- Students assigned as observers can take note of the speaking and listening behaviours that are discussed. Observers could use a class-made observation sheet.
- Discuss when the meetings will be held, e.g. weekly, each fortnight.
- Assessments could be obtained during class meetings, e.g. contribution of ideas, building on ideas, expressing opinions, raising issues or matters to discuss, etc.

3 Persuade Me/Persuade Me Not

This activity is designed to draw students' attention to the spoken language used to persuade by analysing a television advertisement. This activity is best completed with a partner.

- Video-tape advertisements that are aimed at the age level of students in the class.
- Students watch the advertisement for the first time without any specific direction so that they gain a general impression of the spoken text.
- Ask students to list:
  - the product that is being sold.
  - how the characters were portrayed, e.g. **real people, cartoons.**
  - the intended audience.
  - who was speaking in the advertisement.
  - who was listening in the advertisement.
- Students then watch the advertisement a second time to add any information to the above list.
- Direct students to notice specific words in the third viewing and to list them as they are listening, e.g. **list words that try to persuade you that the product is cool, fun or healthy.**
- Compile a class list of the words and phrases that were used to persuade and display the list for future reference.
- Compile a class list of devices that were used, e.g. **analogy, testimony, jargon, repetition** (see Chapter 2, *Speaking and Listening Resource Book*).

How Might This Activity Be Used in Your Class?

- Make class charts of advertising slogans or catchphrases.
- Ask students to interpret these slogans and to state the meaning in their own words
- Involve students in discussions on whether or not they would buy the product and why.

4 Reviews

Reviews is an activity that promotes an understanding of points of view and developing opinions. It is important that students understand that others may have different opinions based on their point of view. It is also important that students understand how a point of view develops and what influences people's thinking, values and beliefs.

- Decide on a text to review (consider age appropriateness), e.g. **a book, a movie, a TV show, an advertisement (television or radio).**
- Have students work in a group to discuss guiding questions such as the following questions which are based on reviewing a movie.

Questions to guide evaluation of content:
- What was the movie about? List the main ideas.
- Who were the main characters? List the main characters.

Questions to develop opinion:
– Who was the intended audience?
– What was the trouble in the movie? Did you care?
– Were the characters interesting?
– Who liked or didn't like the movie? List the reasons why.

Ask students to rate the movie, giving it a score out of ten. Students could then be allocated to different groups to give their review. Students will need to summarise the information that supports their opinion and share their rating.

How Might This Activity Be Used in Your Class?

- Students could practise language to persuade by building onto review discussions, e.g. they could plan a short speech to persuade others to see a movie or read a book they recommend.
- Class charts could be made to record reasons for likes and dislikes.

5 Which Words? Which Actions? Which Voice?

This activity develops awareness of the need to adjust vocabulary choice, tone of voice and body language to suit particular contexts. It uses role play to explore choices and the likely consequences. Introduce this activity to the whole class. Students will progress to working in small groups with the aid of prompt cards.

Introduce this activity by modelling. Choose a scenario and use words, tone of voice and actions that students would recognise as being inappropriate for the context, e.g. role play buying food from the canteen. Shout your request using an aggressive tone and body stance.

Invite students to suggest more appropriate behaviours and record these on a chart or whiteboard, e.g. Context: Ordering food from the school canteen.

Which words?	Which actions?	Which voice?
Please may I have ... Could you tell me how much ... ? Thank you.	Looking directly at canteen worker Leaning forward Smiling	Friendly Loud enough to be heard easily

Involve students in scenarios that will encourage decisions regarding choice of words, actions and voice, e.g. asking an older student for help in the playground (perhaps a student councillor); asking an adult for help in an emergency; offering help to a younger student who has been hurt in the playground.

How Might This Activity Be Used in Your Class?

- Video some of the role plays to share with parents or another class.
- Video some of the role plays to use in a reflection, e.g. ask students how they could improve their speaking or listening.

6 Who Can I Talk to? Who Can I Listen to? How Do I Do It?

Refer to Chapter 5, Early Speaking and Learning Phase, p. 109.

7 Personality Phones

Refer to Chapter 5, Early Speaking and Learning Phase, p. 110.

Personality Phones is designed to give students practice in adjusting speaking and listening for different audiences and for different purposes. It is explained in detail in Chapter 5. This activity can be adapted for students in the Exploratory Phase by adapting it to fit the needs of students, e.g. to express feelings or explain an issue.

Figure 6.18

How Might This Activity Be Used in Your Class?

- Direct students to use a personality phone to practise what they will say, e.g. You need to apologise so use a phone to practise what to say.
- Direct students to use a phone to rehearse their report. Students could use a phone to pretend they are telling a parent about how they told a story at school.

8 Exploring Speaking and Listening

Refer to Chapter 5, Early Speaking and Listening Phase, p. 111.

CONVENTIONS

Major Teaching Emphases

■ **Provide opportunities for students to develop, refine and use new vocabulary.**

■ **Teach structures and features that help students extend and sustain communication,** e.g. using text connectives and conjunctions to indicate cause and effect, maintaining the topic, taking turns.

■ **Teach speaking and listening behaviours that support meaning making,** e.g. body language, facial expression, building on other's ideas.

■ **Teach conversational skills,** e.g. turn-taking confirmation, clarification.

■ **Teach skills of listening and responding in whole-class, partner and small-group discussion,** e.g. how to disagree agreeably.

Teaching Notes

Teaching and learning experiences for students in the Exploratory phase are organised under the following headings:
• Building Vocabulary
• Understanding the Conventions of Spoken Texts
• Understanding the Behaviours Associated with Speaking and Listening
• Understanding the Conventions of Listening

Building Vocabulary

Research has shown that vocabulary acquisition is crucial to academic development (Baker, Sinnons & Kameenui 1998), so it is important for teachers to ensure that students in the Exploratory phase have every opportunity to expand their vocabulary across a broad range of contexts and experiences.

Developing Vocabulary

By creating a rich language environment that includes reading aloud, storytelling, conversations, discussions, inquiries, poetry, rhymes and songs, Exploratory Speakers and Listeners will be immersed in a variety of models and purposes for speaking and listening. Students can be supported to develop their vocabulary in the following ways:

- Jointly construct charts of interesting words, unusual or favourite words (from stories, games, television, movies, songs, etc.)
- Value play, social interactions and unplanned talk.
- Value and build on students' home language.
- Model choice of words for different purposes.
- Introduce subject-specific language and provide opportunities for students to explore and use new vocabulary. Add word charts to learning centres or displays.

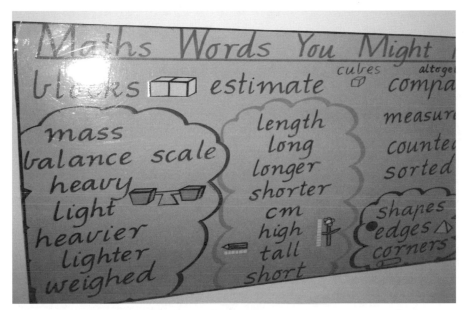

Figure 6.19 Learning centre word charts

Elizabeth:	First you … you … get your tin and make **lines** for… for … showing how … how much you need to cut. Then you **roll** … roll the ball into … the **clay** into a ball then you … you … **flatten** it with a **roller**. You … then you get your piece of **paper** that you **cut** out and lay it onto the clay and cut it … cut it with a **special tool** that … that … that … that cuts the clay.
Teacher:	What other things do you need to do, Elizabeth?
Elizabeth:	You make it into a round **shape** and you … and then you make the bottom and you **decorate** it and then you make the top with … put a hole in it and … and … then you put it in the **kiln**.

Figure 6.20 A transcript of student using subject-specific language (art)

- Provide experiences that require students to use talk to inquire, explore and manipulate language e.g. solve a maths problem, explain the findings of a science experiment.
- Organise activities, such as excursions, outside the classroom to introduce new vocabulary for authentic purposes.
- Provide experiences such as inviting visitors to the classroom, e.g. design questions for a visiting community member.

Understanding the Conventions of Spoken Texts

Understanding the conventions of speaking is linked to understanding the functions of spoken language (see Chapter 1). Language structures and features are selected to make what is said clear and comprehensible to the listener. Choices for unplanned, informal conversations will differ to choices made when students are investigating a problem or a procedure. These choices will again be different to those of planned speaking. At all phases of development, it is essential that students are exposed to different models of speaking so that attention can be drawn to the structures and features needed to suit the purpose.

The *structure* of spoken text refers to the way information is organised and presented in a text. These could include:
– describing an event
– giving directions
– retelling a story.

The *language features* of a spoken text refer to the type of vocabulary, grammar, tone and pace chosen. For example:
– using colloquial words or sayings when conversing with friends
– recognising emotive language to persuade in an advertisement
– stressing certain words or altering volume to gain impact.

Teachers can involve students in a variety of challenging experiences that will promote an understanding of the choices required for speaking and listening for different purposes.
- Explore chants and rhymes where students can explore the repetitive structures as well as the features of these texts.
- Use audio or video tapes to focus on talk as an object, e.g. **What interesting words did they use? How did we know what (the character) wanted? Did you hear a question? Did you hear an explanation, description, request, etc? How did you know?**
- Model Standard English where appropriate, e.g. **How will we explain this science experiment to parents when they visit? How will we give directions to people on the day of the fete?**
- Provide opportunities for students to discuss the different structures and features of speech used for different purposes and for different audiences, e.g. **planning for assembly.**
- Model how to use conjunctions when speaking to extend sentences, e.g. **justify an opinion during a discussion using 'because', 'as', 'since'** …
- Model the use of the correct tense. Jointly construct charts to act as reminders.

Figure 6.21 Ways to speak in a group

Purpose	Language Features
Introduction	Greeting, mention names, use a slow loud voice
Entertainment	Poem — choral speaking, slow down, listen to each other and keep together, use loud and soft voices for effect
Awards	Read certificates, rehearsed speaking, practise tricky pronunciations

Figure 6.22 Purpose and style of speaking

- Provide opportunities for students to plan speaking tasks, e.g. take turns to be reporter for group investigations, give a book report, take part in a Reader's Theatre, dramatise a story, etc.

Conversations

Conversations are important in establishing and maintaining relationships through expressing feelings and sharing experiences. Conversations enable us to give and receive information and compare ideas. This type of unplanned speaking and listening not only develops self-awareness and interpersonal skills; it helps to build topic knowledge and processes for learning.

Figure 6.23 Students in conversation

Teachers can provide opportunities for students to engage in uninterrupted, sustained conversations by:
- modelling conversations.
- allowing students to converse about topics of personal interest.
- providing time each day for conversations.

- encouraging students to participate in conversations with children and adults from other areas of the school.
- encouraging conversations in response to books, movies, unplanned visitors or events.
- teaching prompts to help students initiate conversations.

Understanding the Behaviours Associated with Speaking and Listening

Students need to be aware of the behaviours associated with speaking and listening and how it affects meaningful communication in a variety of contexts. Teachers can involve students in choosing appropriate speaking and listening behaviours through modelling, explicit teaching and discussion. Jointly constructing Y charts or T charts will provide meaningful reminders.

Teachers could involve students in reflecting on what they know about speaking and listening before commencing a series of activities. Take time later to stop and ask students to record their reflections on what they have learned as a result of engaging in a series of activities. (See the Speaking and Listening CD-ROM, Early Phase: Conventions, for an example of a 'Before and After' recording format.)

The following list may provide some useful starting points when considering effective behaviours.

- Suggest students speak clearly and with enough volume so those in the audience can hear and understand.
- Discuss body language when speaking, e.g. **appropriate eye contact, proximity to listener.**
- Discuss body language when listening, e.g. **nodding your head, proximity to speaker.**
- Interpret body language for emotional cues, e.g. **Is the person interested in what you are saying or do you need to change the subject?**
- Discuss how an audience behaves, e.g. **when listening as a group member in order to contribute to a discussion; to instructions; to a grandparent telling a story.**
- Talk about ways to acknowledge what a person has said in a discussion and how to build on their ideas.
- Discuss ways to encourage shy people.
- Discuss ways to approach an adult to ask for help.
- Discuss ways to behave in difficult situations, e.g. **when someone feels angry or upset.**

Understanding the Conventions of Listening

Listening is an active, constructive process concerned with making meaning from verbal and non-verbal cues. Effective listening depends on the expectations and predictions about content, language and genre that the listener brings to the text (Gibbons 2002). The way in which we listen is also linked to the context of the communication. We listen differently during unplanned, spontaneous situations (e.g. in casual conversations) than we do when speaking and listening is planned and formal, e.g. in the classroom when instructions are being given. The structures and features of listening can be considered using the following framework.

Type of Listening	Features
Appreciative listening	• Notices sound quality (pitch, volume, tone). • Interprets mood and emotion. • Notices rhyme, alliteration, onomatopoeia.
Critical listening	• Prepares to respond, to agree or disagree. • Demonstrates attention through body language, e.g. nodding or eye contact. • Remembers key ideas. • Paraphrases or summarises a spoken text. • Distinguishes between fact and opinion. • Detects bias and prejudice.
Empathic listening	• Notices underlying emotions and the speaker's intent. • Uses sympathetic questioning to clarify and understand key messages.

Figure 6.24 Types of listening

Teachers can assist students to become familiar with and use the conventions of listening by providing opportunities for students to:
• engage in conversations.
• listen to speech constructed for different purposes.
• respond to spoken texts, e.g.
  – retell a favourite part of a story
  – encourage drawing, painting and sculpting
  – join in and remember songs, chants and poems
  – answer requests
  – follow directions
  – answer questions
  – listen for key words and ideas
  – comment on another person's ideas
  – join in a game.

Figure 6.25

Involving Students

1 Take a Picture

Take a Picture helps students to enhance their vocabulary and practise the structures and features of spoken language. Prepare a series of pictures from magazines, postcards, commercial posters or photographs taken in and around the classroom.

Students could work in pairs or small groups, using the pictures to create a narrative by brainstorming possible settings, characters, problems and events. The narrative could be rehearsed and presented to another group. Students could take photographs to help clarify a procedure, e.g. during a science experiment or when constructing a sculpture.

2 Sorting and Classifying Activities

Sorting and Classifying Activities develop students' vocabulary to describe objects and their attributes. Students learn the features of descriptive language and develop the ability to structure their talk effectively by describing similarities and differences. Students do this by using phrases such as:

- more than …
- less than …
- it is similar/ different because …
- it belongs here because …
- it is the same as …
- it is different to …
- although …
- instead of …
- so that …

Teachers may design sorting and classifying activities based on the following criteria:

- Perceptual criteria: size, shape, colour, texture, parts, materials or features.
- Knowledge criteria: location, function, operation, characteristics, habits, action, properties or family group.
- Evaluative criteria: usefulness, value, attractiveness, interest level, durability, quality, condition, safety, suitability or fashion.

Students can determine for themselves the number of groups for the classification. It may be useful to have a 'NOT SURE' group. Students then share their ideas with a larger group and the classifications can be discussed.

It is important to teach the conventions of giving feedback or an opinion in this type of sharing so that comments are made about the idea rather than the person, e.g. I agree with… I disagree with

… I would like to add to what Joshua said … I challenge the idea …
I agree with part of what you said but…

See the Speaking and Listening CD-ROM, Exploratory Phase:
Conventions for sorting and classifying sheets.

How Might This Activity Be Used in Your Class?

- Do the students need practice in sorting and classifying concrete
  materials or are they ready to deal with more abstract ideas?
- Do students justify their reasons for grouping? Does the class need
  a visual reminder of the types of phrases they could use to justify
  their thinking?
- Small groups can classify materials and come to an agreed rule.
  One member of the group stays at this location while the rest of
  the group rotates to another position. Newly arrived students try
  to guess the classification rule.

3 Guessing Games

Refer to Chapter 5, Early Speaking and Listening Phase, p. 119.

4 Comparison Activities

Comparison Activities are described in detail in Chapter 5 (see
p. 119). They can be adapted to suit students in the Exploratory
phase by structuring the activity to complement a unit of work.
For example, ask students to work in pairs. Have students draw a
diagram of the water cycle, a story map or the life cycle of a frog.
Students then engage in speaking and listening to compare.

How Might This Activity Be Used in Your Class?

- Ask students to note the main differences between the
  comparisons. Ask: Was any important information left out? (e.g.
  an important label in a drawing of a life cycle.)
- Ask the partners to share their findings with a larger group or
  the whole class so they can prepare a planned talk and have the
  opportunity to share them with a different audience.

5 Barrier Games

Refer to Chapter 5, Early Speaking and Listening Phase, p. 123.

6 Watch Your Tone

Watch Your Tone is explained in detail in Chapter 5 (see p. 125).
This activity can be adapted for students in the Exploratory phase
by drawing on a wider range of examples.

Brainstorm and chart a list of phrases that could be said using a different tone of voice. Add labels to describe the tone, e.g. **happy, angry, frustrated, confused, sad, nervous, impatient, pleading.**

See the Speaking and Listening CD-ROM, Early Phase: Conventions (Watch Your Tone) for an example of a recording idea.

How Might This Activity Be Used in Your Class?

- Ask students to repeat phrases using different tones of voice, e.g. **angry, surprised, curious, sad, happy,** etc. Try using whispers and loud voices.
- Invite students to reflect on times they have noticed that the *tone* in someone's voice 'speaks louder' than the words.
- Ask students to reflect on how they can use tone to improve their communication.
- Select a poem to read aloud. Jointly decide on the words that should be emphasised. These words could be highlighted in some way. Decide where the pauses should be or where the volume and pace should change.

7 Body Talk

This activity promotes awareness of what attentive listening looks like and why it is important in particular contexts. It may provide a springboard for making class agreements on how students should behave when attentive listening is expected. Teachers could involve students in making charts as reminders.

Make a set of cards that have words to describe behaviour, e.g. **fidgeting, looking around, mumbling to yourself, yawning and stretching, rocking back and forth,** etc. See the Speaking and Listening CD-ROM, Early Phase: Conventions for an example of cards.

Students work in pairs. The whole class could participate or a teacher may choose one pair to demonstrate the process for the rest of the class. The speaker will be asked to talk about something familiar, e.g. **to describe a recent event.** The listener is given a card telling them how to behave.

Allow the activity to continue for about thirty seconds. Stop the class and debrief the activity by asking guiding questions, e.g.
Speaker: How did you feel when … *(listener)* … was fidgeting, looking around …

Listener: Were you able to understand … *(speaker)* … when you were fidgeting, looking around …

Have students brainstorm behaviours that would assist communication. Discuss the contexts when attentive listening is expected. Ask them to role play these new behaviours and discuss the different effects. Students could record their findings in a journal.

How Might This Activity Be Used in Your Class?

Introduce the role of observer. Students could observe speaking or listening behaviours in activities for a range of learning areas.

8 Analyse a Video

Analyse a Video is described in detail in Chapter 5 (see p. 127). It can be adapted for students in the Exploratory phase by increasing the complexity of the activity. Choose a video segment to complement a current classroom topic, e.g. choose a text that demonstrates a procedure or gives an explanation.

This activity is also suitable for the Consolidating, Conventional and Proficient phases.

How Might This Activity Be Used in Your Class?

Students watch the video without sound. They then work in small groups to create a script to accompany the video or they work in a small group to 'set the scene', e.g. What happened before the action in this video clip? What will happen next?

9 Role Plays

Role Plays can be used to develop skills of entering or leaving a conversation or a game. Introduce a scenario to the class and engage students in brainstorming possible responses. Discuss ways to include people. Discuss ways of politely refusing a request. After brainstorming, assign roles and allow students to act out the scene.

Scenario	Things to Say *(Example)*
Sam is eating lunch on his own because his best friend is away. He wants to join another group.	*'Hi'* (say names). *'Can I sit with you today?'* Use names. Keep voice friendly.
John wants to join a game of handball with Emma and Ben. How should he ask? What should Emma and Ben say?	*'Hi Emma and Ben, could I play, too?'* *'We're just finishing this game, then you can play.'* *'John, we're playing the best out of three so we won't be finished for a while.'* Use names. Keep voice friendly. Give short explanations.
Jan has arrived at school late and has missed the first part of a sharing circle. How can the other group members help her to feel included?	*'Hi everyone. Sorry I'm late.'* *'Hi Jan. Sally has just been telling us about her dancing class last night.'* *'They are going to put on a concert. You can have a turn after Dan.'* Jan joins the group quickly. The others tell her what is happening and how she can join in.

Figure 6.26 Role play scenario cards

Make up scenario cards as a result of these discussions and add to them for future use (see Figure 6.26 and also the Speaking and Listening CD-ROM, Exploratory Phase: Conventions, Role Play Scenario Cards).

10 Telephone Talk

Telephone Talk develops an understanding of the way conversations are structured for using the telephone, by matching phrases and responses.

Prepare sets of cards with a conversation starter and a matching response. Cut out the cards and distribute. Students must move around the room, find a person and read their part until they find the person who has the matching half of their card. See the Speaking and Listening CD-ROM, Exploratory Phase: Conventions, (Telephone Talk) for a sample set of cards.

This activity is also suitable for the Consolidating phase.

How Might This Activity Be Used in Your Class?

- Involve students in discussions about when, where and why people use the telephone.
- Discuss the important nature of emergency calls. Teach students how to make an emergency call, giving essential details, e.g. name and address.

11 Take a Turn

Refer to Chapter 5, Early Speaking and Listening Phase, p. 121.

12 Ask an Expert

This activity involves students in preparing and responding to questions. Students should decide on a topic that they know a lot about, e.g. a sport they play, a collection they have, a game they know well, a series of books they have been reading or a favourite subject.

Prepare students by immersing them in the idea of an expert panel. Show an excerpt from a television sports commentary or a quiz program where contestants choose a category. Ask students to note the structure of the program, e.g.
- How were questions asked?
- How long were the answers? How much detail was given?
- How were turns organised?
- What type of listening was needed?
- What tone of voice was used?
- Would you change anything?

– Was anyone in the audience inspired to learn more about one of the subjects?

Group students according to common interests; they will become members of the 'expert panel'. Help the class to generate lists of 'open' questions that could be directed to the experts.

Students should prepare and rehearse a short introduction giving the audience background information on their subject and why they have become interested. The audience will listen carefully and respond with probing questions.

How Might This Activity Be Used in Your Class?

- Use the idea of experts when developing a unit of work. Groups of students could be responsible for researching different aspects of a topic. They would be responsible for sharing their knowledge with the class through some form of presentation.
- Invite another class to visit your group of experts. How will the students adjust their presentations for a different audience?
- Use expert groups to present to parents on an open night, or a learning journey.

PROCESSES AND STRATEGIES

Major Teaching Emphases

- **Discuss and reflect on the use of thinking to make meaning in speaking and listening.**

- **Provide opportunities for students to engage in sustained conversations,** e.g. with peers, teachers and known adults.

- **Teach a range of planning tools for speaking,** e.g. how to share ideas.

- **Teach planning tools that focus on listening before, during and after activities,** e.g. identify key ideas, record ideas in a graphic organiser.

- **Model responses to miscommunication,** e.g. how to stop, rephrase and repeat.

Organisation of the Processes and Strategies Aspect

There are several differences in the organisation of the Processes and Strategies aspect. Both the Teaching Notes and the Teaching and Learning Experiences (Involving Students) are in the *Speaking and Listening Resource Book*, Chapter 4: Processes and Strategies.

The rationale for this difference in organisation is that the processes and strategies of speaking and listening are not conceptually hierarchical and therefore not phase-specific. In all phases, a variety of speaking and listening processes and strategies need to be introduced, developed and consolidated.

What varies from one phase to the next is the growth in the:
- number and integration of strategies used throughout the processes of speaking and listening.
- awareness and monitoring of speaking and listening processes.
- efficiency in the uses of the speaking and listening processes.
- ability to articulate the use of the strategies used in the process of speaking and listening.
- awareness of how the use of processes helps with composing and listening to texts.

Supporting Parents of Exploratory Speakers and Listeners

GENERAL DESCRIPTION

Exploratory Speakers and Listeners have been learning to use Standard English appropriately in different settings. They are developing knowledge needed to choose appropriate ways of speaking to suit different people and circumstances.

They communicate successfully in both structured and unstructured situations. They explore ways of using words, tone and body language for different speaking and listening purposes.

Teachers will find that parents are able to support their children effectively when they have an understanding of how children learn and if they are aware of what happens in the classroom. Teachers can help build parent awareness of the learning program in which their child is involved in these kinds of ways:

- Invite parents to join in class activities and talk to them before and after the activity, e.g. **The children are … The adult's role in this task is to … How did the children enjoy this task? What did you find was effective in helping them to understand?**

- Conduct parent/caregiver workshops on learning e.g. **Learning Through Play, Learning with Technology, Helping Children to Learn.**

- Make a video/DVD/CD-ROM with the children to demonstrate certain features of the learning program. Each family can take it home to view with their children. A viewing guide can be created with the student's input.

- When creating displays of student work, add information about the context of the activity and list the important learning that took place during the task.

- Provide students with home-learning tasks that involve them sharing their learning with family members.

Supporting Exploratory Speakers and Listeners in the Home

Exploratory Speakers and Listeners will benefit from a range of these experiences in the home setting. Ideas for providing these appropriate experiences are available on Parent Cards located on the *First Steps* Speaking and Listening CD-ROM. Teachers can select appropriate cards for each Exploratory Speaker and Listener and copy them for parent use.

Parent Cards

1 General Description of Exploratory Speakers and Listeners

2 Developing an Understanding About Different Types of Speaking and Listening

3 Developing an Understanding About Contexts

4 Developing Vocabulary

5 Listening

6 Family Meetings

CHAPTER 7

Consolidating Speaking and Listening Phase

Unplanned	Planned

Unplanned

(Some overlapping)

Martin: On mine, I have to put safety tips,'cos it's more dangerous.

Sam: I'd say like, you know, include other tips and steps included, what about you?

Martin: Well, I'm going to do the title, the same title as you, but I'm going to do steps harder and move a tyre off a bike. And I'm gonna do what materials you need, like you need a spanner and etc.

Sam: Oh yeah.

Martin: I'll do safety tips, because you never know, you could hurt yourself while you're fixing it. Your finger could get stuck in something get jammed or anything, and umm, so I'm gonna do steps to show and maybe some tips, yeah.

Sam: Well, with the safety tips, would you like … do you think you could … Are you gonna write some tips if your finger did get jammed or something?

Martin: Oh, I might do that, but that might …

Sam: It might be a bit difficult.

Martin: Yeah.

Figure 7.1

Planned

Martin: I wanted to teach you how to remove the front tyre of your bike. Well, the materials … You need two spanners, adjustable or the special size, WD 40, that um … loosens um … the a bearings, and a cloth to wash and wipe your hands if you're…. Tips: wear dirty clothes 'cos WD 40 can go over you once you …
OK, the steps are, turn your bike upside down, you know how it turns it upside down, that's pretty easy, then get your WD 40 and spray the bearings on the two sides off your bike

Teacher: So WD 40 is a spray?

Martin: Yeah it ah … prevents rust and it loosens. Step 3 put your spanner on one of, one of the bearings on either side. You have to hold it, and then you put your other spanner on the other side and then turn it clockwise, um … once the bearing has fell off you have to take off the other one, 'cos it is still there, um … pull the tyre through the gap, 'cos there's a gap which you can push the tyre up. And that's how you remove a front tyre if you'd like to. And safety tips when you spray WD 40, pretty obvious, don't drink it and try not to put fingers in small places in the bike.

Figure 7.2

Global Statement

In this phase, students use most language structures and features of Standard Australian English appropriately when speaking in a range of contexts.

They show increasing awareness of the needs of their audience. They experiment with ways to adjust listening and speaking to suit different purposes.

Consolidating Speaking and Listening Indicators

Use of Texts

◆ **Listens effectively to obtain specific information from informational and expressive spoken texts.**

◆ **Composes spoken texts using most text structures and features appropriately in planned situations.**

◆ **Uses a range of unplanned spoken texts effectively as ideas are being developed.**

• Listens and responds to peers in problem-solving groups, showing attention to the task, e.g. extend others' suggestions, generate plans for completing a task.

• Reports briefly to the class on a group discussion or activity, e.g. present a list of group generated ideas.

• Attempts to persuade others in the class to a point of view or action, presenting a few reasons, e.g. why a classroom rule should be changed.

• Combines personally significant opinions with information to interest their audience.

• Conducts brief interviews to obtain information about an issue or topic, e.g. preferences for the canteen menu.

Contextual Understanding

◆ **Is aware that certain forms of spoken text are associated with particular contexts and purposes.**

◆ **Is aware that speaking and listening can be adjusted for different purposes,** e.g. socialising, informing.

◆ **Understands the need to provide background information to enhance meaning,** e.g. give examples.

◆ **Understands that people may represent their own points of view through spoken texts.**

◆ **Uses a small range of devices to enhance meaning,** e.g. rephrasing, adjusting volume and speed of speech, negotiating meaning.

• Compares the features of different spoken texts and talks about how these are related to purpose or context, e.g. compares a telephone conversation with a face-to-face discussion.

• Recognises the importance of Standard English.

• Knows when Standard English is required.

• Recognises alternative interpretations of the same spoken texts.

Conventions

◆ **Varies vocabulary to add interest or to describe with greater accuracy.**

◆ **Uses most language structures and features appropriate to purpose,** e.g. indicates cause and effect, adjusts level of formality according to context.

◆ **Responds appropriately to spoken language in informal and some formal situations for different purposes,** e.g. attends and contributes to small group discussions, by building on others' ideas, providing feedback.

◆ **Selects listening and speaking behaviours to suit the purpose and audience in familiar situations,** e.g. more formal with teachers than peers, adds more detail when listener is unfamiliar with context of speech, uses more comprehension checks when providing unfamiliar information.

• Begins to adopt grammatical patterns for formal speaking.

• Listens to share and compare information.

• Listens to give explanations, draw conclusions, present an argument.

• Listens for words that signal fact or opinion.

Processes and Strategies

◆ **Reflects on speaking and listening activities and uses this knowledge in an attempt to improve communication.**

◆ **Uses a variety of processes and strategies when speaking,** e.g. justifies and explains statements.

◆ **Uses a variety of processes and strategies when listening,** e.g. asks questions to seek confirmation.

◆ **Selects and adjusts verbal and non-verbal behaviours for particular groups,** e.g. younger children.

• Uses scaffolds to plan listening strategies, e.g. graphic organisers, talk diary.

• Discusses with peers and the teacher strategies for communicating with others in different situations.

• Begins to monitor and responds to miscommunication, e.g. stops, rephrases, repeats.

Major Teaching Emphases

Environment and Attitude (see p. 180)

- Provide opportunities for relevant, challenging and purposeful communication.
- Create a supportive environment which values the diversity of students' speaking and listening development (in their home languages).
- Encourage students to see the value of effective listening and speaking for community, school and family life.

Use of Texts (see p. 184)

- Discuss and explore a range of functional spoken texts composed in Standard English.
- Provide opportunities for students to participate in authentic unplanned and planned speaking and listening.
- Provide opportunities for students to participate in extended talk.
- Teach students to extend ideas logically and coherently in spoken texts to suit a particular purpose.
- Teach students to locate and interpret complex information from spoken texts on new and familiar topics.
- Teach students the metalanguage associated with speaking and listening and encourage its use, e.g. orientation, conclusion, dialect, terms for forms of Australian English, e.g. slang, colloquial, negotiate, attend, facial expression, gesture, strategy, comparison, monitor.

Contextual Understanding (see p. 195)

- Discuss ways in which spoken texts can be constructed and adjusted for different purposes, e.g. through register, dialect, vocabulary choices.
- Provide opportunities for students to reflect upon the way in which they interact with particular audiences, e.g. degree of formality, type of vocabulary, topics discussed, code-switching/code-mixing.
- Teach students to include relevant details and information of interest to their listeners when speaking.
- Teach students how to contribute to discussions of matters that interest or affect them.

- Provide opportunities for students to analyse the way people's beliefs and opinions influence the construction of spoken texts.
- Teach students to reflect upon the way in which they express their opinions.
- Teach the use of devices and discuss how they influence meaning, e.g. volume, tone, pace, emphasis, vocabulary choices, amount of detail, type of examples provided.

Conventions (see p. 206)

- Provide opportunities for students to develop, refine and use new vocabulary.
- Teach structures and features that extend and elaborate communication in informal and formal contexts, e.g. how to state and justify an opinion.
- Continue to teach conversational skills, e.g. turn taking, negotiating meaning, managing topic changes.
- Teach students to recognise the different speaking and listening behaviours that are needed for different contexts.
- Teach students listening skills needed to respond appropriately in a variety of situations, e.g. how to offer alternate viewpoints sensitively, how to identify different points of view.

Processes and Strategies (see p. 217)

- Provide opportunities for students to reflect on thinking strategies used for speaking and listening, e.g. encourage students to set goals to improve speaking and listening, consider evidence to support an opinion, think through an issue before raising it with others.
- Provide opportunities for students to engage in sustained conversations and discussions, e.g. how to build on the ideas of others, paraphrasing, giving and seeking opinions.
- Teach students to select planning tools to help them speak effectively in a range of contexts, e.g. debates, in group contexts related to school contexts, with peers and unknown adults in social contexts.
- Teach students to use scaffolds to plan for listening, e.g. how to set goals for listening, how to make accurate notes, how to summarise key ideas from a spoken text.
- Teach strategies to repair miscommunication, e.g. by seeking feedback (confirmation check), clarifying message, rephrasing.

Teaching and Learning Experiences

ENVIRONMENT AND ATTITUDE

Major Teaching Emphases

- Provide opportunities for relevant, challenging and purposeful communication.

- Create a supportive classroom environment which values the diversity of students' speaking and listening development (in their home languages).

- Encourage students to see the value of effective listening and speaking for community, school and family life.

Teaching Notes

A classroom community that supports and nurtures students in the Consolidating phase is one that promotes problem-solving, sharing, cooperative and collaborative experiences to develop skills needed for more complex activities and social contexts. By providing a variety of authentic purposes and audiences for speaking and listening, students will become confident and enthusiastic communicators. The focus for developing positive attitudes towards speaking and listening is organised under the following headings:

- Creating a Supportive Classroom Environment
- Opportunities for Relevant, Challenging and Purposeful Communication
- Speaking and Listening for Community, School and Family Life

Creating a Supportive Classroom Environment

A supportive classroom environment is one that takes into account both the physical aspects and the culture of the classroom. A positive classroom climate is one in which students have opportunities to speak and listen; for a range of purposes where others show an interest and value what they say.

Physical Environment

When organising the physical environment of the classroom, teachers need to consider the grouping arrangements for different speaking and listening purposes. Teachers can involve students in making decisions regarding efficient ways to move in and out of groups and to arrange furniture and resources. Other considerations for an effective physical environment are listed below.

- Provide space for small-group/whole-class interactions, e.g. class meetings, games, partner and small-group work.
- Provide time and suitable areas that cater for independent activities that will stimulate conversation and discussion. Have students share responsibility for the care and storage of materials and equipment.
- Provide a Listening Post with a variety of books and audio tapes, CD-ROM and computer software. Students can also engage in repeated listening experiences as an aid to remembering or discussing texts.
- Provide hand-held dictaphones or MP3 players to enable students to record their speaking that can be shared with others. The recordings could also help students to reflect on their speaking and assist them in their goal setting.
- Provide recordings of a variety of radio segments for students to listen to and analyse for a variety of purposes, e.g. interview, sports commentaries, advertisements, etc.
- Provide recordings of television segments for students to listen to and analyse the spoken language used in advertisements, documentaries or information programs.
- Involve students in developing classroom displays that showcase their work, illustrate new concepts or support their learning of new skills. Encourage students to use these displays when explaining or describing classroom experiences to visitors.

Figure 7.3

Classroom Culture

It is important to develop a classroom culture where students can confidently explore new ways of speaking and listening. Teachers can create a supportive environment for speaking and listening in a variety of meaningful ways. These may include:

- Remain sensitive to cultural difference.
- Maintain an emphasis on enjoyment.
- Communicate your high expectations to students.
- Value social talk and the use of home language.
- Assist students to experiment with new ideas and vocabulary.
- Provide genuine purposes to speak to different audiences.
- Encourage students to choose different speaking formats.
- Motivate students to speak to all members of the class.
- Provide opportunities for students to review and reflect on their learning.

Opportunities for Relevant, Challenging and Purposeful Communication

Students in the Consolidating phase will need to be supported as they engage in speaking and listening to a wide range of audiences for a variety of purposes. Teachers will assist students to use their skills in the following ways.

- Teach students when to use Standard English to achieve a particular purpose.
- Model attentive listening and rephrasing to clarify meaning of texts.
- Expose students to a variety of informational texts, e.g. news reports, panel discussions, interviews or lectures.
- Provide resources for students to record own spoken texts, e.g. video and audio recordings.
- Tell stories and invite guest storytellers.
- Involve students in exploring ideas in all learning areas, e.g. explain the findings of a social survey.
- Develop skills to promote social interactions e.g. how to join a conversation or a game, how to sustain a conversation, change a topic or negotiate meaning.

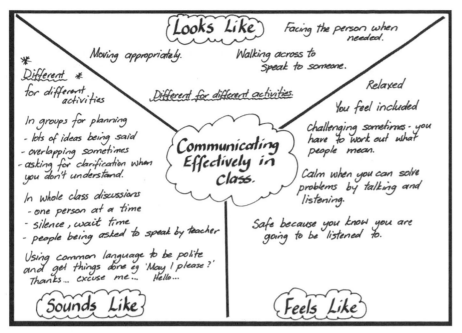

Looks Like

Facing the person when needed.

Moving appropriately.

Walking across to speak to someone.

Different for different activities

Different for different activities

Relaxed

You feel included

Communicating Effectively in Class.

Challenging sometimes - you have to work out what people mean.

Calm when you can solve problems by talking and listening.

In groups for planning
- lots of ideas being said
- overlapping sometimes
- asking for clarification when you don't understand.

In whole class discussions
- one person at a time
- silence, wait time
- people being asked to speak by teacher

Using common language to be polite and get things done eg 'May I please?' Thanks... excuse me... Hello...

Safe because you know you are going to be listened to.

Sounds Like

Feels Like

Figure 7.4 A Y chart developed with students about communicating

Speaking and Listening for Community, School and Family Life

Students in the Consolidating phase are showing an increased awareness of how different situations, purposes and audiences, require different styles of spoken language. They are starting to reflect on how they and others vary speaking to suit different purposes.

Teachers can support the students' language development at this phase by helping them to develop an awareness of how language is used in different situations. For example, students need to know:

- that certain types of speech are used by themselves and others in different community settings.
- how to talk to a person in authority.
- how to adapt speech for the elderly or very young.
- how to sense a person's need from a hint or question.

Teachers can also guide students by:

- using group discussion behaviours, e.g. turn taking, Think-Pair-Share.
- encouraging them to use their negotiation skills in group discussions, class meetings or social conversations.
- inviting them to explore appropriate ways to request something of peers and adults.
- enabling them to explore ways of acknowledging another person's point of view.
- helping them develop competence in giving and following directions.

USE OF TEXTS

Major Teaching Emphases

- Discuss and explore a range of functional spoken texts composed in Standard English.

- Provide opportunities for students to participate in authentic unplanned and planned speaking and listening.

- Provide opportunities for students to participate in extended talk.

- Teach students to extend ideas logically and coherently in spoken texts to suit a particular purpose.

- Teach students to locate and interpret complex information from spoken texts on new and familiar topics.

- Teach students the metalanguage associated with speaking and listening and encourage its use, e.g. orientation, conclusion, dialect, terms for forms of Australian English, e.g. slang, colloquial, negotiate, attend, facial expression, gesture, strategy, comparison, monitor.

Teaching Notes

The focus for supporting Consolidating Speakers and Listeners in this aspect is organised under the following headings:
- Exposure to a Range of Spoken Texts
- Participation in Unplanned and Planned Spoken Texts
- Using Spoken Texts Purposefully
- Developing Topic Knowledge
- Developing Metalanguage

Exposure to a Range of Spoken Texts

Consolidating Speakers and Listeners use most language structures and features appropriately as they speak for different purposes. As they are now experimenting with various ways of modifying listening and speaking, it is important that they have the opportunity to engage with a variety of functional spoken texts in the context of different learning experiences. These texts can be face-to-face or multi-modal including films, radio programs, DVDs, CD-ROMs, the PA system or the telephone.

Spoken language may include greetings, conversations, giving directions and using talk to explore new learning. Teachers also need to consider the specific needs of students when selecting texts.

Teachers can use Familiarising Teaching and Learning Practices to support students' development in using a range of spoken texts. (See Effective Teaching and Learning Practices in the *First Steps Linking Assessment Teaching and Learning book*, p. 124.)

Participation in Unplanned and Planned Spoken Texts

Consolidating Speakers and Listeners need frequent opportunities to interact with each other in different group sizes. By participating in different activities and receiving informative feedback, students will be able to reflect on their use of language and will develop an increased awareness of the specific requirements of different forms of spoken text.

Below are some suggestions that will allow Consolidating Speakers and Listeners to participate in unplanned and planned speaking and listening.

- Getting organised with a partner or small group
- Meeting and greeting people
- Independent inquiry learning tasks
- Personal learning time
- Lunch and recess times
- Packing away resources or equipment
- Science and maths activities
- Partner or small-group reading
- Collaborative tasks
- Reading conference
- Reader's circle
- Writer's conference
- Writer's circle
- Class meeting
- Learning goals
- Inquiry groups.

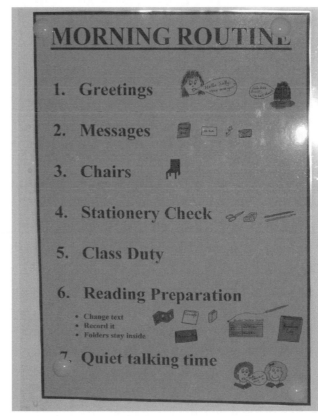

Figure 7.5 A morning routine negotiated with students provides speaking and listening opportunities

It is valuable to provide students with the time to participate in extended talk in the previous situations as it enables them to socialise and to put their thoughts into words. Socialisation, exploration of ideas and experimentation with materials are important components of students' learning at school.

Students' understandings about spoken texts develop over time through Modelled, Shared and Guided Speaking and Listening sessions. Below are some key understandings.

- Speaking and listening is useful for different social and learning purposes.
- Australian English varies.
- Speakers may put forward their own points of view.
- Speaking and listening changes according to how well you know the people involved, the purpose of the communication and the situation in which it occurs.
- Speakers and listeners organise spoken texts for different purposes.
- Listening behaviours may change in different school and community situations.
- Non-verbal language varies according to the context.
- Planning can help speakers to communicate effectively.

Using Spoken Texts Purposefully

Through carefully scaffolded discussions about specific spoken texts, students develop an awareness of the language structures and features of a range of text forms used for different purposes such as:

- meeting and greeting with a familiar or unfamiliar adult.
- sustaining conversations with unfamiliar audiences.
- making decisions in group work.
- accepting another person's point of view.
- providing an introduction to engage the listener when giving instructions about a popular game.
- using key words for headings, and expanding on them when presenting a description.
- comparing new events with previous events and other details to assist the listener to visualise the recount.
- summarising at the end of a report.

It is important that students realise that spoken language is influenced by the context, with the audience and purpose determining the structure of a spoken text. The examples provided in Figure 7.6 offer a starting point for teachers to consider how they might direct students' attention to text functions that suit particular purposes.

Beginning students communicate for …	Students in the Consolidating phase speak and listen to …	Teachers can do these things to draw students' attention to the different purposes and how to extend ideas logically and coherently.		
		Provide Direction	**Give a Comment**	**Ask a Question**
Getting things done.	• work with peers to plan and set up a new game for sport. • let a visiting teacher know how to find the library.	Tell your group about the game bocce and ask them to help you set it up for sport today.	You organised yourselves well to get the game set up so we can play it for sport.	What do you think you need to tell your group about bocce so that they can help you to set it up?
Influencing the behaviour, feelings or attitudes of others.	• prove to the group that an event did occur.	Use details to convince the group that your recount was a true account.	Now that you've given us more information, it does sound like that actually happened!	What did you say to convince your group that your recount of what happened was true?
Getting along with others.	• greet and depart. • join in conversations or tasks. • organise leisure time.	When you greet your kindergarten buddy, ask them a question about their week.	When you are developing a friendship with your buddy, it is good to find out about them.	What would you like to know about your buddy when we visit his/her class today?
Expressing individuality and personal feelings.	• explain what they want to do in a group play or project. • share their plans for their new skateboard with friends.	Include the ideas of everyone in your group to create your display.	It's good to see that you have been able to include each person's suggestions. You must have communicated well.	What is one thing that you want included? How can your group ensure that everybody's ideas are used for the display?
Seeking and learning about the social and physical environment.	• form questions to guide an inquiry into a new topic.	With a partner, pose questions you have about the main ideas of our topic.	I'd like to find that out, too. I'm not sure how that happens.	What else do you need to know to be able to talk about the main ideas of our topic?
Creating stories, games, new worlds and new texts.	• make a voice-over for the model for an interactive display. • create a skit for an assembly.	Your voice-over needs to demonstrate how the model is to be used in the future.	The voice-over matched the display and had details to let the visitors know what it was for.	What do you need to include to show that the model has been created to solve a problem?
Communicating information.	• let others know how they planned a project. • explain the class timetable to a parent.	Explain how you planned your project. Include what you did and why you chose to do it that particular way.	You organised your explanation and you gave a number of reasons, making it easy for the group to see the way you had planned your project.	What will you need to include when you explain how you planned for your project?
Entertaining others.	• discuss entertaining media and topics with peers. • retell stories, jokes and riddles.	Choose a text and topic to talk about that would make your kindergarten buddy feel happy.	You look like you enjoyed telling that story; it was very entertaining.	What can you do to make this topic entertaining or amusing for the junior class?

Figure 7.6 Examples for focusing on the functions of spoken texts

Developing Topic Knowledge

Students in the Consolidating phase are being challenged to understand new information and concepts. Teachers can support students by assessing and building on current knowledge and interests. Teachers can do this by:

- Talking and listening to students in informal situations, e.g. in between tasks, at recess and lunch times, during group work.
- Discussing student's responses to KWL (What do I know? What would I like to know? What have I learnt?). This can be done individually, as a group or a whole class.
- Observe students as they engage in open-ended tasks. Assess what they already know and what they do with the information.
- Interact with students after they have completed an inquiry, e.g. **Ask: How did you find that out? What do you need to do tomorrow with this activity?**
- Conduct one-on-one or group interviews with students about what they learnt.
- Negotiate topics to study with the students, e.g. **Ask: What would you like to learn about next? What do you know about …?**

(Overlapping is occurring in some sections.)

Joshua:	What do you know about frogs?
Elizabeth:	That they're amphibians.
Joshua:	I know they can breathe trough their skin and lungs.
Carl:	Can they? I didn't know that!
Joshua:	Yeah, that they are amphibians, that's all I know, oh yeah, and that they jump for bugs and flies and stuff.
Elizabeth:	I know that they can be lots of colours.
Joshua:	Red-eyed tree frogs have all the colours of the frogs on them … And they can poison us.
Elizabeth:	And they can fly.
Carl:	They can fly?
Elizabeth:	Some of them can fly.
Joshua:	Frogs can't fly.
Carl:	I wonder why they're called tadpoles.
Joshua:	*(reading from a book)* Tree frogs have group of fingers and … some can use their toes for swimming and some use 'em for digging and some use 'em for flying.
Carl:	How do frogs fly?
Elizabeth:	They jump pretty high, but sometimes they jump too a bit too high so they fly.
Joshua:	Is the … That's because they're a webbed, like their feet are webbed so they like, kind of glide.

Figure 7.7 Informal and unplanned discussion about frogs between Consolidating students and an Exploratory student

Developing Metalanguage

The language used to describe language is known as metalanguage. When students are able to use metalanguage to talk competently about their own speaking and listening, it allows them to understand how language operates. Teachers are encouraged to model the use of metalanguage in their daily interactions with students. Students can then demonstrate their understanding of metalanguage in a range of different ways. For example, when students identify different ways to greet people or use different ways to make a request from a friend and an adult, they are demonstrating metalinguistics awareness.

To help Consolidating Speakers and Listeners use the terms associated with speaking and listening, it is important to use metalanguage as part of everyday teaching — across learning areas, during subject-specific and topic-related discussions, during one-on-one conversations with students or as part of planned Modelled, Shared or Guided Learning sessions. For example, teachers may explicitly teach terms such as:

- Use of Texts: terms for particular text forms, e.g. **orientation, conclusion**
- Contextual Understanding: *dialect, Australian English terms*, e.g. **slang, colloquial**
- Conventions: *negotiate, attend, facial expression, gesture*
- Processes and Strategies: *strategy, plan, compare and contrast, infer, reflect.*

For further information about the Use of Texts aspect, see *Speaking and Listening Resource Book*, 2nd Edition.
- Chapter 1: Use of Texts
- Chapter 4: Processes and Strategies

Involving Students

1 Time for Talk

Time for Talk is an activity that encourages students to reflect on the text form, topic and audience they are using when talking to their partners. This activity is explained in detail in Chapter 6, p. 149, and can be easily adapted for students in the Consolidating phase by adapting some of the ideas outlined in that chapter. See the Speaking and Listening CD-ROM, Chapter 6, Exploratory Phase: Use of Texts (Time for Talk Student Records).

2 Conversation Starters

Conversation Starters is a partner activity that develops students' ability to initiate and sustain a conversation on a chosen topic. This activity helps to develop an understanding of how different text types are composed for different purposes.

Introduce Conversation Starters by providing students with a topic. Discuss the purpose for speaking on a particular topic to encourage students to think about the type of details that should be included. Keep a class chart of topics that have been discussed already as students will soon develop skills to choose topics independently. Choose from some of the ideas listed in the following table.

Purpose	Conversation Starters
To exchange personal information	*Tell your partner about:* • one person in your family. • what you usually do when you get home from school. • people and places your family likes to visit.
Sharing likes and dislikes	*Tell your partner:* • things you like to do on the weekends or on the holidays. • what your favourite TV program is and why. • things you like to do on a rainy day. • about your most treasured possession.
Recounting experiences	*Tell your partner what you remember about:* • last Christmas. • the last movie that you saw. • what happened at the last party that you went to. • something that happened on your favourite TV show.
Expressing opinions	*Tell your partner about:* • the one thing that makes you very angry. • what you think about kids' TV at the moment. • your favourite author. • how you would feel if all the trees around your school were cut down.
Describing and explaining	*Tell your partner:* • how to get from school to your house. • what your dream house would look like. • what your favourite sandwich is and how to make it. • how to play your favourite card game.
Entertaining	*Tell your partner:* • a joke or a few jokes. • a story that one of your grandparents has told you about when they were kids. • a tall tale, e.g. when you were a superhero. • part of a book that you have just read.
Imagining	*Tell your partner:* • what you would do if school was cancelled for the day. • what animal you would like to change into and why. • what the world would be like if you fell asleep for a hundred years and then woke up. • about a marvellous invention of yours.

Figure 7.8

3 Listen to Learn

Refer to Chapter 5, Early Speaking and Listening Phase, p. 99.

See the Speaking and Listening CD-ROM, Exploratory Phase: Use of Texts (Listen to Learn — Thinking Frameworks).

This activity is suitable for all phases.

How Might This Activity Be Used in Your Class?

- Choose spoken texts that will help students identify complex information.
- Use some visual headings or props to support students in extending their ideas logically and clearly when representing their learning.

4 Talk to Teach

Refer to Chapter 5, Early Speaking and Listening Phase, p. 101.

5 What's My Opinion?

This activity provides students with the opportunity to locate and interpret key information. It requires students to distinguish between fact and opinion and to evaluate how a speaker justifies an opinion. It also involves students in responding to the ideas and opinions of others.

Prepare an audio or video recording of people discussing a current issue or a topic. This may be from a television current affairs program, talk-back radio or a documentary.

- Students should listen to the recording and note the main information expressed by speakers. (Refer to Figure 7.9 as an example of a recording format.)
- Provide time for students to think about the opinions they have heard and to reflect on the way the speaker justified his or her thinking.
- Ask students to evaluate the strengths and weaknesses of the justifications/reasons given. Suggest they consider if the speaker was convincing.
- Students can prepare to take turns so they can express their ideas with others. Suggest prompts to help students initiate a response, e.g. **One point that I agreed with was ... because ... ; I disagreed with the idea that ... because ... ; I had never thought about ... before ... and I think ...**
- Decide on a way to take turns, e.g. **sharing circle, toss a foam ball around the group, toss around a ball of wool to make a conversation web.**

- Have students record a reflection on the activity in a journal, e.g. How well did they take part in the discussion? Did they have enough knowledge of the topic? Were they able to express ideas clearly? Did they have the appropriate vocabulary to express their feelings clearly?

Structure of Spoken Text	Comment or Example
Was the issue or problem clearly stated?	Did the person give a personal opinion? Did the speaker support their opinion? Did the speaker present any facts? Did the speaker offer a solution or a suggestion?

Figure 7.9 Recording Format

6 Reflect and Respond

Refer to Chapter 6, Exploratory Speaking and Listening Phase, p. 147.

7 What Comes Next?

Refer to Chapter 5, Early Speaking and Listening Phase, p. 97.

8 Getting to Know You

Getting to Know You is an activity designed to provide students with practice in asking and answering questions. It will help students to develop their interviewing skills.

Students work in pairs. Discuss the nature of questioning to gain information then how to listen carefully to respond with a related question or comment. Teach students to ask open-ended questions and to encourage the speaker to include details and points of interest, e.g. students could say, 'Tell me about: Your hobbies, sporting interests, favourite book, favourite movie, best holiday, favourite school subject, pets, etc.'

Allow students many opportunities to practise interviewing class members on familiar topics.

How Might This Activity Be Used in Your Class?

Have one student assume a different identity to role play in an interview, e.g. a sporting identity, a pop star or a movie actor. Questions could be designed to elicit information on their achievements or the pros and cons of being famous.

9 Mini Debate

A mini debate provides an opportunity for students to generate alternative arguments for a given topic. It allows students to see that there can be differing points of view surrounding a topic and that opinions need to be supported with reasons or evidence.

- Students can work in small groups of about four and sit in a circle.
- Introduce a topic, e.g. **the school day should be longer.**
- Students will take turns to give reasons as to why they agree with the statement.
- When everyone has had a turn, the group then suggests why they disagree with the statement.
- Reflection — discuss statements that seemed to support the statement and the opposing argument effectively.
- Discuss the word *rebuttal*. Teach students how to acknowledge a point of view but then suggest an argument that refutes that particular view.

How Might This Activity Be Used in Your Class?

- Involve students in discussing the difference between facts and opinions.
- Discuss with students how opinions and points of view are developed, e.g. **ask students questions such as, Where does evidence come from? Whose opinions do you value?**

10 Radio Play

Radio Play provides students with an opportunity to listen in order to analyse the structures and features of spoken narrative. This activity also asks students to compare and contrast the way that spoken language is used to entertain, now and from the past. Ask students to imagine a time before television and to list reasons why radio would have been an important part of people's lives, e.g. **news, music, entertainment such as plays, serials, quiz shows.** Provide a recording of a radio play or part of a serial program. Radio serials from the past may be found in national library archives, e.g. **National Library of Australia.** (Visit The National Collection of Screen and Sound website; www.nla.gov.au.)

Provide students with guiding questions to help them focus on their listening. Students should record answers to these questions as they are listening. Choose from some of the following ideas and questions.

- List the sound effects used in this story or play. How do you think the sound effects were created?

- Choose one sound effect. Describe how it adds to the meaning of the story.
- How does expression and tone of voice help to tell the story?
- List key words to describe the structure of the story, e.g. setting, main characters, problem, resolution.
- List any words or sayings that you heard in the historical recordings that may not be used in the same way today.
- Note the way words are pronounced and list any words that sound different to you.
- Identify attitudes, values or beliefs in the historical play or version. Consider if any are different from those that you hold.

How Might This Activity Be Used in Your Class?

- Have students create their own radio play with added sound effects. Record and share with another class.
- Ask students to interview older people to discover the role that radio may have played in their lives.

CONTEXTUAL UNDERSTANDING

Major Teaching Emphases

- **Discuss ways in which spoken texts can be constructed and adjusted for different purposes,** e.g. through register, dialect, vocabulary choices.

- **Provide opportunities for students to reflect upon the way in which they interact with particular audiences,** e.g. degree of formality, type of vocabulary, topics discussed, code-switching/ code-mixing.

- **Teach students to include relevant details and information of interest to their listeners when speaking.**

- **Teach students how to contribute to discussions of matters that interest or affect them.**

- **Provide opportunities for students to analyse the way people's beliefs and opinions influence the construction of spoken texts.**

- **Teach students to reflect upon the way in which they express their opinions.**

- **Teach the use of devices and discuss how they influence meaning,** e.g. volume, tone, pace, emphasis, vocabulary choices, amount of detail, type of example provided.

Teaching Notes

The focus for supporting Consolidating Speakers and Listeners in this aspect is organised under the following headings.
- Understandings About Context
- Reflecting on Interactions
- Considering the Needs of the Audience
- Contributing to Matters of Importance
- Investigating the Way Ideas and People Are Represented
- Use of Devices

Understandings About Context

Students in this phase are more aware of the impact of context on speaking and listening. Through their involvement in learning and teaching experiences across the curriculum, students learn about appropriate speaking and listening conventions for different situations. For example, students learn how to adjust speaking and listening when interviewing the principal as part of a class survey or when explaining a game to a younger student. Students need to be involved in planning before they encounter unfamiliar situations so they are aware of the adjustments that may be required when they speak and listen.

It is important that teachers allocate time for reflecting on the effectiveness of student language use. This will include discussions on situations that required a change in register, adjusting volume or vocabulary. Engaging in these types of discussions assists students to identify the language requirements of different contexts.

Reflecting on Interactions

Students in the Consolidating phase will benefit from opportunities to reflect on the way they interact with unfamiliar audiences in new situations. This will involve discussing how to judge the degree of formality required, choice of vocabulary, topic, etc.

Teacher:	Do you think your speaking changes?
Sarah:	Yeah, 'cos sometimes there's different people. Some people are important like not important, like adults you need to speak politely and with children it's kind of you speak like how you would speak to yourself … and … casual.
Erica-Jayne:	At school your language changes because, obviously you're not allowed to use inappropriate language at school, but some people might be allowed to at home. And with, like, little toddlers you have to, you wouldn't say very long words, you'd just say, like instead of saying, this way you would feel confident about something, to a toddler you would say this way you would feel good about doing this.
Tristan:	To your friends it's more, like, not so formal.

Figure 7.10 Transcript of students' discussions about listening and speaking

The meaning students make from a spoken text is influenced by their life experiences, their knowledge of spoken language (the words and the behaviours) and the relationship with the speaker. Teachers may find it helpful to learn about the way in which students' culture influences their speaking and listening. Teachers can use discussions with parents/caregivers to help find out about the cultural and social knowledge of their students. (See the Speaking and Listening CD-ROM Consolidating Phase for parent/caregiver survey.)

As students reflect on their interactions, teachers can acknowledge and value students' own language use, and help them to gain confidence to communicate effectively in different situations.

Some students may benefit from discussions about code-switching when considering the ways language is used in different situations.

In this way, students develop an awareness that will help them choose a dialect that will best serve the students' needs in a particular context.

Teachers can support students to reflect upon the way in which they interact with particular audiences in the following ways:

- Ask questions that show a genuine interest in what the student wants and needs to communicate, e.g. How do you think we can work this out together? Can you tell me in another way?
- Acknowledge students' feelings, e.g. I can see that you are annoyed. You sound really happy about that.
- Refer to class decisions about speaking and listening, e.g. We decided we would express our opinions calmly in our class. We were going to use a PMI to help the group come to an agreement. We agreed that when we are making a decision in a group, we should stop what we are doing and join in.
- Give guidance to students who have difficulty adjusting their speaking and listening so they know what to do in future situations, e.g. We know that didn't work this time, what could you say and do differently if something like this happened again? Let's listen to some different ways we can say that. That's one way of saying that. What's another way?

Considering the Needs of the Audience

Consolidating Speakers and Listeners are gaining confidence when interacting with familiar audiences and are becoming more aware of the needs of a wider audience. They need support to include relevant details and information of interest to their listeners when speaking and to reflect upon the way they express their opinions.

Figure 7.11

Modelled, Shared and Guided Speaking and Listening are ideal practices for teaching students to consider the needs of their audience. Teachers can also provide direction, responses and questions to students and draw their attention to appropriate verbal and non-verbal language, as shown below:

- Tell your buddy from Room 4 something you think they will like to hear.
- What background information will the other groups need when you tell them about your investigation?
- What kinds of talk will you need to use in your story so that we have a good mental picture of what is happening?
- How do you think we should speak when the principal/director comes to visit our class?
- What things will we do when the visiting footballer talks to us?
- I think your group was amazed when you told them that recount. They know more about you and your favourite hobby.
- What do you think your partner liked listening to?
- How will we show that we are interested when our visitor comes to tell us about water conservation?
- You used the slides on the PowerPoint to help us see what we would need to do before we started learning how to skate.
- What do we need to do when certificates are being presented at the assembly?
- What are some different ways we can start our project reports?
- How will we make sure that our visitors know that we want to listen to them?

Consolidating Speakers and Listeners also need continued support to develop their interpersonal and collaborative skills. For example, beginning and ending a conversation, asking for help, giving and receiving compliments, joining in, saying thank you, negotiating, turn taking, disagreeing in an agreeable way, expressing empathy, understanding others' feelings, apologising.

Contributing to Matters of Importance

It is valuable for students in this phase to contribute ideas, offer opinions, express feelings, and give feedback to others. They learn that speaking and listening is useful for raising awareness of issues and identifying actions that can be taken to solve problems. Teachers can support students in the following ways.

- Negotiate with students and invite them to express their ideas and opinions when planning, reviewing and organising tasks.
- Have open-ended tasks that allow students to choose topics and materials.

- Provide time for students to raise issues of concern in regular sessions such as class meetings.
- Provide space (such as pin-up boards) for students to display work such as posters, flow charts and artwork. These displays will help when students discuss learning with visitors to the class.

Investigating the Way Ideas and People Are Represented

Students in this phase will need to be supported through careful teacher scaffolding in understanding the different ways that their own and other people's beliefs and opinions can be represented in spoken texts. A range of electronic spoken texts are available to use for discussions of how people and ideas are represented in various ways. CD-ROMs, films, television programs and audio tapes include spoken texts such as stories, recounts, advertisements and reports. Consolidating Speakers and Listeners will benefit from discussions that focus on the following kinds of questions:

- Why do you think the people or ideas were explained in that way?
- How did it make you feel about the ideas or people as you listened?
- Who might like the way the ideas or people are shown in this? Why? Who might not?
- Do you think these things are true about the ideas or people? Why?
- Did you hear a point of view that was the same as yours?
- What does the spoken text mean for you?
- What do you think is the main message about the people or ideas?
- What other messages are there?
- Is the speaker using a dialect different to yours?
- Does the spoken text make sense?
- Does it sound right? Why?
- What words have been used?
- What body language has been used?

Use of Devices

Consolidating Speakers and Listeners use a small range of verbal and non-verbal devices to convey meaning. Teachers can explicitly guide students to reflect on how students, as speakers and listeners, adjust their spoken and non-verbal language to enhance meaning in school situations. Teachers can also encourage students to discuss how the use of these devices differs from those used in the home and community contexts. The focus for Consolidating Speakers and Listeners includes:

- How prosodic features (volume, tone, pace, clarity and intonation) and vocabulary alter when conversing at home with a familiar adult compared to discussing school work with the principal or speaking in a small group.

- How non-verbal language (facial expressions, body position, posture, eye contact, gestures, and movement) alter when conversing with a peer compared to an unknown adult.
- How verbal devices can be used to create an effect, e.g. asking a rhetorical question when introducing an item to be performed at assembly.
- How the conventions of Standard English are more powerful in certain contexts, e.g. requesting consent for an activity from the principal is more likely if these conventions are observed.

For further information about the Contextual Understanding aspect, see *First Steps Speaking and Listening Resource Book*, 2nd Edition, Chapter 2: Contextual Understanding.

For further information on the teaching and learning practices referred to in this section, see Chapter 7 in the *First Steps Linking Assessment, Teaching and Learning* book.

Involving Students

1 Communicating in the Community

Refer to Chapter 6, Exploratory Speaking and Listening Phase, p. 156.

2 Speaking and Listening Grids (Oliver, Haig and Rochecouste 2003)

Speaking and Listening Grids help students consider the ways their speaking and listening is adjusted for different audiences. Students think of different audiences and situations and then place them onto a grid for speaking and a grid for listening. Copies of the grids are reproduced and given to students. They record words they would use for speaking onto the Speaking Grid; they record listening behaviours and responses onto the Listening Grid.

Students can also use the grids in a Reflect and Respond session.

	Friends	Family friends	New people you meet	The principal or teachers	Shop assistants	Your friend's parents
How do you ask for help from … ?						
How do you share exciting news with … ?						
How do you solve a problem with … ?						

Figure 7.12 A sample of a grid made by a class

Ask students the following questions:
- Who do you interact with? How would you group them?
  e.g. **friends who are boys, other classmates, family friends**
- What are some of the interactions you might have throughout the day? e.g. **greeting, apologising, asking for something, planning**
  - Record the students' responses onto a grid.
  - Reproduce and copy the grids for students.
  - Model the first two grid sections, e.g. **How do I greet teachers? How do I greet friends I know really well? What do I do when a teacher greets me? What do I do when a friend greets me?**

– Ask students to complete their grids.

– Discuss questions, e.g. **Why do we use different words for some people? Why do we look at some people more than others when we are listening?**

– Ask students to record some of their reflections in a journal, e.g. **What did you learn about speaking and listening after hearing about other people's grids?**

3 Speech Pyramid
(Hymes 1974 and Oliver, Haig and Rochecouste 2003)

Speech Pyramids involve students observing and noting what happens in a speech situation. These observations are then discussed and placed in a Speech Pyramid. The speech situation is recorded at the top of the pyramid, speech events in the middle and speech acts at the bottom. Students share their Speech Pyramids and explore the speaking and listening behaviours they need for different situations. This helps students to develop the ability to make appropriate adjustments when speaking and listening in different contexts.

Model the activity using a familiar speech situation at school, e.g. **class meetings, discussion groups, literature circle.** Have some observation notes about a speech situation on hand. Think aloud, refer to the observation notes and record the speech situation, speech events and speech acts onto a prepared pyramid on a whiteboard, data projector, overhead or a large sheet of paper. This step can be repeated at a later time with students contributing in a shared session.

- Ask students to think of speech situations that they have participated in.
- Have students work in small groups or individually to select and complete observations of a speech situation.
- They can then complete their own Speech Pyramid.

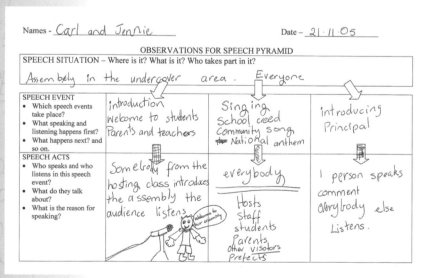

Figure 7.13 Observation samples

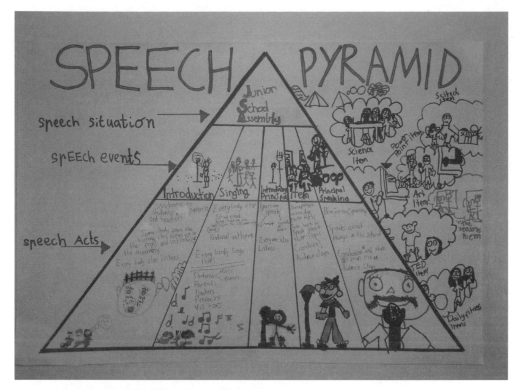

Figure 7.14 Speech pyramid of school assembly

– Ask students to share their Speech Pyramid with each other. Provide discussion points, e.g. **Are any speech acts similar to speech acts in different Speech Pyramids? What are the different kinds of reasons or purposes for the speech acts? Who is controlling the speech acts? What do you think would control the speech acts in a different speech situation?**

4 Time Machine

Time Machine is an activity that allows students to investigate the way English usage changes over time. Students will investigate recordings from the past in order to compare and contrast the way that spoken language is used today.

Locate recordings from the past such as old movies, oral histories or archived recordings (see National Film and Sound Archive, www.screensound.gov.au)

Have students listen to recordings from the past in order to focus on particular features. Students could list features such as:
• unknown vocabulary
• words that are used in a different way to the way they are used today
• pronunciation — ask students to describe the pronunciation or accent used

• pace and pausing – ask students to describe what they notice.

How Might This Activity Be Used in Your Class?

Ask students to prepare a Reader's Theatre script from an old novel, e.g. Enid Blyton's Secret Seven or Famous Five.

5 Class Meetings

Refer to Chapter 6, Exploratory Phase, p. 157.

6 Graffiti Groups

Graffiti Groups provides students with an opportunity to discuss matters that interest or affect them. Students learn to express opinions and consider other points of view.

Introduce the idea of a graffiti board as an avenue that students can use to record issues as they arise. Issues may be of a social nature, e.g. **We should have tables and chairs outside for eating during class breaks.** Issues may arise through investigating topics in a variety of curriculum areas, e.g. **The government should make recycling compulsory.** A graffiti board can be a whiteboard or a large sheet of paper that students can easily access.

• Choose a time to discuss the issues that have been collected on the graffiti board.
• Introduce the session by reading through the listed ideas for discussion. Group any ideas that may be similar.
• Students form groups based on the issue or idea they would like to discuss.
• Students should keep a journal to record ideas as they are discussed. The journal should be organised into two columns. One column will be for recording summarised opinions that others in the group give. In the other column, students should make their own personal comments.

7 Changing Views

Changing Views provides students with the opportunity to discuss a text, identify the point of view from which it is presented, and consider how it would change if presented from a different point of view. Following discussions, students are encouraged to re-create texts or excerpts from a different point of view.

• After students have listened to a text, discuss whose point of view is represented in it. Ask students to identify sections of the text that lead them to their conclusions e.g. **they need to consider elements such as choice of language, tone of voice, body language, etc.**
• Discuss with them whose point of view is not represented.

- Arrange students in small groups and have them discuss a particular event from a different point of view e.g. **one not heard in the text.**
- Have students brainstorm how to present the event from the different points of view. Invite groups to share their findings,
- Students may be encouraged to deliver the alternative text to the class; the class can then reflect on its effectiveness.

This activity is also suitable for the Consolidating, Conventional and Proficient phases.

How Might This Activity Be Used in Your Class?

Students could choose a text to listen to, e.g. a talking book, extracts from TV news, current affairs shows, talk-back radio, formal speeches, political broadcasts, etc.

CONVENTIONS

Major Teaching Emphases

- **Provide opportunities for students to develop, refine and use new vocabulary.**

- **Teach structures and features that extend and elaborate communication in informal and formal contexts,** e.g. how to state and justify an opinion.

- **Continue to teach conversational skills,** e.g. turn taking, negotiating meaning, managing topic changes.

- **Teach students to recognise the different speaking and listening behaviours that are needed for different contexts.**

- **Teach students listening skills needed to respond appropriately in a variety of situations,** e.g. how to offer alternate viewpoints sensitively, how to identify different points of view.

Teaching Notes

Teaching and learning experiences for students in the Consolidating phase are organised under the following headings:
- Building Vocabulary
- Understanding the Conventions of Spoken Texts
- Understanding the Behaviours Associated with Speaking and Listening
- Understanding the Conventions of Listening

Building Vocabulary

Students in the Consolidating phase will have developed an extensive vocabulary through experiences at school, at home, in the community and through the media. The challenge for them lies in finding words that 'best fit' the situation. This becomes essential when students are discussing understandings about particular subjects. Subject-specific vocabulary needs to be learned and practised in both informal and formal settings. Students should also develop a precise vocabulary in order to communicate feelings and needs in a clear, succinct manner.

Opportunities to develop, refine and use vocabulary can be drawn from many sources. By analysing a range of spoken texts, students will identify vocabulary used for a range of purposes.

These texts may be from movies, television, radio, literature, the Internet, everyday conversations and encounters with friends and community members. Students in the Consolidating phase could be supported in developing their vocabulary in the following ways:

- Encourage students to keep individual lists to extend their spoken vocabulary.
- Analyse segments of news reports or current affairs programs. Jointly construct charts of:
  – interesting or unusual words
  – descriptive words
  – words or phrases that signal attempts at providing a balanced view
  – words or phrases that signal a particular point of view.
- Analyse spoken texts to discuss speakers' choice of words; Do they achieve words that are the 'best fit' in the context?
- Introduce subject-specific language and provide opportunities for students to explore and use new vocabulary.
- Involve students in analysing spoken language used outside the classroom to determine the types of vocabulary used in different social situations.

Understanding the Conventions of Spoken Texts

At all phases of development it is important that students are exposed to different examples of spoken language so that attention can be drawn to structures and features that suit different purposes.

The *structure* of a spoken text refers to the way information is organised and presented in a text. For example:
- turn taking in a conversation
- making an apology, e.g. state name and reason
- introducing people.

The *language features* of a spoken text refer to the type of vocabulary, grammar, tone and pace chosen. For example:
- using colloquial words or sayings when conversing with friends
- recognising emotive language used to persuade in an advertisement
- stressing certain words or altering volume to gain an impact.

Students in the Consolidating phase can be encouraged to consider the way language is used in the following ways:
- Involve students in discussions about styles of speech, e.g. research the way they speak when talking to friends, talking to known adults, talking to unknown adults, talking to those much younger or older than themselves.

- Involve students in examining different types of speaking used for different purposes, e.g.
  - How is the spoken language of a news program different to a documentary?
  - How is the spoken language of a soap opera different to a lifestyle program?
  - What is Standard English and who uses it?
- Provide opportunities for students to plan before speaking in formal situations, e.g. to make an announcement over the speaker system; to deliver a speech of thanks at a sporting event; to a visiting performer; to a guest speaker; to ask questions on an excursion.

Conversations

Conversations are important in establishing and maintaining relationships through expressing feelings and sharing experiences. It is through conversations that we give and receive information and compare ideas. This type of unplanned speaking and listening not only develops self-awareness and interpersonal skills; it helps to build topic knowledge and processes for learning. Conversations can be between partners or within small groups. Discuss likely issues with students and negotiate agreed behaviours for interacting during conversations. The following list of questions may provide a starting point.

- What are the implications of making 'personal' comments?
- How can differing opinions be stated in a respectful manner?
- How can likes and dislikes be expressed sensitively?
- How can confrontation and argument be avoided?
- How can everyone be included in the conversation?
- What needs to be considered when someone new joins a group?
- How can we ensure that everyone who wants to speak gets the opportunity?
- When and how is it appropriate to interrupt?

Understanding the Behaviours Associated with Speaking and Listening

Students need to be aware of the behaviours associated with speaking and listening and how it affects meaningful communication in a variety of contexts. The expectations of school and community may differ to those that students experience at home. Learning new ways of communicating will build on students' prior knowledge and add to their repertoire of skills, helping them to choose behaviours that meet the expectations of different contexts. Knowing when to choose certain behaviours is complex and students may need the support of their teachers to do this effectively. Teachers can support students in some of the following ways.

- Teach students to speak clearly and with enough volume so that those in the audience can hear and understand.
- Discuss body language when speaking, e.g. appropriate eye contact, proximity of speaker and listener.
- Discuss body language when listening, e.g. nodding your head, proximity to the speaker.
- Discuss how to interpret body language for emotional cues.
- Teach students to observe and reflect on the body language portrayed by others, e.g. when watching video footage.
- Discuss how an audience behaves, e.g. when listening to the teacher, when listening to another student, at assembly, at the theatre.
- Teach students to ensure that everyone has a chance to contribute to a discussion, e.g. invite a shy person to speak and give them time to think.
- Teach students how to encourage group members in a discussion, e.g. teach students to use prompts such as, 'Go on!'; 'Do you have an example?'

Figure 7.15 Student using body language to enhance meaning

Teacher:	So can you say it is a little bit more than just speaking, isn't it, Joshua?
Joshua:	Aaah, yeah and well, it's, it's also got to do with your tone of voice, and …
Teacher:	What do you mean by that?
Joshua:	I mean like if ….like, say if your mum said, 'Emily and Joshua, we're going to Whiteman Park today,' and Emily said, 'Oh, great.' (*Student uses a bored tone of voice:*) Do you think she really means it?
Teacher:	Probably not.
Joshua:	Yeah, but if, if she said, 'Oh, cool, I'd like to go to Whiteman Park. Can I take Pinky Pie?' (*Student uses a happy tone of voice.*) Do you think she does mean it?
Teacher:	That sounds more like she wants to go.
Joshua:	So it's got a lot to do with the tone of voice.
Teacher:	Anything else?
Joshua:	Um ... yeah, the look, the … your facial expressions. If you were um …, in a bored kind of expression, which would go with the first kind of example of voice tone, we wouldn't really wanna go to it, but if you actually have a smile on your face and looked really excited, you would wanna go, 'cos that's what it would look like anyway.

Figure 7.16 A transcript of student discussing facial expression and tone

Understanding the Conventions of Listening

Listening is an active, constructive process concerned with making meaning from verbal and non-verbal cues. Effective listening depends on the expectations and predictions about content, language and genre that the listener brings to the text (Gibbons 2002). The way in which we listen is also linked to the context of the communication. We listen differently during unplanned, spontaneous situations, e.g. in casual conversations, than we do when speaking and listening is planned and formal, e.g. in the classroom when instructions are being given. The structures and features of listening can be considered using the following framework.

Type of Listening	Features
Appreciative Listening	• Noticing sound quality (pitch, volume, tone). • Interpreting mood and emotion. • Noticing rhyme, alliteration, onomatopoeia.
Critical Listening	• Preparing to respond, to agree or disagree. • Demonstrate attention through body language, e.g. nodding or eye contact. • Remembering key ideas. • Paraphrasing or summarising a spoken text. • To distinguish between fact and opinion. • To detect bias and prejudice.
Empathic Listening	• Noticing underlying emotions and the speaker's intent. • The use of sympathetic questioning to clarify and understand key messages.

Figure 7.17

Teachers can assist students to become familiar with and use the conventions of listening in some of the following ways.
• Provide time for students to engage in conversations.
• Provide opportunities for students to listen to speech constructed for different purposes, e.g. to be entertained, to gain information, to build relationships.
• Provide opportunities for students to respond to spoken texts, e.g. through discussions, questions, using journals, artwork, etc.
• Provide opportunities to develop active listening skills, for example:
  – know when it is important to stay silent and let a person speak uninterrupted.
  – acknowledge the contributions others make in a discussion, e.g. Jo had an idea that we can build on.

- Provide opportunities for students to explore and analyse different types of listening inside and outside the classroom. Use students' findings' to clarify the conventions of listening needed for different purposes.
  - When is listening easy?
  - When is listening difficult?
  - When do I change the way I listen?
  - How do I know when I should respond to a speaker? When should I stay quiet?

Involving Students

1 Eye Contact (Miyata 2004)

This activity promotes the use of eye contact as a convention to convey sincerity and to establish rapport when speaking in a group or to a large audience. Students work in small groups. Have students prepare for the activity by mentally rehearsing a short recount. Explain that students will take turns to speak in the group. The speaker should tell their recount as he or she slowly scans the faces of the members in their group. (Suggest that the speaker starts with the person sitting opposite and then move to those students on one side, then slowly move to those students sitting on the other side.) As the speaker finishes the recount, he or she should make direct eye contact with one person and say, 'What do you think of that?' The person gives a brief response, maintaining eye contact as they speak.

Ask students to reflect on the use of eye contact during the activity and ask questions, e.g. **Did the use of eye contact make everyone feel included? Did it help you to concentrate? Was the eye contact uncomfortable in any way?**

Vary the activity by asking students to tell tall tales as an alternative to a recount.

2 Let's Negotiate

Let's Negotiate provides students with an opportunity to practise the conventions associated with negotiating and reaching decisions in a group. This activity will include turn-taking, initiating discussion, attentive listening behaviours and accepting the ideas of others. Group members are required to discuss an issue or idea in order to reach a collective decision. It is essential to stress that all members of the group should contribute to the discussion and the final decision.

Organise students into small groups, of about four students. Ask students to think of ways that all group members can be included. Explain that there will be a time limit (three to five minutes). In that time, the group will need to discuss the issue or idea and arrive at a decision that can be shared with the rest of the class. Some ideas for discussion could be:

- You never seem to get a chance to choose the TV programs that are watched in your house. Decide what you could do to have a turn to choose a program.
- You were the only person to see someone accidentally break a window at school. The person ran away without telling anyone. What will you do?
- You are having trouble crossing a busy road when you walk to school and again when you walk home. What can you do about it?
- It is your job to give the dog a bath at home but the dog seems to hate water and you always have a battle on your hands. Can the group invent a solution?

Provide time for students to share their decisions with the class. Invite students to comment on the way conventions were observed, e.g. **Did everyone get a turn? How did the group arrive at the final decision? If decisions were difficult to make, what created the difficulty?**

3 Guessing Games

Refer to Chapter 5, Early Speaking and Listening Phase, p. 119.

4 Comparison Activities

Refer to Chapter 5, Early Speaking and Listening Phase, p. 119.

5 What Did You See? (Gibbons 2002)

This is a memory game that practises vocabulary. It could be played with a small group or the whole class. Place objects or pictures relating to a topic being studied on a table. After students have looked at them for a few moments, cover the objects with a cloth and see how many objects the students can remember. Also refer to Chapter 5, Early Speaking and Listening Phase, p. 120.

How Might This Activity Be Used in Your Class?

Relate this game to a science topic, e.g. equipment such as magnifying glass, thermometer, measuring jugs, scales, ruler, stopwatch, etc. This will help to reinforce vocabulary that may be needed for a unit of work.

6 Take a Turn

Refer to Chapter 5, Early Speaking and Listening Phase, p. 121.

7 Let Me Introduce You

This activity allows students to explore the conventions associated with making introductions. Students learn how to choose the appropriate conventions to suit different contexts.

Ask students to think of situations that require an introduction. Have students brainstorm these ideas and record them.
- Note which introductions are made in informal situations and those that are made in formal situations.
- Note situations where people introduce themselves and when another person makes the introduction.
- Jointly construct the steps to make an informal introduction, e.g. informally introduce yourself: 'Hello, my name is ... ' ; informally introduce another, 'Hi ... I'd like you to meet ... '

To create steps for a formal introduction, have students listen to a radio or television recording where a host introduces a guest. Jointly record the steps used, pointing out the way that a listener is orientated by the inclusion of pertinent background information.

How Might This Activity Be Used in Your Class?
- Introduce this activity prior to inviting a guest speaker. Allow students to role play the conventions of introductions.
- Compare introductions made for entertainment purposes and those made for everyday purposes.

8 Generic Games

There are many common games that can be used to support understanding of the conventions of spoken language. See *First Steps Reading Map of Development*, 2nd Edition, and *First Steps Writing Map of Development*, 2nd Edition, for descriptions of games.

9 Barrier Games

Refer to Chapter 5: Early Speaking and Listening Phase, p. 123.

10 Role Plays

Role plays can be used to develop an understanding of the conventions used for a variety of purposes. This activity is explained in detail in Chapter 5 (see p. 124). See the Speaking and Listening CD-ROM, Chapter 7, Consolidating Phase, Conventions: for scenarios cards.

11 Say It Again

This activity explores the structure of recounts. It also makes students critically aware of appropriate vocabulary, tone, pace and the use of descriptive language.

Choose a scenario that will be familiar to the students, e.g. **While walking home from school, some students witnessed an accident in the car park of the local shopping centre. A blue van reversed and hit a new yellow Volkswagen.**

Have the students work in small groups to brainstorm the details of the accident. They can pose questions such as: Who was driving? What were they doing before the collision? How did they react? What action did the students take? Was anyone hurt?

The students choose an audience for their recount, e.g. **a police officer, their parents, friends at school, a passer-by.** Students rehearse their recount and share it with their group.

How Might This Activity Be Used in Your Class?

- Ask students to reflect on their choice of vocabulary. How did it differ in each recount and why?
- Ask students to reflect on their use of pace, intonation and expressive language. What affected their choices?

12 Watch Your Tone

This activity focuses on tone of voice and provides an opportunity for students to develop an understanding of tone and pitch variation.

Model an example for students, e.g. **Say, 'Have you seen my new pens today?'** in an excited tone or as an accusation.

Ask students to reflect on one of the following sentences. Ask students to say the sentences in different ways and record adverbs to describe the tone of voice used.
- What time did you get home?
- The principal called me at work today.
- That was a nice thing to say.

Ask students to reflect on times we need to be careful about choosing our 'tone of voice'. Ask: How do we adjust our tone when we need to negotiate or disagree when emotions are in danger of clouding the message we want to convey? Consider ways to record students' reflections for future use, e.g. **in journals, class charts or posters.**

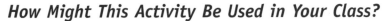

How Might This Activity Be Used in Your Class?

- Ask students to repeat phrases using different tones of voice, e.g. angry, surprised, curious, sad, happy, etc. Try using whispers and loud voices.
- Invite students to reflect on times they have noticed the *tone* in someone's voice 'speaks louder' than the words.
- Ask students to reflect on how they can use tone to improve their communication.

13 Who's Listening?

Who's Listening is an activity that emphasises students' awareness of certain behaviours that accompany speaking and listening, such as the factors that assist and hinder communication. The behaviours of turn-taking and body language are explored in this activity. This activity could take place prior to jointly constructing charts of speaking and listening behaviours. (See the First Steps Speaking and Listening CD-ROM, Exploratory Phase, Conventions for Listening Behaviours cards.)

This activity can be performed in pairs. The first part is very noisy so make sure that students know how to stop on a given signal. Tell the students that they will have three tasks and thirty seconds to complete each task and that speaking should stop on a given signal. Ask the students to decide who will be A and who will be B. Stop after each task and debrief.

Student A and Student B should talk about their family members. They will talk at the same time.

Debrief: Could you hear your partner? Could you tell what your partner was saying? Did it affect the way that you spoke?

- Student A should talk about their family members. Student B says nothing, but conveys the attitude of not listening.

Debrief: What did Student B do to show that listening wasn't happening? How did that make Student A feel? How did that affect the way that Student A spoke?

- Student B should talk about their family members. Student A should say nothing but should convey that they are listening attentively.

Debrief: What did Student B do to show that listening was happening? How did that make Student A feel? How did it affect the way that Student A spoke?

How Might This Activity Be Used in Your Class?

Use this activity to introduce the role of observer. An observer could be appointed to look for certain behaviours and then present feedback to the group, e.g. observe the behaviour of asking a clarifying question in a group discussion, observe the behaviour of following instructions in a group science experiment.

14 Analyse a Video

Refer to Chapter 5, Early Speaking and Listening Phase, p. 127. (See the Speaking and Listening CD-ROM, Exploratory Phase, Conventions, for frameworks.)

15 Ask an Expert

Refer to Chapter 6, Exploratory Speaking and Listening Phase, p. 172.

PROCESSES AND STRATEGIES

Major Teaching Emphases

- **Provide opportunities for students to reflect on thinking strategies used for speaking and listening,** e.g. encourage students to set goals to improve speaking and listening, consider evidence to support an opinion, think through an issue before raising it with others.

- **Provide opportunities for students to engage in sustained conversations and discussions,** e.g. how to build on the ideas of others, paraphrasing, giving and seeking opinions.

- **Teach students to select planning tools to help them speak effectively in a range of contexts,** e.g. debates, in group contexts related to school contexts, with peers and unknown adults in social contexts.

- **Teach students to use scaffolds to plan for listening,** e.g. how to set goals for listening, how to make accurate notes, how to summarise key ideas from a spoken text.

- **Teach strategies to repair miscommunication,** e.g. by seeking feedback (confirmation check) and clarifying message, rephrasing.

Organisation of the Processes and Strategies Aspect

There are several differences in the organisation of the Processes and Strategies aspect. Both the Teaching Notes and the Teaching and Learning Experiences (Involving Students) are in the *Speaking and Listening Resource Book,* 2nd Edition, Chapter 4: Processes and Strategies.

The rationale for this difference in organisation is that the processes and strategies of speaking and listening are not conceptually hierarchical and therefore not phase specific. In all phases, a variety of speaking and listening processes and strategies need to be introduced, developed and consolidated.

What varies from one phase to the next is the growth in:
- the number and integration of strategies used throughout the processes of speaking and listening.
- the awareness and monitoring of speaking and listening processes.
- the efficiency in the uses of the speaking and listening processes.
- the ability to articulate the use of the strategies used in the process of speaking and listening.
- the awareness of how the use of processes helps with composing and listening to texts.

Supporting Parents of Consolidating Speakers and Listeners

GENERAL DESCRIPTION

Consolidating Speakers and Listeners are learning to use Standard English appropriately. They think about the needs of their audience when communicating in order to make their message clearly understood. They try different ways to adjust their vocabulary, tone and body language to suit different purposes.

Teachers will find that parents are able to support their children effectively when they have an understanding of how children learn and if they are aware of what happens in the classroom. Teachers can help build parent awareness of the learning program in which their child is involved in these kinds of ways:

- Invite parents in to join in class activities and talk to them before and after the activity, e.g. **The students are … The adult's role in this activity is to … How did the students enjoy this activity? What did you find was effective in helping them to understand?**
- Conduct parent/caregiver workshops on learning e.g. **Learning with Technology, Helping Children to Learn, Making Learning Fun.**
- Make a video, DVD, CD-ROM with the students to demonstrate certain features of the learning program.
- Each family can take it home to view with their students. A viewing guide can be created with the student's input.
- When creating displays of student work, add information about the context of the activity and list the important learning that took place during the activity.
- Provide students with home learning tasks that involve them sharing their learning with family members.

Supporting Consolidating Speakers and Listeners in the Home

Consolidating Speakers and Listeners will benefit from a range of experiences in the home setting. Ideas for providing appropriate experiences are available on Parent Cards located on the *First Steps* Speaking and Listening CD-ROM. Teachers can select appropriate cards for each Consolidating Speaker and Listener and copy them for parent use.

Parent Cards

1 General Description of Consolidating Speakers and Listeners

2 Developing an Understanding About Different Types of Speaking and Listening

3 Developing an Understanding About Contexts

4 Developing Vocabulary

5 Listening

6 Family Meetings

CHAPTER 8

Conventional Speaking and Listening Phase

Unplanned	**Planned**

(Reflection on planning with teacher) Teacher: Carl, how did you remember what to tell about the MP3™ Player. Carl: I just looked at my pictures that I drew. Teacher: So you've got lots of writing there, did the writing … did that help you at all? Carl: The writing, well some of it, 'cos I didn't draw the … some of the writing … umm, it helps you remember. Teacher: Do you think your grandad would have understood it? Carl: Maybe not, probably because he's not used to all the technologies, so … Teacher: What might you have done there? Carl: Explain what it means and perhaps have the computer on, he could sit, so he could sit and, umm, watch what I was doing as I, umm, explained it. I'd need to go quite slow for him … so he could work out, work out what I was doing.	*(Carl uses his plan to tell a familiar adult how to use an MP3™ player.)* Carl: Well, an MP3™ player is like a music downloader thing, yeah, it's small, so you can just carry it around, and when you buy one you should get a cord with it that plugs into your computer as well and your MP3™ player or an IPod. And you have to go to Windows media player, if you have music on that you can download onto your MP3™ player. You go to synchronise list and you choose the music that you want on it, and on the box it should say how many, how many megabytes you have on it, that there's the memory of it, aah, and it's practically the same as just a little CD player, but you don't carry around heaps of CDs, and, um … so you practically use it as a CD player so it has a playing button, stop button, fast forward, rewind and a pause button. So the play button is obviously just to play music, the search button is to choose the music.
Figure 8.1	**Figure 8.2**

Global Statement

In this phase, students recognise and control most language structures and features of Standard English when speaking for a range of purposes. They select and sustain language and style appropriate to audience and purpose. They are aware of the value of planning and reflecting to improve the effectiveness of communication.

Conventional Speaking and Listening Indicators

Use of Texts

◆ **Identifies main ideas and supporting details of a range of spoken informational and expressive texts.**

◆ **Develops and presents familiar ideas and information, and supports opinion with some detail, in a variety of classroom situations.**

◆ **Controls text features and structures effectively in planned and unplanned texts.**

◆ **Uses Standard English effectively in a range of contexts.**

• Presents a strong point of view to peers in a group, offering some considered reasons or arguments.

• Listens and responds to short presentations or arguments that offer alternative viewpoints on a familiar issue.

• Prepares and presents accurate summaries of decisions reached in group activities.

• Responds constructively to other points of view in groups and class discussion.

• Includes text features and structures that enhance meaning for their audience, e.g. vocabulary choices.

Contextual Understanding

◆ **Considers the appropriateness of text form and register in relation to audience when speaking and listening in familiar situations.**

◆ **Adjusts speaking and listening appropriately for different familiar contexts.**

◆ **Includes information and text features to maintain audience interest,** e.g. choice of vocabulary, appropriate level of detail.

◆ **Understands that people's points of view and beliefs influence the construction of spoken texts.**

◆ **Uses a range of devices when attempting to influence a listener,** e.g. tone, volume, expression, choice of style.

• Considers the needs of a familiar audience when preparing a spoken presentation.

• Recognises and discusses some indicators of socio-cultural bias or prejudice.

• Recognises alternative interpretations of the same spoken text.

Conventions

◆ **Selects vocabulary to enhance meaning and effect.**

◆ **Recognises and controls most language structures and features appropriate to the purpose in informal and some formal situations,** e.g. can express and justify own opinion succinctly, can rephrase others' contributions to group discussions.

◆ **Uses appropriate speaking and listening behaviours in informal and some formal situations,** e.g. can style-shift when conversing with unfamiliar people, listens for general or specific information according to purpose.

◆ **Is aware of the audience needs when responding,** e.g. offers alternate viewpoints sensitively.

• Selects and sustains language style appropriate to a range of purposes, contexts and audiences

• When listening, begins to explore and recognise structures and conventions that enable speakers to influence an audience, e.g. statements of attitude, opinion, through tone and expression.

Processes and Strategies

◆ **Draws on a range of strategies and deliberately adjusts speaking and listening to meet the needs of the task.**

◆ **Adjusts information or adjusts tone of voice in response to a listener's reaction.**

◆ **Selects appropriate strategies when listening,** e.g. asks questions to elicit additional information.

◆ **Identifies a range of strategies used to enhance a talk.**

• Independently uses strategies to plan listening, e.g. makes accurate notes, graphic representations, summaries.

• Plans and rehearses speech for informal and some formal purposes, e.g. adjusts speaking to communicate effectively and persuasively.

• Monitors and adjusts communication, e.g. seeks feedback to ensure they have been understood.

Major Teaching Emphases

Environment and Attitude (see p. 223)

- Provide opportunities for relevant, challenging and purposeful communication.
- Create a supportive environment which values the diversity of students' speaking and listening development (in their home languages).
- Encourage students to see the value of effective speaking and listening for community, school and family life.

Use of Texts (see p. 226)

- Discuss and compare a range of functional spoken texts.
- Provide opportunities for students to participate in authentic unplanned and planned speaking and listening.
- Provide opportunities for students to participate in extended talk.
- Teach students to incorporate text features and structures effectively in a range of spoken texts.
- Teach students to recognise and evaluate complex and challenging information on familiar and unfamiliar topics.
- Teach students the metalanguage associated with speaking and listening and encourage its use, e.g. functional, literary, informational, multi-modal, recasting, contexts, style, pitch, active listening.

Contextual Understanding (see p. 236)

- Teach students to make appropriate choices when speaking and listening to suit the context, e.g. style, content, dialect, text form.
- Teach students to reflect upon the way in which they interact with particular audiences.
- Teach students to consider the needs and background knowledge of their audience when selecting suitable content for spoken texts.
- Provide support for students to contribute to discussions about matters of personal and social interest.

- Teach students to analyse the different ways in which values and beliefs can be represented in spoken texts.
- Provide opportunities for students to justify their selection of spoken texts for different audiences.
- Teach students to select devices to influence a particular audience, e.g. irony, humour, counter-argue, rebuke and respond to others' comments.

Conventions (see p. 250)

- Provide opportunities for students to develop, use and refine vocabulary.
- Teach structures and features to compose spoken texts for informal and formal contexts, e.g. how to greet unfamiliar adults, how to open and close a conversation, how to plan and present a formal speech.
- Teach speaking and listening behaviours that facilitate communication (in unplanned and planned situations), e.g. how to build on the ideas of others, effective use of body language.
- Continue to teach students the skills needed to communicate with others with critical awareness.

Processes and Strategies (see p. 262)

- Teach students to plan and monitor their use of thinking strategies when speaking and listening, e.g. determine importance, compare information.
- Provide opportunities for students to engage in sustained conversations and discussions.
- Provide opportunities for students to choose appropriate processes and strategies, e.g. analyse the requirements of the task.
- Teach students to select tools for listening, e.g. use graphic organisers to synthesise information from several texts.
- Teach students to anticipate and address possible points of miscommunication.

Teaching and Learning Experiences

ENVIRONMENT AND ATTITUDE

Major Teaching Emphases

■ Provide opportunities for relevant, challenging and purposeful communication.

■ Create a supportive environment which values the diversity of students' speaking and listening development (in their home languages).

■ Encourage students to see the value of effective speaking and listening for community, school and family life.

Teaching Notes

A classroom community that supports and nurtures students in the Conventional phase is one that offers challenging experiences that enable students to analyse and reflect on a wide variety of spoken texts. Students in the Conventional phase will be involved in planning speaking and listening for a range of purposes and audiences as they engage in more challenging topics. Students are encouraged to choose different ways of speaking and listening appropriate to informal and formal purposes.

The focus for developing positive attitudes towards speaking and listening is organised under the following headings:
• Creating a Supportive Classroom Environment
• Providing Opportunities for Relevant, Challenging and Purposeful Communication
• Speaking and Listening for Community, School and Family Life

Creating a Supportive Classroom Environment

A supportive classroom environment is one in which both the physical aspects and the culture of the classroom are considered. A positive classroom climate is one in which students have opportunities to speak and listen; where others show an interest and value what they say. These opportunities develop a confidence and enthusiasm to engage in speaking and listening activities.

223

Physical Environment

An environment that supports Conventional Speakers and Listeners is intellectually stimulating as students are able to actively engage in a variety of speaking and listening situations. Teachers can create a supportive environment in consultation with students in the following ways.

- Provide areas for students to display charts and posters.
- Provide hand-held dictaphones so students can record their speaking when rehearsing and reflecting on presentations and for peer- and self-assessment.
- Provide a video camera to record group discussions or individual presentations.
- Provide audio or video recordings so students can analyse their speaking.
- Teach students to utilise visual aids such as PowerPoint software, models, posters or videos.
- Display jointly made charts that support planning for speaking and listening.

Classroom Culture

As well as providing appropriate material and a carefully planned physical environment, it is important to develop a supportive environment where students can confidently explore new ways of speaking and listening. Teachers will:

- Assist students to experiment with new ideas and vocabulary.
- Provide authentic purposes for speaking and listening.
- Provide genuine purposes to speak to different audiences.
- Establish and teach procedures for solving problems when listening or speaking for different purposes.
- Encourage students to take responsibility for planning and refining speaking for formal purposes.
- Involve students in developing criteria for assessments.
- Invite students to develop and participate in reasoned arguments during discussions and debates.
- Encourage students to set personal goals to improve their speaking and listening skills.
- Encourage students to set goals to understand the needs of listeners.

Providing Opportunities for Relevant, Challenging and Purposeful Communication

Students in the Conventional phase control most language structures and features of Standard English but will still need to be supported in making appropriate choices for the new situations that may be encountered. Teachers can support students in some of the following ways.

- Encourage students to examine situations that require code-switching or style-shifting. (Code-shifting is switching between dialects, for example from Aboriginal English to Standard English. Style shifting means adjusting style from casual (may use slang, etc.) to a more formal style of Standard English.)
- Provide a variety of speaking situations, e.g. informal and formal, pairs, small group, large group.
- Provide variety in speaking purposes, e.g. to inform, persuade, entertain, respond, request.
- Model attentive listening and paraphrasing to clarify meaning.
- Read a variety of fiction and non-fiction texts every day.
- Provide a range of ICT resources for students to plan and develop their spoken texts.
- Tell stories and invite guest storytellers. Invite local indigenous storytellers. Read stories and poems written by indigenous people and discuss the 'voice' that can be heard.
- Invite students to explore ideas in all learning areas, e.g. discuss responses to music or works of art.
- Model language to promote social interactions, e.g. how to give appropriate feedback.

Speaking and Listening for Community, School and Family Life

The demands of interacting in school and in the broader community require students to be aware of different ways of speaking and listening in different contexts. Students also need to understand the use of Standard English in order to operate effectively in a variety of situations.

Teachers can assist students in the Conventional phase to develop the knowledge, skills and attitudes to:
- speak confidently to a range of familiar and unfamiliar teachers, adults and peers.
- engage in group discussion.
- give and follow directions confidently.
- share their knowledge and understanding through peer tutoring.
- discuss topics of increasing complexity.
- monitor their own listening and ask questions to clarify meaning.

Figure 8.3 Students participating in an informal conversation

USE OF TEXTS

Major Teaching Emphases

- Discuss and compare a range of functional spoken texts.

- Provide opportunities for students to participate in authentic unplanned and planned speaking and listening.

- Provide opportunities for students to participate in extended talk.

- Teach students to incorporate text features and structures effectively in a range of spoken texts.

- Teach students to recognise and evaluate complex and challenging information on familiar and unfamiliar topics.

- Teach students the metalanguage associated with speaking and listening and encourage its use, e.g. functional, literacy, informational, multi-modal, recasting, contexts, style, pitch, active listening.

Teaching Notes

The focus for supporting Conventional Speakers and Listeners in this aspect is organised under the following headings:
- Discussing and Comparing a Range of Spoken Texts
- Participation in Unplanned and Planned Spoken Texts
- Using Spoken Texts Effectively
- Evaluating Complex Information
- Developing Metalanguage

Discussing and Comparing a Range of Spoken Texts

Conventional Speakers and Listeners need to experience a range of different spoken texts. These texts should include everyday, literary and informational texts. Some of these texts will be multi-modal or hybrid text forms that will fit into more than one category. For example, interactive web pages, documentaries, video games and talking books can include a combination of voice-overs, films, texts and images. Literary and informational spoken texts may include poems, raps, plays, interviews, stories, recounts, songs, debates, descriptions, procedures and reports.

It is essential that students in the Conventional phase be exposed to a wide range of mass-media texts, such as television and newspaper reports. Students need to understand how to use, interpret and analyse these texts.

Conventional Speakers and Listeners will benefit from ongoing opportunities to discuss and compare a wide range of functional spoken texts; and to also compare Standard English to spoken texts composed in other forms of English.

Teachers can use the Familiarising Teaching and Learning Practice to support students' development in using a range of spoken texts. (See Effective Teaching and Learning Practices, in the *First Steps Linking Assessment Teaching and Learning* book (LATL), p. 124.)

Participation in Unplanned and Planned Spoken Texts

Conventional Speakers and Listeners need to be given frequent opportunities to experience and compose a diverse range of spoken texts in both planned and unplanned situations. The spoken language of students will be enhanced by teachers providing explicit instruction and supportive feedback as well as opportunities to use speaking and listening across all the curriculum areas. Interaction with others in whole-class and small-group situations is also essential.

There are many instances where Conventional Speakers and Listeners participate in unplanned and planned speaking and listening, such as the following:

- collecting and distributing materials
- independent study or group projects
- meeting and greeting
- lunch and recess times
- sport/Physical Education/ Outdoor Education
- collaborative tasks
- school events
- social situations.

Socialisation, exploration of ideas and experimentation with different spoken texts are important components of students' learning.

Small-group or partner work activities are vital to the development of speaking and listening at this phase as it provides students with the opportunity to practise some of the skills from the structured speaking and listening sessions, skills such as asking questions when interviewing an expert or arriving at a consensus when solving a group problem.

Modelled, Shared and Guided Speaking and Listening sessions (see *LATL*, p. 126–129) provide ideal opportunities for Conventional Speakers and Listeners to compose a range of unplanned and planned spoken texts. These sessions can be one-on-one, small group or whole class. They can be mini sessions within another activity, part of the planned learning for the day, or occur incidentally as the opportunity arises. Some of the understandings about spoken texts that students develop over time will include:

- People make assumptions when they speak and listen.
- Listeners can agree with or challenge points of view.
- Different language patterns and vocabulary exist for formal and informal situations.
- Non-verbal language may be different from non-verbal language used at home and in the community. It may be interpreted differently by different people.
- There are strategies for speaking and listening to help in unplanned and planned interactions.
- The combination of verbal and non-verbal language makes meaning.
- Planning can help speakers to consider and include effective text features in everyday, informational and literary spoken texts.

Using Spoken Texts Effectively

In the Conventional phase, students continue to recognise and have an understanding of the structures and features of spoken texts. Students need the opportunity to independently create and comprehend texts in a variety of ways for different purposes. Reflection and review are essential components in developing these abilities, and teachers should consider this when planning. (See Figure 8.4.)

Students need to be aware that spoken language will be influenced by the context, with the audience and the purpose determining the structure of the text. Spoken language is structured differently to written language, as it is more variable and responsive to the audience. Facilitated class discussion about these differences will provide an excellent starting point for teachers and students to consider how they might effectively use text structures and features to suit particular purposes. Students in this phase will encounter new situations that require different ways of communicating. For example, they may need to discuss the difficulties of various situations such as explaining how they want their hair styled or cut at the hairdresser's, how to disagree appropriately with a teacher, how to talk to people they don't agree with when participating in a group project, etc.

Conventional students communicate for …	Conventional students speak and listen to …	Teachers can do these things to draw students' attention to the different purposes and how to incorporate text features and structures effectively.		
		Provide Direction	**Give a Comment**	**Ask a Question**
Getting things done	• show a visiting teacher the guidelines for the class. • plan a fund-raising activity with a peer.	Explain the five guidelines of this class for our visiting teacher. Introduce and give details for each guideline.	You defined some of the words, used examples and then restated the guidelines. It was very clear.	What information will a visiting teacher need to know about our class guidelines before they start working with us?
Influencing the behaviour, feelings or attitudes of others	• convince the group to present their information as a play. • debate.	Work out a way to convince your group that a play would be an effective text to use.	There are some good reasons for doing a play. I am sure that you will persuade the others.	What did you say to persuade your group to create a play?
Getting along with others	• greet/depart. • join in conversations. • seek the well-being of others. • organise leisure time.	In your group, discuss things you can say to find out about how your friends/teachers/parents feel.	Socialising can be a lot of fun as you find out about other people and maintain friendships.	When a friend asks you if you are well, how do you feel? What if an unfamiliar adult asks if you are well?
Expressing individuality and personal feelings	• interview peers and others about opinions, e.g. **on sun protection products**. • recount own experiences.	Use your own opinions to answer the survey questions about sun protection.	I wonder if all ages would have similar views.	What information will you tell your peers when you do the survey with them? Why?
Seeking and learning about the social and physical environment	• find out about the camping and clothing requirements for a camp. • form own questions.	Find out about the kind of clothing that will be need for our camp.	That is a good question to ask. You will need to know if the weather varies.	Now that you have your questions, where will you go? Do you need to contact anyone?
Creating stories, games, new worlds and new texts	• create own role play scenarios. • develop content for school radio.	Design a short radio play that will run over the week.	Your radio play has captured the interest of the other students.	What would be an appealing topic for your radio play?
Communicating information	• show senior citizens how to use an electronic device, e.g. **mobile phone**. • teach some younger students how to find information about …	Plan how you will tell the senior citizen about the … Consider which words you might need to define.	I think the definitions will be very helpful to your audience and your examples gave me a good idea of how it works.	What did the senior citizens ask you after your instructions? What features helped them to understand the steps to take?
Entertaining others	• discuss topics of interest to peers. • retell and create narratives. • recount own experiences.	Plan a talk to entertain your group for five minutes. Consider your topic and style.	Your choice of topic for your recount was suitable to entertain your group.	How can you make the style of your text entertaining for the audience?

Figure 8.4 Examples for focusing on the functions of spoken texts

In the Conventional phase, there is a continued focus on encouraging students to use the full range of functions when speaking and listening (see Chapter 1, Figure 1.11). Teachers will provide learning experiences in which students can use functional spoken texts.

Evaluating Complex Information

Students in the Conventional phase need to be supported to recognise and evaluate complex and challenging information from a range of spoken texts. For example, they will need to learn how to determine the importance of the information they hear, what are the key words or main ideas, do they have to be remembered and if so, how will they be remembered.

Teachers can establish students' current knowledge and interests in a range of ways:

- Observe students as they engage in open-ended tasks during independent study time, e.g. **ask students to design a means of promoting sun smart behaviour for people of their age.** Observe what they already know and what they do with the information.
- Observe and listen to students' representations, e.g. **writing, role play, PowerPoint presentations, movies, etc.**
- Interact with students after their independent study time, e.g. **How did you find that out? What do you think you will do next with this project? Why? Who did you decide to work with? How did you convince her/him to join you?**
- Conduct interviews about the students' learning on an individual basis or in small groups.
- Negotiate further topics to study with the students, e.g. **What do you need to further research for this project? What do you know about … ?**
- Ask students to summarise new information by recounting main ideas. Observe how students interpret the information.
- Ask students to explain a newly learned concept to a partner. Observe whether they adapt their vocabulary correctly to give a clear explanation.

Louis:	And, um, then, if you're doing your nose, you draw like this little faded line coming off your eyebrows, and then like, sort of doing a little loop on the end and then coming back to the other one. Um, if you get what I mean. All right?
Teacher:	So it's like this big long tunnel thing?
Louis:	Yeah, and then you can like just, you can like, you draw this little, like an arch sort, um, on the sides of it and you sort of ... What you can do for a technique like, you make it sort of look like you haven't just drawn a line there and make it look realistic, you can smudge it a bit and it gives sort of an effect like it looks like it's actually round or something, or like shadow and all that. And, um, then you can just like colour it between these little corners here to sort of, like, the nostrils, and then you draw two short lines going down from the nostrils to these two points of the um, of the mouth! And it is sort of like when you're drawing a wave etc. you just go like that.

Figure 8.5 Students discussing art concepts

Developing Metalanguage

The vocabulary used to talk about language is known as metalanguage. Students need to use metalanguage so they can discuss their knowledge of spoken language. It is expected that students will demonstrate their understanding of metalanguage. For example, when students are able to say that they heard a speaker pause before presenting a main point in their argument, they are demonstrating metalinguistic awareness.

To help Conventional Speakers and Listeners continue to use the terms associated with speaking and listening, teachers can use metalanguage as part of everyday teaching and across all learning areas. It can be incorporated into targeted discussions, during explicit demonstrations, during one-on-one conversations with students or as part of planned Modelled, Shared or Guided Speaking and Listening sessions.

Below are some words and terms that are associated with speaking and listening in the Conventional phase.
- Use of Texts: *literary, informational, functional, text structures, text features, multi-modal*
- Contextual Understanding: *dialect, recasting, contexts, style*
- Conventions: *pitch, tone, syntax*
- Processes and Strategies: *refining, extending, active listening.*

For further information about the Use of Texts aspect, see the *Speaking and Listening Resource* Book,
- Chapter 1: Use of Texts
- Chapter 4: Processes and Strategies.

Involving Students

1 The Speech of the Century

The Speech of the Century requires students to listen to public speeches in order to identify the structure of a formal speech and the features used. This activity also provides an opportunity for students to discuss the way spoken language can be composed to persuade, inspire or motivate the listener. Students will need to take notes to prepare before imitating a speechmaker.

Prepare an audio or video recording and transcripts of a speech. (These may be obtained through history websites or from current events reported on radio or television websites.) Students can use a transcript to focus on particular language features by highlighting words or phrases that are emphasised through volume, tone or a change in pace. Students should also highlight devices such as idioms or repetition.

• Have students listen to the recording several times.
• Provide time for students to think about and discuss the way in which the speech has been structured, e.g. the sequence of main ideas.
• Allow time for students to rehearse the speech as they attempt to imitate the speaker, using similar pace, expression, etc.
• Have students share their version of the speech with a partner.
• Reflect on the devices used and the effects they create, e.g. ask students to discuss their favourite part of the speech, the part that was most powerful or moving, etc. Ask students to discuss the devices that they could use when doing performance speaking.

Students may record their responses to discussions in a reflective journal.

2 Rate the Reporter

Rate the Reporter promotes awareness of interviewing techniques. This activity provides students with an opportunity to examine the types of questions that reporters ask and to evaluate the effectiveness of different types of questions.

Prepare an audio or video recording of an interview from radio or television. Have students discuss the types of questions that need to be asked in an interview, e.g. open questions, clarifying questions and probing questions.

Have students discuss the role of the reporter. Discussions could centre around what the role should be if the report was to be objective and what the role could be if the reporter wanted to manipulate a story in a certain way, e.g. to encourage people to 'open-up', to elicit the facts or to support a particular point of view. Invite students to develop a rubric that could be used to assess a particular reporter.

Students can listen to an audio or video recording of an interview and make their assessments. They can then form small groups to discuss their assessments.

Students may record their reactions to this activity in journals.

How Might This Activity Be Used in Your Class?

- Students could role play interview scenarios based on imaginary or current issues. They could assume different characters with different points of view that may surround an issue.
- Students could innovate on an interview that they have listened to. The reporter could ask the same questions but the interviewee could give alternative answers based on a different point of view, e.g. a reporter may have asked the Prime Minister questions about sending troops overseas. When innovating, the student who is assuming the Prime Minister's identity answers from the point of view of a pacifist.

3 Listen to Learn

Refer to Chapter 6, Exploratory Speaking and Listening Phase, p. 145.

4 Talk to Teach

Refer to Chapter 6, Exploratory Speaking and Listening Phase, p. 146.

5 Reflect and Respond

Refer to Chapter 4, Beginning Speaking and Listening Phase, p. 63.

6 Independent or Collaborative Study Time

Refer to Chapter 9, Proficient Speaking and Listening Phase, p. 275.

7 Time for Talk

Refer to Chapter 7, Consolidating Speaking and Listening Phase, p. 189.

How Might This Activity Be Used in Your Class?

- Students can keep a record of their daily Time for Talk over a set period of time. They can then reflect on the complexity of their topics and consider the effectiveness of text types. Students can also use the review time to set goals.
- Collate, graph and analyse records of text types and topics. Ask questions, e.g. What is the most popular text type used by students in our class? What social talk is taking place? What information talk is happening?
- Use Time for Talk to assess students' skills using a particular text type, e.g. tell students that they must tell a recount this week to you and a small group of students.
- Explore the differences between writing and speaking and listening, e.g. spoken recount and a written recount. Consider the potential for combining texts in spoken language.

8 Report Talk

Report Talk is an activity that develops an understanding of the way information is structured when giving an oral report. Students analyse a television current affairs program in order to investigate the text types that are used and how information is organised. This activity could involve the whole class or students could form discussion groups after taking notes.

- Prepare a recording of a current affairs program and decide which story will be the focus of the activity.
- Have students listen carefully in order to record key words and main ideas. The video will need to be paused and rewound from time to time so that students have the opportunity to re-listen to significant information.
- Students should record information on the following structures and features of a television report.

Introduction
- Who introduces the segment?
- What background information is provided?
- Are their attempts to build knowledge of the topic for the listener?
- Are any attempts made to introduce and explain technical or specialised vocabulary?

Involving Others
- How is the reporter in the field introduced?
- How are other people connected with the segment introduced?
- How does the reporter introduce him/herself?
- How does the reporter introduce interviewees to the television audience?
- What type of questions does the reporter ask, e.g. **open or closed questions, probing questions or clarifying questions?**

Conclusion
- How is the interview concluded?
- How does the reporter conclude the segment?
- How does the studio reporter conclude the segment, e.g. **Are the main points summarised? Are personal opinions or comments given?**

Allow time for students to discuss the information they have collected. Have students reflect on the effectiveness of the structure and features of this type of report, asking them to note elements that they could use when planning to give a report.

9 Storytelling

Storytelling is a very powerful activity to use with students. Telling stories to and with students helps them to discover themselves and make sense of the world around them. Through listening and telling stories, Conventional students develop an extensive understanding of how texts are structured and presented to suit particular, audiences and purposes.

The following activities suggest ways to involve students in storytelling.

Personal Stories: These stories provide students with the opportunity to listen to people reflecting on the past and telling personal anecdotes. Invite guest speakers to the class or students can listen to a range of recorded oral histories. These are available at libraries or via the Internet.

Students can be invited to tell 'their story'; it should be planned using storyboards and presented orally. Conventional students should be encouraged to use a range of different presentations, e.g. PowerPoint presentations, digital story maker , Microsoft™ Photo Story 3, Dream Weaver, video footage, radio scripts, podcasts, etc.

Photo Fun: This activity requires students to collect photographs of past or significant events in their life. They use these photographs to prepare a storyboard and tell a story. This activity can be used in a small group and students can plan the writing and presentation of the story.

CONTEXTUAL UNDERSTANDING

Major Teaching Emphases

- **Teach students to make appropriate choices when speaking and listening to suit the context,** e.g. style, content, dialect, text form.

- **Teach students to reflect upon the way in which they interact with particular audiences.**

- **Teach students to consider the needs and background knowledge of their audience when selecting suitable content for spoken texts.**

- **Provide support for students to contribute to discussions about matters of personal and social interest.**

- **Teach students to analyse the different ways in which values and beliefs can be represented in spoken texts.**

- **Provide opportunities for students to justify their selection of spoken texts for different audiences.**

- **Teach students to select devices to influence a particular audience,** e.g. irony, humour, counter-argue, rebuke and respond to others' comments.

Teaching Notes

The focus for supporting Conventional Speakers and Listeners in this aspect is organised under the following headings.
- Understandings About Context
- Reflecting on Interactions
- Considering the Needs of the Audience
- Contributing to Matters of Importance
- Investigating the Way Ideas and People Are Represented
- Justifying Selections
- Use of Devices

Understandings About Context

It is important that students are supported to consider the context — audience, purpose, situation and topic — when making speaking and listening choices. Students need to know how to choose appropriate speaking and listening conventions and behaviours to suit different contexts. Analysing and Reflecting are ideal teaching practices for teaching students to make appropriate speaking and listening choices according to the purpose and the audience. In the Conventional phase, students will benefit from opportunities to make appropriate speaking and listening choices in the Simulating and Applying sessions. (See *Linking Assessment, Teaching and Learning* book for sections on Analysing p. 130, Reflecting p. 140, Simulating p. 139, and Applying p. 132.)

Conventional Speakers and Listeners are supported as teachers discuss with students the suitability of spoken texts for different audiences and purposes. This can occur before, during and after participation in unplanned and planned speaking and listening as shown in the following example.

Task: Visiting a class of younger students to play some games that the students have made in small groups.		
Examples of Teacher Interactions		
Before	**During**	**After**
The children in Kindergarten are looking forward to our visit. However, since you are unknown to most children, there may be some children who do not want to join in your group's game. What could you say and do to encourage them? How would this be different to what you might say to a younger child you know well?	Provide feedback and encouragement to students with comments such as *The children are joining in and playing your game really well. I can see that you showed the children what to do as you explained it for them.* *Have you tried … ?*	*What helped the children understand the game we made?* *Did we have to restate any of our instructions?* *Were there any words that the children did not understand?* *Did you change anything else such as tone?* *Did you move closer?* *Did you sit down so you could see the children's faces?*

Figure 8.6

Reflecting on Interactions

Students in the Conventional phase will be interacting with people they are not familiar with. For example, they may be asked to teach a concept to a group of younger students, they may play host to students visiting from another school or be involved in a survey to collect information or opinions from adults. Unfamiliar audiences place challenging demands on students as they need to know how to adjust speaking and listening for different contexts.

When guiding students to reflect on their interactions, teachers acknowledge and value students' own language use, building their confidence to communicate in different situations. Some students may benefit from discussions about code-switching when considering the ways language is used in different situations.

Teachers can support students to reflect upon the way in which they interact with particular audiences in the following ways:

- Ask guiding questions, e.g. **Do you feel as though you achieved your purpose? Do you think the listeners understood your main points? Could you control your emotions effectively enough to state your different point of view?**
- Use questions that show a genuine interest in what the student wants and needs to communicate, e.g. **How do you think we can work this out together? Can you tell me in another way?**
- Acknowledge the student's feelings e.g. **I can see that you are annoyed. You sound really happy about that.**
- Wait before offering support. Students may be able to work out the meaning together and then teachers can give positive comments.
- Refer to class decisions about speaking and listening, e.g. **We decided we would respond to other opinions calmly in our class. We decided that we needed to include all ideas in a small-group brainstorm. We agreed that we would use Standard English for this session.**
- Use positive statements when students adjust their speaking and listening, e.g. **I liked the way you rephrased what you had said in response to a question from the audience.**

When students are having difficulty adjusting their speaking and listening, teachers will support them in generating alternative responses, e.g. **We know that didn't work this time, what could you say and do differently if something like this happened again? Let's listen to some different ways we can say that. I wonder why it is difficult to understand what is meant by that. That's one way of saying that. What's another way?**

Considering the Needs of the Audience

Students in the Consolidating phase are aware that speaking and listening needs to be adjusted to suit particular audiences. They consider factors such as the age of the audience and the formality of the situation, choice of topic, level of detail, vocabulary, tone and pace. Teachers can support students to make considered choices by discussing some of the following points.

– What do you think your parents would like to hear about when they come for your Learning Journey?

– I noticed that you are planning to show your parents how you learnt to include video clips on a PowerPoint. What do your parents already know about using PowerPoint?

– What kinds of talk will you need to use in your story so that we can visualise the events?

– The principal/director is coming to visit our class to find out about what we are learning. What text forms could we use to talk about the Science Investigations or solving maths problems?

– How will we show our interest when our visitor comes to tell us about water conservation?

– It was good that you found out what some of the class knew about skateboards before you started your planning for your class presentation on hobbies.

– What background information can you give about the fund-raising event at the school assembly? What do you think people need to know?

Conventional Speakers and Listeners benefit from continued support in developing their interpersonal and collaborative skills to help them consider the needs of their audience and to learn to adjust their spoken language for different contexts. For further information refer to Chapter 3, in the *First Steps Speaking and Listening Resource Book,* 2nd Edition.

Figure 8.7 Students interacting in small groups

Contributing to Matters of Importance

Conventional Speakers and Listeners need daily opportunities to contribute to matters of interest or issues that affect them. When students do this, they learn that speaking and listening helps to raise awareness of particular situations and that action can be taken to solve problems. Students also develop their abilities to express ideas, opinions and feelings. Teachers can support students in the following ways.

- Negotiate with students and invite their ideas and opinions when planning, reviewing and organising tasks in the classroom.
- Have open-ended tasks that provide students with choices about topics and materials.
- Provide effective feedback when students do raise matters or issues.
- Include regular sessions such as Class Meetings, Personal Learning Time, Time for Talk and Graffiti Groups.
- Have displays that capture students' interests and invite discussion.
- Allow students to create and share their own displays in areas around the room or school.

Investigating the Way Ideas and People Are Represented

Conventional Speakers and Listeners will need support in investigating the different ways ideas and people can be represented in spoken texts. A range of electronic spoken texts are available to use, e.g. **CD-ROMs, films, television programs and audio tapes that include spoken texts such as stories, recounts, advertisements and reports.** It is also possible to record some of the spoken texts from the school and classroom to use as a starting point for discussion. Students' discussions in reading and writing will also support the development of critical awareness in speaking and listening. Conventional Speakers and Listeners will benefit from Analysing, Reflecting and Discussion sessions that focus on the following kinds of questions:

- Why do you think the people or ideas were explained in that way?
- How did the spoken text make you feel?
- Would this spoken text work as recount or procedure? Why?
- Why did you select that text? Who might agree with the way the ideas or people are shown in this? Why? Who might not?
- Do you think ideas or people have been excluded? How?
- Whose is the main point of view?
- What does the spoken text mean for you?
- Does the spoken text make sense?
- What do you think is the main message about the people or ideas? What other messages are there?

- Does it sound right? Why?
- Are these words subject-specific?
- What devices have been used to get the message across?
- What would be another way to say this about that idea or person?
- Is the choice of style appropriate for this context?

Justifying Selections

It is beneficial for Conventional Speakers and Listeners to explain or justify why they have chosen a particular text. When students have to justify their choices, it allows them to explain and elaborate on what they know about speaking and listening.

Teachers can support students to discuss the choices they make by using some of the guiding questions outlined in Figure 8.8.

Features Students Can Choose to Enhance Meaning	Examples of Questions and Statements by Teachers
Text form	• Why did you choose a recount for your planned talk to the class? • Your narrative appeared to begin with the ending, which was an effective way to gain the audience's attention. Describe your planning process, including the decision to begin the narrative in that way. • Why did you choose that combination of text types for your presentation?
Content	• What helped you to organise the content you needed to include in your group's report? • When you introduced your new friend to the art teacher, what did you say? Why? • The anecdotes helped you to influence the audience in your planned talk. Why do you think they were so effective in gaining the audience's attention and input?
Delivery	• Your volume changed throughout the story. Did you plan that? If not, why do you think that happened? • When you were helping your group to make a decision about which task to do, you gave examples of how it might feel if you did the art activity. Why?
Language	• Why did you choose that style? Dialect? • I noticed you used a dialect of English for that section of the story. Why was it important to use it there? • Why did you use those subject-specific words?

Figure 8.8

The following suggestions will give students the opportunity to express and justify their selections of texts.

- Reflect and Respond sessions (see Use of Texts in this chapter)
- Self-assessment (see the Speaking and Listening CD-ROM, Chapter 8: Conventional Phase, Contextual Understanding)
- Journal entries after unplanned and planned speaking and listening.

Use of Devices

In the Conventional phase, emphasis is placed on speakers and listeners selecting devices for maximum effect when constructing messages. Teacher-guided discussions on the use of these devices and their reasons for choosing them will help Conventional Speakers and Listeners determine their effectiveness. The focus for Conventional Speakers is on experimenting with the purposes and effects of:

- Body language, tone, pace, inflection and emphasis in family, school and community situations, e.g. **style shift takes place when conversing with peers or unfamiliar adults such as choice of vocabulary,**
- Varying pitch, pace, phrasing, pronunciation, facial expression, gestures, sound and silence to deliberately influence the interpretation of spoken texts, e.g. **utilising the persuasive language and manipulative devices used in commercials.**
- Using humour and irony in planned presentations to engage the interest of the audience.
- Using code, dialect, technical terms, slang and jargon to exclude others, e.g. **political, computer or surfing jargon.**
- Different varieties of English that are appropriate according to different contexts, e.g. **knowing that Standard English is more appropriate when looking for employment or requesting a service.**

For further information about the Contextual Understanding aspect, see *Speaking and Listening Resource Book*, 2nd Edition, Chapter 2: Contextual Understanding.

For further information on the teaching and learning practices referred to in this section, see Chapter 7: *Linking Assessment, Teaching and Learning* book.

Involving Students

1 Mock Trials

Mock Trials provide students with the opportunity to practise using spoken language for formal situations. Students are required to plan persuasive texts that include the use of devices that will strengthen an argument. Students can role play the judge, the accused, lawyers for the defence and prosecution, witnesses, members of the jury and court officials.

Introduce mock trials by showing students a recording of court proceedings from a suitable movie. Ask students to observe the way speaking and listening is organised in a formal manner, e.g. people are instructed to take turns by the judge, and those listening do not interrupt. Students should note how lawyers ask questions of witnesses and present arguments to the jury. The jury makes a decision and the judge either dismisses the case or imposes a sentence.

- Mock trials could be based on issues arising from fictional texts or matters relating to social studies, e.g. The Big Bad Wolf could be on trial for breaking and entering, a mining company could be on trial for environmental damage.
- Allow time for students to prepare for their part in the mock trial and for the trial to take place.
- Have students reflect on the way that language was used, e.g. Could students maintain a formal style of speech? Did those presenting arguments use persuasive language effectively?

2 Class Meetings

Refer to Chapter 6, Exploratory Speaking and Listening Phase, p. 157.

3 Graffiti Groups

Graffiti Groups provide students with an opportunity to contribute to matters that interest or affect them. Students add ideas to a Graffiti Board which is displayed for easy access. When the board is full, the ideas are grouped together and students form groups according to their interest. Students may do this activity with a partner or in small groups. They should feel that they can express their opinions confidentially and participate in sustained conversation.

Groups decide on a system to ensure all members have their say. The students are given a time frame for their talk and then they write their reflections in their journals. A page is divided. On one side of the page, they record the ideas and statements they have heard about the topics and, on the other side, they write their reflections and personal comments about the issue.

Figure 8.9 A sample of a Graffiti Board

- Introduce the Graffiti Board activity and discuss some guidelines for its use, e.g. general topics are included, brief statements, clear messages, etc.
- Model appropriate comments and place on the Graffiti Board.
- When the board is full, model and talk through the following process:
  - Form a group with others who also want to discuss the same topic.
  - Decide on how turns will be taken.
  - Discuss the topic in the stipulated time.
  - Complete a journal entry about the discussion. Record observations of what was said on one side; reflect and make personal comments on the other side.

Ask students to choose an item on the Graffiti Board and follow the above steps.

- Negotiate with the students to decide those items that should be removed from the board.
- Discuss the process and consider ways to improve it for the next session.
- Have students assess their own participation in this activity over time.

How Might This Activity Be Used in Your Class?

- Keep copies of the Graffiti Boards and compare the kinds of matters raised, e.g. **What topics appear regularly on Graffiti Boards in our class?**
- The class could compare their topics with other classes participating in this activity.
- This activity could be used as a preparation for debating.

4 Context Game

Context Game helps students to discuss ways in which speaking and listening changes according to the situation. This activity teaches students to consider the background knowledge and needs of the audience when selecting content. It also assists students to consider the choices they make about verbal and non-verbal devices to improve their speaking.

Students make a set of cards for different purposes, audiences and situations. The cards are used to create a random set of contexts. Students work in pairs of small groups to develop the spoken language that suits the context.

– Model the activity first.
– Have students work in pairs to record a range of audiences (who?), purposes (why?) and situations (where? how?) on three different-coloured cards, e.g. red cards for audiences, blue cards for purposes, and yellow cards for situations. Share and discuss. Place the cards upside down into three piles.
– Use the cards to play a game in pairs or small groups.
– One card from each pile is drawn and displayed.
– The team discusses and decides how to demonstrate the interaction for this context, within a specified time limit, e.g. two minutes. For example, students may draw out four cards labelled grandparent, thank-you speech, anecdote and birthday party.
– Teams share their ideas and compare their interpretations, e.g. How and why were the interactions different? Does this happen in real life?
– Return the cards to the piles, shuffle and repeat.

How Might This Activity Be Used in Your Class?

• The ideas can be used for role-play sessions.
• Have students design a different game or use for the cards.

5 Time Machine

Refer to Chapter 7: Consolidating Speaking and Listening Phase, p. 203.

How Might This Activity Be Used in Your Class?

Have students create transcripts for particular times and places; the activity could be incorporated into Society and Environment, e.g. a study of a historical event.

6 Speaking and Listening Grids

Refer to Chapter 7: Consolidating Speaking and Listening, p. 201.

7 Speech Pyramid

Refer to Chapter 7: Consolidating Speaking and Listening, p. 202.

8 Networks

Refer to Chapter 9, Proficient Speaking and Listening Phase, p. 284.

9 Communicating in the Community

Refer to Chapter 6, Exploratory Speaking and Listening, p. 156.

10 Come On! (Abbot & Godhino 2004)

It is important that students in the Conventional phase develop an understanding of how different factors can influence the way people construct meaning from a spoken text. The following activity will provide an opportunity for students to experience and reflect on how the choice of tone of voice, pace, stress, intonation, volume, body language, etc. can affect the way a message is delivered and received.

- Students are given a statement on a card and they then have to express the words in a particular way, e.g. 'Come on!' could be expressed in a tone registering shock, fear, surprise or pleading.
- The teacher asks for a volunteer.
- The students try to guess what feeling was expressed.
- The volunteer student or the teacher asks the students why they guessed that particular feeling. Answers might be, e.g. the way you were standing, the look on your face, the tone of your voice.
- Students can explore how differing contexts will affect the meaning of a statement.
- Repeat the activity with different statements. It can be performed by the whole class, in small groups or in pairs.

11 Listening Between the Lines (Abbot & Godhino 2004)

Listening Between the Lines provides students with an opportunity to explore implied meaning in relation to different audiences, situations and purposes. In spoken language there is often a significant meaning contained in what is left unsaid. Being able to recognise this implied or inferred meaning is an essential skill. Many communication breakdowns occur through the inability of people to read all the signs in a conversation.

Teachers can develop students' ability to recognise implied or inferred meaning by:

- Explaining the meaning of 'reading between the lines'. When people 'read between the lines', they are constructing a meaning that is implied rather than stated or obvious.
- Discussing the different meanings that people construe even though they are hearing the same words. Model this by using words or expressions that have different meanings, e.g. wicked,

real, gay, fine, or a question such as 'What are you doing?' or statements such as 'Nice shoes', 'Oh my God', 'Hurry up', 'Come on', etc. All these expressions take on different meanings depending on who is saying them, e.g. parents, friends, teachers, police, etc.

- Students can present their findings to other groups or to the class.
- Allow students to consider why meanings are different. Typical responses might be, e.g. meanings vary depending on age groups, cultural groupings, the purpose of the speaker, and the intention of the listener.
- Encourage students to collect examples of expressions used in different contexts where there may be a number of different meanings, e.g. home, school, advertising, the Internet, TV, etc.

12 Adjusting My View

This is a role play activity that makes students aware that speaking must be adjusted to suit different social and situational contexts. Ask students to think of a time when they have deliberately adjusted the way they spoke because of a particular situation or because they had to consider the person or people they were talking to. Students can do this activity in pairs. Provide scenario cards.

Each pair is to create a two-minute role play, acting out the scenario. They need to consider the way they should speak and the scenario must be in the appropriate social context, e.g. thanking a grandparent/peer/boy or girl friend for a present, asking an employer for time off, asking a teacher for an extension on an assignment, asking a bank/parent/friend for money.

- During the role plays, the class can reflect on whether the role plays were an accurate representation.
- As a class, discuss the ways people deliberately adjust the way they talk to meet the needs of the audience, situation and context. Remind students of the devices that are used when constructing spoken text.

13 Consumer Quandaries!

Consumer Quandries! is designed to make students aware of how advertising uses language to persuade or convince consumers to buy a product or service.

- Students view and listen to a variety of different advertisements.
- They describe their favourite advertisement and explain their choice.
- Discuss how language is used in advertisements to promote products or services.

- Make a class chart with the devices that have been used, e.g. testimonial.
- Discuss the meaning of the devices that have been used and how these strategies are designed to influence people's thinking.
- In pairs or small groups, students can think of other persuasive advertisements that meet the strategies that appear on the class chart.
- Share findings of groups. Discuss the spoken language strategies that they think are the most powerful. Ask: how much does this depend on the social/cultural/age context of the consumer?
- Students can create a storyboard, then record a range of advertisements and present them to the class to analyse.
- Students can explore the impact of sound in advertisements, e.g. background music, voice-overs, tone, pitch, pace, etc.

14 Advertising Avalanche

This activity is an extension of the previous activity. Students are required to review their previous learning and create their own advertisements using techniques and devices that were discussed.

Students can work in pairs or small groups. They can select advertisements from the following ideas.

Cause: e.g. anti-smoking, preserving old-growth forests
- *Product:* e.g. consumer goods — clothing, food, video and computer games, sporting equipment.
- *Event:* e.g. Big Day Out concert, live bands, sporting event community fund-raiser, etc.
  - Students will have to take into account the target audience, e.g. adult, child, specific age or gender group.
  - They can select the most appropriate devices or techniques to use.
  - Students then develop a plan, e.g. a storyboard for presentation.
  - Groups are encouraged to use a range of multi-media, e.g. video, PowerPoint, sound effects, to enhance the delivery of their presentation.
  - Groups can present their advertisements to the class.
  - The class reviews and provides feedback on the effectiveness of the presentation, and the devices and techniques that were chosen.

Links to Other First Steps Materials

These activities will also support the development of Contextual Understanding for Conventional Speakers and Listeners.

Reading Map of Development, Picture the Author p. 227; Interviews p. 222; Do You Get It? p. 225; Text Innovation p. 226; Spot the Devices p. 278; Panel Discussion p. 277; What's Missing? p. 280.

CONVENTIONS

Major Teaching Emphases

■ **Provide opportunities for students to extend, refine and use vocabulary.**

■ **Teach structures and features to compose spoken texts for informal and formal situations,** e.g. how to greet unfamiliar adults, how to open and close a conversation, how to plan and present a formal speech.

■ **Teach speaking and listening behaviours that facilitate communication (in unplanned and planned situations),** e.g. how to build on the ideas of others, effective use of body language.

■ **Continue to teach students the skills needed to communicate with others with critical awareness.**

Teaching Notes

Teaching and learning experiences for students in the Conventional Phase are organised under the following headings:
• Building Vocabulary
• Understanding the Conventions of Speaking
• Understanding the Behaviours Associated with Speaking and Listening
• Understanding the Conventions of Listening

Building Vocabulary

Students in the Conventional phase understand the potential of words to persuade, clarify, solve problems and entertain. They will continue to need practice in refining and using vocabulary that 'best fits' a particular purpose. They will also continue to need explicit teaching in order to learn and use new technical and subject-specific words.

Opportunities to develop, refine and use vocabulary can be drawn from many sources. By analysing a range of spoken texts, students will identify vocabulary used for a range of purposes. These texts may be from movies, television, radio, literature, the Internet, everyday conversations and encounters with friends and community members.

Students in the Conventional phase could be supported in developing their vocabulary in the following ways:

- Encourage students to read widely and to discuss the word choice of various authors.
- Involve students in poetry readings and discussions.
- Analyse segments from television, e.g. news reports or current affairs programs. Jointly construct charts of:
  - interesting or unusual words
  - descriptive words
  - subject-specific words
  - words that signal attempts at providing a balanced view
  - words that signal a particular point of view.
- Analyse spoken texts to discuss speakers' choice of words. Ask: Do they achieve words that are the 'best fit' in the context?
- Make charts of synonyms, antonyms, adjectives and adverbs.
- Encourage students to keep individual lists to extend their spoken vocabulary.
- Analyse popular songs and discuss word choice. Ask: Who does the song appeal to and why?
- Introduce subject-specific language and provide opportunities for students to explore and use new vocabulary.
- Involve students in analysing spoken language needed outside the classroom to determine the types of vocabulary needed in different social settings.

Understanding the Conventions of Speaking

Students in the Conventional phase will benefit from analysing a wide variety of speaking and listening situations. This will develop an understanding of the way spoken language is structured and how features are chosen to meet the needs of different audiences and purposes.

The *structure* of spoken text refers to the way information is organised and presented in a text. These could include:
- seeking and giving clarification
- giving and justifying an opinion
- explaining cause and effect.

The language features of a spoken text refer to the type of vocabulary, grammar, tone and pace chosen. For example:
- using colloquial words or sayings when conversing with friends
- emotive language used to persuade in an advertisement
- signal words in a formal presentation, e.g. first of all, finally.

Teach students the skills needed to extend discussions, e.g. model ways to extend a discussion by elaborating on other people's ideas, model how to give and justify an opinion, model how to offer viewpoints sensitively, model ways to include all the people in the group.

Teachers may work with a small group of students to facilitate a discussion. These sessions may be video-taped. The video can then be used to highlight the type of speaking and listening skills that were used to progress the discussion and then to generate a framework that will guide them during independent discussions.

Conversations

Conversations are important in establishing and maintaining relationships through expressing feelings and sharing experiences. It is through conversations that we give and receive information and compare ideas. This type of unplanned speaking and listening not only develops self awareness and interpersonal skills; it helps to build topic knowledge and processes for learning. Teachers can discuss likely issues with students and negotiate agreed behaviours for interacting during conversations. The following list of questions may provide a starting point.

- What are the implications of making 'personal' comments?
- How can differing opinions be stated in a respectful manner?
- How can likes and dislikes be expressed sensitively?
- How can confrontation and argument be avoided
- How can everyone be included in the conversation?
- What needs to be considered when someone new joins a group?
- How can we ensure that everyone who wants to speak gets the opportunity?
- When and how is it appropriate to interrupt?

Understanding the Behaviours Associated with Speaking and Listening

Students need to develop a critical awareness of the behaviours associated with speaking and listening and how it affects meaningful communication in a variety of contexts. Teachers can involve students in choosing appropriate speaking and listening behaviours through modelling, explicit teaching and discussion. Jointly constructing Y charts or T charts will provide meaningful reminders. The following list may provide some useful starting points when considering effective behaviours:

- Speak clearly and with enough volume that everyone can hear and understand.

- Discuss body language when speaking, e.g. appropriate eye contact, proximity of speaker and listener.
- Discuss body language when listening, e.g. nodding your head, proximity to speaker.
- Discuss how to interpret body language for emotional cues.
- Provide opportunities for students to observe and reflect on the body language portrayed, e.g. watch an interview with the sound turned off.
- Discuss how an audience behaves, e.g. when listening to the teacher, when listening to another student, at assembly, at the theatre.
- How to take turns in a discussion.

Journal entries in response to:

Speaking is more than words. What else do you do to get your message across?

*We use body language, like smiling or crying and we also use different tones, if we are serious or trying to make somebody feel better. If we are bored, we may use a monotone and look around, not paying attention or focusing on what the person is saying.

Molly

" You could also write down your message on paper, or you can use a code. Emotions are also a way of talking, crying is a way of saying you're sad. Body language is also a way of communicating. Or you could draw what you want to say, and there is probably more, but that's what I can think of.

Tayla

Figure 8.10 Journal entries about speaking and listening

Teacher:	What do you do when you listen?
Tayla:	You make eye contact. You have to let them know you're listening.
Molly:	You kind of treat the person how you wanna be treated, if you like it when you want them to listen to what you wanna say.
Tayla:	Sometimes you don't listen properly 'cos you don't want to learn about that subject or something like that.
Molly:	When you're listening, you might, you don't overlap too much, but you say things like, yeah, but you don't really talk over them.
Teacher:	Do you think your listening changes? We talked about speaking changing from home and school, how does listening change?
Tayla:	(overlapping) We'll like we've said before, when you're at school you listen more so you get the full instructions.
Molly:	And yeah, so …
Tayla:	And if the teacher's telling you to do an essay or something it's a really big deal, then you might wanna listen to make sure you get it right.
Teacher:	A lot of people think you need to be looking to be listening. Do you think that is true?
Tayla:	Yes, sometimes. Sometimes if you're not … With me it's … I don't have to look at them to …
Molly:	Nah … sometimes you're not looking but you're listening.
Tayla:	Yeah, I think it helps to look at the person but sometimes it gets too easy to look at something else and …
Molly:	My mum, she could be, like, cooking dinner or something, and I talk to her making sure she's listening even when she's doing something else, 'cos she answers me as well.

Figure 8.11 Transcript of discussion about listening

Understanding the Conventions of Listening

Listening is an active, constructive process concerned with making meaning from verbal and non-verbal cues. By building an awareness of the conventions of listening, teachers assist students to develop and refine communication skills. Effective listening depends on the expectations and predictions about content, language and genre that the listener brings to the text (Gibbons 2002). The way in which we listen is also linked to the context of the communication. We listen differently during unplanned, spontaneous situations, e.g. **casual conversations**, than we do when speaking and listening is planned and formal, e.g. **in the classroom when instructions are being given**. The structures and features of listening can be considered using the following framework based on Nunan 1991.

Type of Listening (Structure)	Features
Surface listening	• Is listening to only the obvious or literal meaning and ignoring other levels of meaning.
Participatory listening	• Is expressive and lets the speaker know that you are tuned in. • Apparent not only in verbal responses, but also through facial expressions, body language, etc. • The speaker may build on to what has been said, may agree or disagree with the speaker, will encourage the speaker to continue.
Passive listening	• Is listening without talking or directing the speaker in any way, verbally or non-verbally. • The listener remains still and silent but indicates attentiveness through body language. • Can be a powerful means of communicating acceptance. • Allows the speaker to develop thoughts with another person who supports but does not intrude.
In-depth listening	• Is listening to detect underlying motives, feelings and needs. • The listener asks clarifying questions.
Non-judgemental listening	• Is listening with an open mind. • The listener is focused on understanding the content.
Critical listening	• Is listening with the intent of making an evaluation of the content. • The listener may ask probing questions.
Empathic listening	• Involves not only understanding the content of a message but also understanding how the other person feels. • The listener indicates understanding and seeks feedback by paraphrasing or restating a message or asking for clarification.
Objective listening	• Is used when there is a danger of allowing the emotional impact of a message to obscure objective reality. • It allows a listener to remain impartial and to think clearly and objectively.

Figure 8.12 The structures and features of listening (Nunan 1991)

Involve students in different types of listening for different purposes in some of the following ways:

- Provide time for students to engage in extended conversations.
- Provide opportunities for students to listen and respond to speech constructed for different purposes.
- Provide opportunities for students to respond to spoken texts through discussions, questions, journals, artwork.
- Provide opportunities for students to explore and analyse different types of listening. Use students' findings to clarify the conventions of listening needed for different purposes.
  - When is listening easy?
  - When is listening difficult?
  - When do I change the way I listen?
  - How do I know when I should respond to a speaker? When should I stay quiet?
- Invite community members into the classroom who rely on good listening skills in their workplace, e.g. health professionals, members of the clergy. How did they learn to listen?

Involving Students

1 Say It Again

This activity explores the structure of recounts. It also makes students critically aware of appropriate vocabulary, tone, pace and the use of descriptive language.

- Choose a scenario that will be familiar to the students, e.g. while they were walking home from school, they witnessed an accident in the car park of the local shopping centre.
- Have the students work in small groups to brainstorm the details of the accident. They can pose questions such as: Who was driving? What were they doing before the collision? How did they react? What action did the students take? Was anyone hurt?
- The students choose an audience for their recount, e.g. a police officer, their parents, friends at school, a passer-by.
- Students rehearse their recount and share it with their group.

How Might This Activity Be Used in Your Class?

- Ask students to reflect on their choice of vocabulary. How did it differ in each recount and why?
- Ask students to reflect on their use of pace, intonation and expressive language. What affected their choices?

255

2 Subjective Versus Objective

This activity develops the use of non-judgemental vocabulary and phrases needed to review and critique spoken language. Students can use this activity to develop criteria that could be followed when giving feedback to their peers. The emphasis is on the need to understand contexts when it is important to use language sensitively and objectively.

Prepare an audio or video recording of a spoken text. This could be a segment from a television interview or a recorded presentation. Ask students to comment on the text and record the words used. Classify these words or phrases into groups that indicate subjective judgements (likes or dislikes) and those that indicate objective statements, e.g. **based on factual statements.**

Students could work in pairs to compile lists of objective descriptors to be used when giving feedback. Consider how feedback could be used for different speaking purposes, e.g.
- contributing to group discussions
- negotiating the allocation of tasks for a group project
- making a planned presentation
- taking part in a formal debate.

Discuss and compare the lists that students compile. Clarify the type of language needed to give effective feedback. These words and phrases could be recorded on class charts, recorded in students' journals or developed into assessment rubrics.

3 Icebreakers and Interrogators

Icebreakers and Interrogators develops an understanding of the structures and features of different types of questions. Students will gain practice in identifying the intentions of a speaker so that they can prepare to respond appropriately.

Introduce the activity by discussing the meaning of questions intended as *icebreakers* and those intended to be *interrogators*. Generally, *icebreakers* are questions that are used to initiate social contact and require only brief responses. *Interrogators* are more probing questions that require thoughtful or extended responses.

Model examples and engage students in discussions to clarify the types of questions as *icebreakers* or *interrogators*, e.g. **How are you? How was school today? How was the disco last night? Did you have a good weekend? What happened at the concert last night? What did you do on the weekend? What decisions did you make in your drama class today? What did you decide to do with your group of friends?**

Class charts could be made to illustrate the differences between these questions and suggested responses. Alternatively, students could reflect on the activity and record their response in a journal.

How Might This Activity Be Used in Your Class?

Ask the students to consider how differing contexts affect the way these questions may be interpreted. For example, Do you respond differently to a friend asking, *'How are you?'* compared to when you are visiting the doctor because you are unwell?

4 Impromptu Speaking

Being asked to give a speech without warning can be nerve-racking experience if a student has had no previous experience. This activity provides practice in structuring language to suit the occasion.

Discuss possible scenarios with students, e.g. you are called upon to thank the coach at the end-of-season wind-up party; you are asked to thank a guest speaker; you receive a trophy or an award and have to thank the organisation.

Discuss the content that each scenario should include and devise a framework to help structure a speech.
- An introduction: e.g. 'I would like to thank ...' 'On behalf of ...'
- Mention names.
- Include an event or a highlight: e.g. 'I particularly enjoyed ...' 'The highlight of the season was...'
- Conclusion: build in a 'future' reference, e.g. 'I hope next season is just as successful ...' 'We wish you all the best in your endeavours ...' 'I hope to continue with ...'

How Might This Activity Be Used in Your Class?

- Produce scenario cards. Students choose a card from a pile and give an impromptu speech. (See the Speaking and Listening CD-ROM, Chapter 8 — Conventional Phase: Conventions.)
- Vary the audience, e.g. you accept an award at a charity ball, you donate a large cheque to a telethon on behalf of your company, your team has designed a solar car and you have won a race and television crews are filming your acceptance speech.

5 Ask an Expert

Ask an Expert is an activity that allows students to organise information for a planned talk. It is explained in detail in Chapter 6 but can be easily adapted to students in the Conventional phase.

How Might This Activity Be Used in Your Class?

- Use the idea of experts when developing a unit of work. Groups of students could be responsible for researching different aspects of a topic. They would be responsible for sharing their knowledge with the class through some form of presentation.
- Invite another class to visit your group of experts. Ask: How will the students adjust their presentations for a different audience?
- Use expert groups to present to parents on an open night, or learning journey.

6 Barrier Games

Refer to Chapter 5, Early Speaking and Listening Phase, p. 123.

7 Take a Turn

Refer to Chapter 5, Early Speaking and Listening Phase, p. 121.

8 Who's Listening?

Refer to Chapter 7, Consolidating Speaking and Listening Phase, p. 215.

9 Telephone Talk

Telephone Talk helps students to understand the conventions of telephone conversations and to build confidence when speaking and listening on the telephone. (See the Speaking and Listening CD-ROM, Conventional Phase: Conventions.)

Involve students in a brainstorming session to find out:
– What are the purposes for telephone conversations?
– When do students find using the telephone easy?
– When do students find using the telephone difficult or uncomfortable?
– Have they experienced any conflicts or issues regarding the use of telephones?
– When should mobile phones be used and when should they not be used?

This session may uncover issues that could be discussed, e.g. the school may have rules prohibiting the use of mobile phones in class, inappropriate messages may be an issue, talking very loudly on a mobile phone while travelling on a train or bus may irritate some people. Other examples for discussion may include some of the following:
– How to introduce yourself and make a request.
– How to politely ask to speak to another person.
– How to make an appointment.

– How to ask to be connected to a person when the call goes via
 a switchboard.
– How to politely refuse requests to donate to charity.
– How to decline a telemarketing call.
– What information needs to be considered when contacting
 emergency services?

How Might This Activity Be Used in Your Class?

- Involve students in making reminder cards to help prompt them
 with what to say when making phone calls. Discuss strategies to
 help organise what you will say on the phone, e.g. make a list to
 order take-away food.

- Involve students in role playing, e.g. receiving a call and taking an
 accurate message. Emphasise the details that should be recorded.
 Investigate different types of commercially made message pads.
 Students could design their own telephone message pad to use
 at home.

- Ask students to collect examples of greetings on answering
 machines. Analyse them and produce a framework to guide people
 on how to create a greeting for an answering machine. Ask students
 to create a greeting for the Prime Minister's Office, the head office
 of ASIO, a movie studio, etc.

10 Radio Ratings

Radio Ratings develops critical awareness of the way conventions
are chosen to suit a particular purpose and audience. This activity
is designed to focus on the conventions chosen for broadcasting.
(See the Speaking and Listening CD-ROM, Conventional Phase:
Conventions.)

Involve students in brainstorming different types of radio
presentations, e.g. talk-back, news reports: sports, weather, music
varieties, advertisements, etc. Students could be responsible for
taping segments of different broadcasts or the teacher could prepare
examples for students to listen to.

Students could analyse particular recorded examples for:
- text type
- vocabulary choice
- length of conversational turns
- pace and intonation of delivery
- intended audience
- introductions
- farewells
- standard and non-standard English.

Students should record their findings in a journal. They could use the language features listed above as headings for journal entries.

How Might This Activity Be Used in Your Class?

Students could use the findings of these investigations to produce their own radio segment. Recordings could be made for particular audiences, e.g. to share with another class, as part of an assembly performance, to share with parents, etc.

11 Listening Matters

Listening Matters develops students' understanding of the importance of listening, how to recognise different listening situations and to adjust behaviours to suit the purpose.

Prepare students by discussing occupations that rely on good listening skills. Brainstorm a list of occupations. Prepare a list of questions, for example:
• How does listening help you in your job?
• What helps you to listen?
• When is listening difficult for you?
• How did you learn to listen?

Invite a community member such as a pharmacist, naturopath, councillor, builder, etc. to visit the classroom. It is essential that well-developed listening skills be a major requirement of their occupation. Students can prepare an interview using the questions generated from class members.

How Might This Activity Be Used in Your Class?

Students prepare a questionnaire or survey to gather information about listening from parents and other family members in the workforce.

12 Running Commentary

Running Commentary allows students to focus on body language and how it is used to convey meaning in communications. Students will become more aware of their own body language, assisting them to make informed choices as to how they wish to convey feelings and emotions through body language.

Show and explain a running commentary to students by playing a video recording of a horse race, football or cricket match or celebrities arriving on the red carpet. Students will need to focus on conventions such as:

- descriptive language used.
- devices, such as analogy.
- the pace of speech, e.g. a horse race is called very quickly.
- the tone, e.g. excitement when a goal is scored or when a celebrity stops to talk to a person in the crowd.

Have students imitate a running commentary style of speaking by working in pairs. Prepare a video recording or access a suitable video clip from an Internet site as the basis for this activity.

Student A should sit with their back to the screen; they will listen to the running commentary.

Student B should watch the screen but without sound. This student should give a running commentary of the action by focusing on information gleaned through observing body language. Limit the speaking time to about sixty seconds to begin with. Student A should then respond to the commentary by summarising the main events.

Both students should then view the video clip, with the sound turned on. The students should discuss the running commentary, noting information that was accurately captured through observing body language and information that may have been misinterpreted.

Students should record their findings in a journal, noting how body language helped them to interpret a communication. These recordings may be organised under headings such as facial expressions, gestures, proximity, eye contact, and posture.

PROCESSES AND STRATEGIES

Major Teaching Emphases

- ■ **Teach students to plan and monitor their use of thinking strategies when speaking and listening,** e.g. determine importance, compare information.

- ■ **Provide opportunities for students to engage in sustained conversations and discussions.**

- ■ **Provide opportunities for students to choose appropriate processes and strategies,** e.g. analyse the requirements of the task.

- ■ **Teach students to select tools for listening,** e.g. use graphic organisers to synthesise information from several texts.

- ■ **Teach students to anticipate and address possible points of miscommunication.**

Organisation of the Processes and Strategies Aspect

There are several differences in the organisation of the Processes and Strategies aspect. Both the Teaching Notes and the Teaching and Learning Experiences (Involving Students) are in the Speaking and Listening Resource Book, 2nd Edition, and Chapter 4: Processes and Strategies.

The rationale for this difference in organisation is that the processes and strategies of speaking and listening are not conceptually hierarchical and therefore not phase-specific. In all phases, a variety of speaking and listening processes and strategies need to be introduced, developed and consolidated.

What varies from one phase to the next is the growth in:
- the number and integration of strategies used throughout the processes of speaking and listening.
- the awareness and monitoring of speaking and listening processes.
- the efficiency in the uses of the speaking and listening processes.
- the ability to articulate the use of the strategies used in the process of speaking and listening.
- the awareness of how the use of processes helps with composing and comprehending texts.

Supporting Parents of Conventional Speakers and Listeners

GENERAL DESCRIPTION

Conventional Speakers and Listeners are confident users of Standard English. They select and maintain language and styles to suit particular purposes and audiences. They know that it is important to plan and reflect on their speaking and listening to communicate successfully.

Supporting Conventional Speakers and Listeners in the Home

Conventional Speakers and Listeners will benefit from a range of experiences in the home setting. Ideas for providing appropriate experiences are available on Parent Cards located on the *First Steps* Speaking and Listening CD-ROM. Teachers can select appropriate cards for each Conventional Speaker and Listener and copy them for parent use.

Parent Cards

1 General Description of Conventional Speakers and Listeners

2 Developing an Understanding About Different Types of Speaking and Listening

3 Developing an Understanding About Contexts

4 Developing Vocabulary

5 Listening

6 Family Meetings

CHAPTER 9

Proficient Speaking and Listening Phase

Unplanned	Planned

(Rebecca speaking about her workplace experience.)

Rebecca: We also had a buddy day which was my absolute favourite where we actually paired up with other women actually working there on the day.

Teacher: So you could follow someone around for the day?

Rebecca: In the morning I paired up with an environmental scientist and she told me that her job was more than planting trees which was quite funny. And we got to wear sexy hard hats with really bright jackets, um, and funny goggles and it was really good fun … and in the afternoon, I worked with a few girls but most were guys in the apprentice workshop they've got there … did some welding and stuff, just shown that.

(An extract form Rebecca's planned description of 'How to Surf')

The first step is to paddle. You have to paddle really hard to get in with the wave and you feel like a push from behind you when you're on the wave. You will know, because it's like a gliding feeling. And when, as soon as you know you are on the wave, it's best to push up with your hands on the board and have your feet follow it up so you are like … you are still holding onto the board but you're in a low crouching position. And then when you think you have got your feet in the right position which is kind of, almost your back foot's almost right at the back of the board and your other foot's almost in the middle, you'll be able to balance, usually test run a few times.

Figure 9.1 **Figure 9.2**

Global Statement

In this phase, students' control of Standard English reflects their understanding of the way language structures and features are manipulated to achieve different purposes and effects. They evaluate the appropriateness and effectiveness of spoken texts in relation to audience, purpose and context. They experiment with complex devices to improve their communication.

Proficient Speaking and Listening Indicators

Use of Texts

- ◆ Processes ideas and information from a range of classroom texts dealing with challenging ideas and issues.
- ◆ Interacts with peers in structured situations to discuss familiar or accessible subjects.
- ◆ Listens to a range of sustained spoken texts on challenging ideas and issues, noting key ideas and information in a systematic way.
- ◆ Uses text features and structures for effect in unplanned and planned texts.
- ◆ Use of Standard English in different contexts shows critical awareness of audience and purpose.
- • Provides considered reasons for opinions and ideas while discussing complex or controversial topics with others.
- • Monitors audience cues and controls responses, e.g. anticipates likely questions, adds humour for effect.
- • Takes part in a range of team-speaking situations, e.g. reader's theatre, debates.

Contextual Understanding

- ◆ Judges appropriateness and effect of text form and register in relation to audience, purpose and context.
- ◆ Makes adjustments in speaking and listening to suit specific purposes and audiences.
- ◆ Includes relevant and appropriate information to orientate their listeners, e.g. acknowledges differing opinions.
- ◆ Discusses ways in which spoken texts can include or exclude the values and beliefs of particular audiences.
- ◆ Selects devices designed to impact or influence a particular audience, e.g. irony, humour.
- • Can critically discuss spoken language use
- • Shows awareness of the difference between writing and speaking.

Conventions

- ◆ Understands and manipulates language structures and features in formal and informal situations, e.g. structures a formal speech, sustains conversation with an unfamiliar adult.
- ◆ Experiments with some language structures and features that enable speakers to influence audiences.
- ◆ Selects vocabulary to impact on target audience.
- ◆ Adjusts speaking and listening behaviours appropriate to the purpose and situation when interacting, e.g. builds on the ideas of others to achieve group goals, invites others to have a speaking turn.
- ◆ When listening, identifies and analyses structures and features that signal bias and points of view.
- • Uses conventions of formal speaking, e.g. introduces and concludes formal speeches, uses staging cues and transition markers, e.g. firstly, finally.
- • Recognises aspects of language use, such as vocabulary, rhythm and imagery which enhances spoken texts.
- • Manages a wide range of registers, e.g. to deliver a sustained, effective argument.

Processes and Strategies

- ◆ Selects and applies appropriate strategies for monitoring and adjusting communication.
- ◆ Monitors and reflects on spoken texts drawing on knowledge of differences in non-verbal behaviours, e.g. facial expression, eye contact, proximity.
- ◆ Plans and selects appropriate processes and strategies when speaking, e.g. uses anecdotes and data to influence an audience.
- ◆ Plans and selects appropriate processes and strategies when listening, e.g. records important data.
- ◆ Develops strategies to improve listening in challenging contexts, e.g. seeks clarification, confirms information.
- • Notices cues such as change of pace and key words which indicate a new or important point is about to be made.
- • Transforms information from one context to another, e.g. uses information gained in an interview as the basis for a written report.
- • Monitors communication and responds to listeners needs, e.g. pausing, rephrasing, questioning, simplifying.

Major Teaching Emphases

Environment and Attitude (see p. 267)

- Provide opportunities for relevant, challenging and purposeful communication.
- Create a supportive environment which values the diversity of students' speaking and listening development.
- Encourage students to see the value of effective listening and speaking for community, school and family life.

Use of Texts (see p. 270)

- Discuss and compare a range of functional spoken texts.
- Provide opportunities for students to participate in authentic unplanned and planned speaking and listening.
- Provide opportunities for students to participate in extended talk for a range of purposes.
- Teach students to use effective text structures and features to suit a range of purposes.
- Teach students to extract and analyse complex and challenging information from spoken texts.
- Encourage students to use the metalanguage associated with speaking and listening independently, e.g. interaction, intertextuality, alternative, style shifts, adjust, position, pace, convention, evaluate, reflection, rephrasing.

Contextual Understanding (see p. 279)

- Provide opportunities that challenge students to carefully consider their choices when speaking and listening.
- Teach students to reflect upon the way in which they interact with particular audiences.
- Teach students to consider the needs and background knowledge of their audience when selecting suitable content for spoken texts.

- Provide support for students to contribute to matters of social interest or concern.
- Teach students to extend their critical analysis to include complex themes and issues.
- Teach students to reflect upon the way in which they interact with their audience.
- Teach students to select and manipulate devices to suit a particular context.

Conventions (see p. 290)

- Support students to take responsibility for expanding, refining and using new vocabulary.
- Provide opportunities for students to compose complex spoken texts for known and unknown audiences.
- Teach skills needed to sustain and facilitate communication in unplanned and planned situations, e.g. to interrupt, intervene, recap or redirect.
- Teach skills needed to respond appropriately to the intellectual and emotional demands of different situations.

Processes and Strategies (see p. 299)

- Teach students to select appropriate thinking strategies to explore complex concepts and ideas.
- Provide opportunities for students to engage in sustained conversations and discussions.
- Provide opportunities for students to adapt a range of processes and strategies to compose complex and challenging texts.
- Provide opportunities for students to interact responsively in contexts where they are required to facilitate discussion.
- Provide opportunities for students to identify and use prompts that anticipate and manage likely disagreements.

Teaching and Learning Experiences

ENVIRONMENT AND ATTITUDE

Major Teaching Emphases

■ Provide opportunities for relevant, challenging and purposeful communication.

■ Create a supportive classroom environment which values the diversity of students' speaking and listening development.

■ Encourage students to see the value of effective speaking and listening for community, school and family life.

Teaching Notes

Students in the Proficient phase will benefit from an environment in which they feel supported, engaged and challenged in meaningful speaking and listening situations. It is important to provide a variety of contexts for speaking and listening that will help extend students' knowledge of a wide range of text forms. Students should be encouraged to solve problems, evaluate their own work and take responsibility for improving and refining speaking and listening skills. The focus for developing positive attitudes towards speaking and listening is organised under the following headings:

• Creating a Supportive Classroom Environment
• Providing Opportunities for Relevant, Challenging and Purposeful Communication
• Speaking and Listening for Community, School and Family Life

Creating a Supportive Classroom Environment

A supportive environment for students in the Proficient phase is one that provides the opportunities for students to analyse, reflect and produce a wide variety of spoken texts. These opportunities enable students to develop a confidence and enthusiasm to engage in speaking and listening activities.

Physical Environment

An environment that supports Proficient Speakers and Listeners is intellectually stimulating as students engage in an increasing variety of complex speaking and listening situations. Such an environment may include:

- A wide range of recorded examples of spoken texts, e.g. television, radio recordings, appropriate Internet sites.
- Equipment such as video cameras and audio recorders to record rehearsals for self-assessment purposes.
- Equipment to aid formal presentations, e.g. digital projectors to assist a PowerPoint presentation, hyper studio, video footage, photographs, etc.
- Displays made by students such as words and phrases to use in discussions, questions to guide critical analyses of spoken texts and guidelines for self-reflection.

Classroom Culture

As well as providing appropriate material and a carefully planned physical environment, it is essential to develop a comfortable climate where students can confidently analyse and participate in a range of speaking and listening experiences.

- Provide opportunities for students to discuss situations where they find speaking and listening difficult.
- Encourage students to make informed choices when speaking and listening in different contexts.
- Provide opportunities for students to express, discuss and reflect on their thinking with others.
- Support students to take responsibility for planning, refining and adjusting speaking and listening for formal situations.
- Establish guidelines to ensure that all class members support each other when speaking and listening in planned situations, e.g. when giving a formal presentation.
- Support students to evaluate their own speaking, both planned and unplanned.
- Encourage students to evaluate their own listening.
- Encourage students to set goals to improve elements of their speaking and listening.

Providing Opportunities for Relevant, Challenging and Purposeful Communication

Students in the Proficient phase have developed a high level of control over the structures and features of Standard English. However, they will need teacher guidance when encountering new

or demanding situations. Support can be provided in some of the following ways:

- Teach students to consider the implications of choosing an inappropriate style or dialect in particular contexts.
- Encourage students to use negotiating skills to deal with conflict situations.
- Teach students to plan for situations where it is likely that people will disagree.
- Teach students how to give constructive feedback and advice to peers about their speaking and listening.
- Involve students in speaking and listening related to complex issues and topics.
- Ask students to reflect on the type of listening chosen for a particular context, e.g. critical, empathetic or appreciative.

Speaking and Listening for Community, School and Family Life

Students in the Proficient phase are able to monitor and control their use of language with confidence in most familiar situations. They will still need to be supported in managing spoken language with unfamiliar audiences. They will also continue to critically evaluate the social and cultural implications of spoken texts.

Teachers can assist students in the Proficient phase by developing the knowledge, skills and attitudes to be able to:

- use language to include all members of an audience, e.g. explain technical terms that may be unknown by some listeners.
- facilitate group discussions.
- make an impromptu speech to a known audience, e.g. an acceptance speech, thanking someone.
- acknowledge different points of view in a variety of situations.
- use spoken language to critically reflect on and analyse a range of texts.
- compare and contrast different points of view.
- choose conventions appropriate to a range of contexts, e.g. choose suitable vocabulary and non-verbal behaviours for friends and for unfamiliar adults, initiate and close a conversation.
- monitor their listening comprehension and know when to take notes and when to ask clarifying questions.

USE OF TEXTS

Major Teaching Emphases

- Discuss and compare a range of functional spoken texts.

- Provide opportunities for students to participate in authentic unplanned and planned speaking and listening.

- Provide opportunities for students to participate in extended talk for a range of purposes.

- Teach students to use effective text structures and features to suit a range of purposes.

- Teach students to extract and analyse complex and challenging information from spoken texts.

- Encourage students to use the metalanguage associated with speaking and listening independently, e.g. interaction, intertextuality, alternative, style shifts, adjust, position, pace, convention, evaluate, reflection, rephrasing.

Teaching Notes

The focus for supporting Proficient Speakers and Listeners in this aspect is organised under the following headings:
- Discussing a Range of Spoken Texts
- Participation in Unplanned and Planned Spoken Texts
- Using Texts for a Purpose
- Understanding Complex Information
- Developing Metalanguage.

Discussing a Range of Spoken Texts

Students in the Proficient phase will need to develop the skills required to meet the demands of complex social and academic contexts. They will benefit from experiences that challenge them to reflect on and critically analyse linguistic structures and features of a variety of spoken texts. These texts will be literary, informational and social and will include narratives, poetry, reports, speeches, interviews and debates. Students require opportunities to develop critical awareness of the social and cultural functions of language, discussing the way in which language can influence attitudes, values and beliefs.

Participation in Unplanned and Planned Spoken Texts

Proficient Speakers and Listeners continue to need frequent opportunities to interact with each other as they work throughout the day. These interactions should occur in both planned and unplanned situations and will allow them to fully experience, analyse, comprehend and produce a diverse range of spoken texts.

At this phase, students' spoken language will be developed through the ongoing combination of explicit instruction and supportive feedback as well as opportunities to use speaking and listening across curriculum areas. Development of Proficient students' speaking and listening will best occur through a mixture of whole-class and small-group interactions.

In the course of everyday interpersonal interactions, students in the Proficient phase will engage in a wide range of planned and unplanned speaking and listening, e.g.

- Social interactions: one-on-one or in groups
- Workplace interactions: co-workers, management, customers
- Collaboration with others: family, school, wider community
- Commercial transactions: retail consumers, banking.

Figure 9.3

Figure 9.4

It is important to allow students to participate in substantive conversations. Talking and listening to others allows students to adjust, refine and even change existing views or misconceptions.

Modelled, Shared and Guided Speaking and Listening sessions (see *First Steps* Linking Assessment, Teaching and Learning book, pages 126–129) provide ideal opportunities for Proficient Speakers and Listeners to compose a range of unplanned and planned spoken texts. Over time, students will develop some of the understandings about spoken texts through Modelled, Shared and Guided Speaking and Listening sessions. Some of these understandings will include the following:

• People use functional spoken texts frequently throughout the day.
• When points of view are explored, other views can be confirmed or extended.
• Speakers make choices about how they will use spoken language according to the situation, audience and purpose.
• Non-verbal language and use of devices can influence the way a listener interprets a spoken text, e.g. a politician may use repetitive words and gestures to highlight a particular point. The listener will need to judge whether they agree or disagree with the underlying message.
• The relationship between language and power, e.g. politicians, advertisers and business executives are accomplished in manipulating language in order to influence decision-making in the community.
• Language and culture are linked, e.g. our attitudes, values and beliefs are influenced by the stories told through generations of family members or by the way families are portrayed through television programs and movies.
• There are different attitudes to varieties of English.
• Meaning is communicated through a combination of verbal and non-verbal language. Planning and rehearsing can help speakers to improve their speaking in both informal and formal situations.

Using Texts for a Purpose

Proficient students need to extend their understanding of how successful speakers and listeners use a range of text forms for different purposes.

In the Proficient phase, students will encounter increased demands on their speaking and listening skills as they engage in unfamiliar speaking and listening situations in different curriculum areas, in wider community settings and in workplace experiences. Therefore, students in this phase will still need to be explicitly taught to use effective text structures and features to suit a range of purposes.

Proficient Speakers and Learners should feel confident to use appropriate spoken language when they need to:

- use social conventions for a range of situations (both in and out of school).
- initiate a conversation with an unknown person.
- maintain a conversation.
- organise information in a report so that the listener is provided with enough information to understand a complicated procedure.
- change a topic.
- clarify and confirm ideas in small-group work.

Teachers can focus attention on the different functions of language and the way that language is structured by using guiding questions and providing feedback before, during and after speaking and listening activities. (See Figure 9.5 for examples of ways to focus on the functions of spoken texts.)

Proficient students communicate for …	Students in the Proficient phase speak and listen to …	Teachers can involve students in these activities to draw their attention to the relationship between structure, text features and purpose.		
		Provide Direction	**Give a Comment**	**Ask a Question**
Getting things done	• instruct parents on where they need to go for a special event. • explain to an unfamiliar teacher what they or their class teacher requires for a particular task or resource.	Ensure that you provide a brief explanation to the teacher of why you have come so that they understand where you are from and the reasons for you being there before you make your specific requests.	You have written down the exact amounts, model number and colours so that you can provide precise details in your explanation. You have also made notes on what you require if you are asked to provide this information.	How do you expect teachers may feel about being interrupted from their work? What words and phrases might we use to acknowledge these feelings before explaining why we are here?
Influencing the behaviour, feelings or attitudes of others	• convince the group to accept a particular identity for a challenge. • present a strong case for a particular point of view on an issue.	Think about which examples would be most convincing in demonstrating your point of view.	You used some very emotive words that conveyed the passion you feel for this topic.	Why do you think others in the group do not view it the same way as you?
Getting along with others	• greet or depart. • initiate and maintain conversations. • seek the well-being of others. • organise leisure time.	In your group discuss the kinds of topics that you might use to initiate a conversation with your group of friends/another group of peers/your friend's parents/a parent of a friend who you have not met yet.	Yes, talking about someone you have in common, or asking about something that you know they have some experience in, can help get the conversation going.	How would you ask these questions so that they feel you are genuinely interested? What would it look like, feel like, sound like?
Expressing individuality and personal feelings	• recount own experiences. • describe personal reactions to and feelings about experiences, people or issues.	Describe your reaction to … e.g. a current event. Include reasons for your personal opinions.	You sounded passionate about what happened. Your personal reaction was conveyed to the group in a convincing manner.	What are some of the language features you used to express your opinion clearly? Did others have similar reactions? How were they expressed?

Seeking and learning about the social and physical environment	• interview peers and others about opinions on a controversial issue. • make a telephone inquiry when organising a pizza day for the class.	To make sure that you have all the information that you require before contacting the pizza place, with a partner write down two lists. (Information that we need, information that the pizza place might need from us). Then, number the items in order of priority.	Writing a brief introduction to yourself and the reason for your call and rehearsing before the call seemed to make you feel more confident.	Do you think it would be appropriate to enquire about a group discount?
Creating stories, games, new worlds and new texts	• create stories for others and self. • design debate topics. • create dramatisations or role plays that demonstrate possible solutions about a controversial issues.	Plan a story to entertain young children. Think about your audience and the style of presentation that will appeal to them.	Your exaggerated facial expressions to show different emotions, and the way you looked directly at the children when telling your story, encouraged them to react to the events with similar emotions.	Why do you think it is important to be expressive in your facial expressions and voice with young children? Did any of the children react differently to how you expected?
Communicating information	• describe details about things as part of an instruction. • show peers how to complete voting slips for student council elections.	Describe the significant features of the different buildings or rooms that will help someone unfamiliar with our school to identify them.	Even if they don't see the signs, they should be able to recognise the school library because you have described its unique features and explained how it differs from the other buildings.	Did you notice the listener repeat any particular details or use hand gestures? How confident were you that they would be able to find it? What signals did you use to make this assessment?
Entertaining others	• discuss topics of interest with peers and familiar adults. • formally introduce a person to a class or a school assembly.	Introduce this WWII veteran at the school assembly by briefly recounting his war experiences. Make sure that you stress the historical significance of these experiences.	Your reference to specific dates and places in the chronological recount of his war experiences really provided the audience with a sense of history.	When recounting his war experiences to your family tonight, how will you alter the details and language you use? Will you still sequence the events in the same time order?

Figure 9.5 Examples for focusing on the functions of spoken texts

Understanding Complex Information

Proficient Speakers and Listeners are expected to select specialised topics to study and to continue to develop and extend their general knowledge. Students can also be encouraged to utilise information from spoken texts to inform opinions, make decisions and share information with others. They can be encouraged to understand complex texts in a range of ways.

• Encourage students to make notes and diagrams when listening to complex information.

• Encourage students to ask questions to clarify their understanding of difficult content or unknown vocabulary.

• Encourage students to ask a speaker to give examples that will assist their understanding.

- Encourage students to retell a spoken text, explaining important information in their own words.
- Provide opportunities for students to use reflective journals to record the main structures or features of a particular text, or their reaction to a particular text.

Developing Metalanguage

The language used to talk about language is known as metalanguage. When students use metalanguage, it helps them to understand how language operates. They also understand the directions and feedback provided by teachers who use the metalanguage in their daily interactions with students.

To help Proficient Speakers and Listeners continue to use the terms associated with speaking and listening, it is important to use metalanguage as part of everyday teaching. This can be incorporated into learning areas, as part of targeted discussions, during explicit demonstrations, during one-on-one conversations with students or as part of planned Modelled, Shared or Guided Speaking and Listening sessions.

When working with Proficient Speakers and Listeners, consider the use of the following terms:
Use of Texts: *interaction, intertextuality*
Contextual Understanding: *alternative, style shifts, adjust, position*
Conventions: *pace, convention*
Processes and Strategies: *plan, monitor, evaluate, reflection, rephrasing.*

> For further information about the Use of Texts aspect, see *First Steps Speaking and Listening Resource Book,* 2nd Edition:
> - Chapter 1: Use of Texts
> - Chapter 4: Processes and Strategies

Involving Students

1 Collaborative Study Time

Collaborative Study Time allows students to use extended talk to discuss their cross-curricula projects in groups. These discussion groups give students the opportunity to discuss complex and challenging ideas. The focus of the activity is for students to speak and listen to make a range of decisions, such as who they will learn with and what their study or inquiry will be about.

- Have students design their independent study tasks. Their focus may be a topic, a text or a learning area inquiry. Students discuss and record details, e.g. **What do we want to find out? How will we find out? When will we do it? How will we share? What we find out? Who needs to know about it? What speaking and listening will we need to do to complete this study?**

- Have students arrange an appointment to discuss their plan with you.
- Interact with students and support their selections and make suggestions where appropriate, e.g. **Have you thought about …? I think that would be a feasible option for that investigation. Ben has some ideas for study in this area. Perhaps you could ask him to share his ideas. They might provide you with a starting point.**
- Support students by providing feedback, suggestions and suitable resources, such as articles to read.
- At the end of the session, students can briefly report on their progress.
- Have students put forward any requests during this time.
- When students have completed the activity, they can reflect upon it before considering a new project or activity.

How Might This Activity Be Used in Your Class?

- Include some journal time in this session.
- Observe the students as they speak and listen during the session.
- Organise a notice board (electronic and physical) so students can submit their requests; however, encourage them to use speaking and listening as much as possible.

2 Listen to Learn

Refer to Chapter 6, Exploratory Speaking and Listening Phase, p. 145.

How Might This Activity Be Used in Your Class?

- Choose spoken texts that will provide an opportunity to help students analyse complex ideas — these may be instructional videos, current affairs programs, teacher lectures, radio programs, radio plays and interviews.
- Encourage students to explore appropriate thinking frameworks to support them in organising and recording their ideas logically and clearly when presenting their learning.
- Students may have questions and selected audio texts that can help their inquiry.
- Students may listen to a number of spoken texts to compare and contrast ideas and information.

3 Talk to Teach

Refer to Chapter 6, Exploratory Speaking and Listening Phase, p. 146.

How Might This Activity Be Used in Your Class?

- Keep a list of 'experts' and draw upon it when you need someone to teach something to the class.
- Arrange a task that students can do in the community on an ongoing basis, e.g. they could teach senior citizens how to use the computer, mobile phone, etc.
- Implement activities that are based on simulation, e.g. students can imagine they are a board of directors for an advertising company and students have to make a collective decision on the target audience and image for their product. Each member of the board has to share their vision and inform the other members of the exact requirements they have for the advertising campaign for their product.

4 Reflect and Respond

Refer to Chapter 4, Beginning Speaking and Listening Phase, p. 63.

How Might This Activity Be Used in Your Class?

- Provide students with opportunities to discuss challenging spoken texts by involving them in discussions using guiding questions, e.g. What attitudes were evident? Were there assumptions about the audience evident? How would this change if it was delivered to …? How was it similar or different to other texts that we have listened to? What information was difficult to understand? How did you work out what it meant? When you were socialising this week, what did you do to keep the conversation going? What were some of the differences between the kinds of topics you talked about and the way that you spoke in these situations?
- Students can focus on the appropriateness of particular strategies for a task, e.g. in an interview, questions need to effective in obtaining specific details about an event, how to phrase certain questions and the tone that should be used; the expected responses of interviewees.
- In discussion times, students can compose charts or 'how-to' guides for particular speaking and listening activities, e.g. 'How to conduct an interview', 'How to convince a young child to brush their teeth'; 'How to choose and order a mobile phone'.
- Set tasks in which students are required to investigate a particular speaking and listening function or situation across a range of contexts. For example, they could 'research' the techniques that different people use to motivate and encourage others, such as sports coaches, parents, and teachers. They could record the actual

words and statements used, the structure of the speech, e.g. the beginning, the middle, the ending and non-verbal gestures. Small groups could evaluate the different situations they observed.

5 Quick Topics

Quick Topics is an activity that requires students to choose a text form suitable for an impromptu speech. Students develop the ability to 'think on their feet' as they present their thoughts in a clear, organised manner with little preparation time.

Decide on an object, statement or word that will become the topic for a talk, e.g. display an unusual contraption such as an antique tool and ask students to describe its use; comment on a statement such as 'the movie series *Star Wars* was based on books that were really accounts of ancient history'; discuss the word 'shock'.

• Decide on the length of time that a student should speak for (perhaps one to two minutes). The students will need to quickly decide what form their speaking will take, e.g. a narrative, description, argument, procedure, etc.

• Ask listening students to give feedback.

• Have students record a reflection in their journals, noting successes and areas for improvement. Ask: Was the text form chosen effective? Were ideas organised effectively?

6 Storytelling

Refer to Chapter 8: Conventional Speaking and Listening Phase, p. 235.

CONTEXTUAL UNDERSTANDING

Major Teaching Emphases

- Provide opportunities that challenge students to carefully consider their choices when speaking and listening.

- Teach students to reflect upon the way in which they interact with particular audiences.

- Teach students to consider the needs and background knowledge of their audience when selecting suitable content for spoken texts.

- Provide support for students to contribute to matters of social interest or concern.

- Teach students to extend their critical analysis to include complex themes and issues.

- Teach students to reflect upon the way in which they interact with their audience.

- Teach students to select and manipulate devices to suit a particular context.

Teaching Notes

The focus for supporting Proficient Speakers and Listeners in this aspect is organised under the following headings:

- A Focus on the Context
- Reflecting on Interactions
- Considering the Needs of the Audience
- Contributing to Matters of Importance
- Analysing the Way Ideas and People Are Represented
- Use of Devices

A Focus on the Context

In the Proficient phase students continue to learn about appropriate speaking and listening conventions for different contexts. Analysing and Reflecting are ideal teaching practices for teaching students to carefully consider their speaking and listening choices according to the context. As students participate in Analysing and Reflecting sessions, they continue to develop skills in using spoken language in different contexts including identifying when the use of different varieties or forms of English is appropriate.

Proficient Speakers and Listeners are supported as teachers guide and support them as they consider speaking and listening choices. This can occur before, during and after students participate in unplanned and planned speaking and listening as shown in the example below:

Task: Students have been placed with an employer for some learning experience in a workplace.		
Examples of Teacher Interactions		
Before	**During**	**After**
• *Your employer knows that you are going to make contact and is looking forward to meeting you. Since this is the first time you will meet, what could you say and do to convince the employer that you are willing to learn and that you will be able to participate in the set tasks?* • *How would this be different to meeting a new class member for the first time?* • *What speaking and listening skills will be important for your work experience?*	• *Do you understand what your employer asks you to do? What can help here? How can you ask for clarification or check that you have understood?* • *I see that one of your goals relates to following instructions. How will listening help here? What can you do to help with focusing on the steps needed?* • *Have you tried one of our school listening strategies?*	• *What speaking and listening skills were important for your work experience? Were they the skills you thought would be important?* • *How did you adjust your speaking and listening for the workplace?* • *At school we use different thinking frameworks to help us with listening and planned speaking. Were any of these useful?* • *How did you manage unplanned speaking and listening?*

Figure 9.6

Figure 9.7

Reflecting on Interactions

Proficient Speakers and Listeners benefit from many opportunities to explore and articulate the way life experience affects the knowledge, beliefs, attitudes and values that they personally hold and how these may be different for other people. Students can be involved in examining assumptions that people may make when communicating and discussing how different cultural experiences may result in misunderstanding. Students in the Proficient phase will also benefit from discussing the way that English language usage changes over time and how the attitudes towards the use of different dialects or styles of English will be interpreted by some people. Students will need to reflect on how they interact with others in some of the following ways:

Making Assumptions
– Discuss the need for providing suitable background information when explaining a problem to a peer, teacher or in a shop.
– Discuss the need to ask questions to make sure a listener has all the necessary details, e.g. what time to meet, what to wear or bring to a party.

Acknowledging Feelings
– Discuss how to control emotions in order to maintain a position in a discussion.
– Discuss how to acknowledge the feelings of others in an emotional situation in order that they have the opportunity to explain.

Making Time
– Discuss the importance of allowing people time to respond to a question or comment.
– Discuss the importance of allowing time to respond personally, e.g. by repeating the question to give yourself thinking time or by saying 'I'll need to think about that and get back to you.'

Considering the Needs of the Audience

Proficient Speakers and Listeners are aware of ways of interacting with different audiences. They continue to need support to consider the needs and background knowledge of their listeners when speaking to unfamiliar audiences or large groups. Teachers can direct students' attention to these matters by discussing questions such as:

• What do you think the exchange students would like to hear about when they come to our school?
• The senior citizens group said that they learnt some valuable information when we helped them in their computers class last week. What did we say and do that was helpful?

- I noticed that you are planning to show your parents how you learnt to include video clips on a PowerPoint presentation. What do your parents already know about using PowerPoint?
- How do you think you will tell your story so that we can visualise the events?
- What suitable text forms could we use to share our ideas about this at the school assembly?
- After Graffiti Groups activity, which speech captured your attention? Why? (See p. 243.)
- What background information can you give about the fund-raising event at the group meeting? What do you think people need to know?

Contributing to Matters of Importance

Proficient Speakers and Listeners need regular opportunities to contribute to discussions about matters of social interest or concern. When students are able to do this, they learn that speaking and listening helps to raise awareness of situations and that action can be taken to solve problems. Students also develop their abilities to express ideas, opinions and feelings. Teachers can support students in these ways:

- Negotiate with students and invite their ideas and opinions when planning, reviewing and organising tasks within learning sessions.
- Have open-ended tasks that provide students with choices about topics and materials.
- Provide effective feedback when students do raise matters or issues.
- Include regular sessions such as Group Meetings, Independent Study Time and Graffiti Groups.
- Allow students to create and share their own displays in areas around the room or school.
- Have displays that capture students' interests and invite discussion.

Analysing the Way Ideas and People Are Represented

Proficient Speakers and Listeners will need support to analyse complex themes and issues when considering the different ways in which ideas and people can be represented in spoken texts. A range of electronic spoken texts are available to use for discussions of how people and ideas have been represented in particular ways. CD-ROMs, films, television programs and audio tapes include spoken texts such as stories, articles, recounts, advertisements and reports. Proficient Speakers and Listeners will benefit from Analysing, Reflecting and Discussion sessions which focus on the following kinds of questions:

- How does this spoken text suit the purpose of the communication?
- How do I react to the text? Why?
- Why was this particular spoken text selected?
- How do groups of people socialise? How do they connect with each other? What common texts do they use?
- Do you think particular people have been excluded? How could they be included?
- Why is that point of view being expressed?
- Do you think particular ideas have been excluded? How could they be presented?
- Who might agree with the way the ideas or people are shown in this? Why? Who might not?
- Is this representation fair? Why?
- Who is privileged in this situation?
- In what way has the background knowledge of the participants been considered?
- How else could that be interpreted?
- How does the choice of style affect me as the audience? How would it affect other audiences?
- How have the subject-specific words been used?
- What do you think is the main message about the people and/or ideas?
- What devices have been used to convince the listener or the speaker?

Use of Devices

Spoken texts comprise a selection of information that can be presented in different ways to position listeners towards certain beliefs, assumptions and points of view. Proficient Speakers and Listeners make many decisions when crafting their spoken texts. It is important to provide them with many opportunities to plan and evaluate the effectiveness of their spoken texts and their manipulation of devices. The focus is on determining:

- What is the purpose of my text? e.g. **Do I want to entertain, inform, or present a particular point of view?**
- Who is the audience for my text? e.g. **Have I taken into consideration the age, socio-economic status, cultural background, academic background and familiarity with the subject content? Is it a familiar audience to me or will I have to make some assumptions about the audience?**
- How I will use non-verbal devices? e.g. **looking at individuals in turn when talking to a room full of people.**
- What devices will I use to best suit my audience and purpose, e.g. **choice of vocabulary—judgemental or emotive?**

Involving Students

1 Networks (Milroy and Milroy 1992)

Networks helps students to consider how the relationship between speakers and listeners affects the way in which they interact.

Students identify and describe their speech networks within a speech community. A speech community is a group of people that see each other regularly and share many common understandings, e.g. a group of friends at school, players on a basketball team.

Prepare students for this activity by providing them with background information about the different kinds of networks (see below).

- Explain the activity and any unfamiliar terminology to students.
  - A network describes the groups of people with whom you interact.
  - A network can be dense. (The people on your network all interact with each other.)
  - A network can be loose. (The people on your network do not all interact with each other.)
  - A network can be interconnected. (The people are connected in more than one way.)
  - A network can have strong ties or links. (People speak to each other frequently.)
  - A network can have weak ties or links. (People speak to each other infrequently.)
- Have students list the speech communities which they belong to, e.g. a sporting team, a youth group, a friendship group.
- Ask students to choose one group and list the people that belong to the group (including their own name).
- Draw a circle and arrange the names of listed people around the outside of the circle. The student rules a line from themself to the other people that they speak to regularly. Choosing another colour, the student then rules lines to show who other people speak to. This will show whether the network is dense, with individuals speaking to many others on a regular basis, or loose, where only some people are spoken to on a regular basis.
- Students should discuss how a speech network assists members to communicate, e.g. some experiences are shared and do not have to be explained, technical terms are well understood and members develop a kind of shorthand to the things they say to each other.
- Have students record the findings for this activity in a journal, noting the type of language that is used only for a speech network.

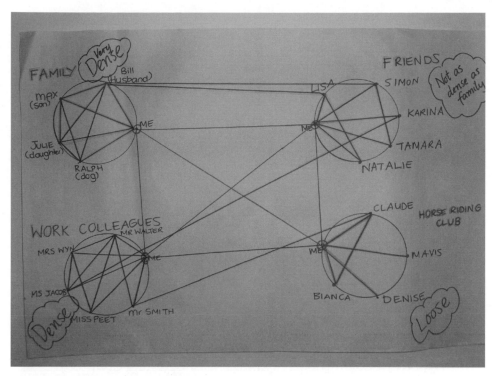

Figure 9.8 A Network sample

How Might This Activity Be Used in Your Class?

- Organise an afternoon in which students teach another class about Networks.
- Students could create displays and guide or inform visitors who visit their displays.
- Consider a multi-modal representation, e.g. **PowerPoint** presentation with film footage.
- Encourage students to reflect upon the kinds of value judgements they are making about people in determining where they fit in the network.

2 Listening Investigations

Refer to Chapter 9: Proficient Speaking and Listening Phase.

3 Class Meetings

Class meetings are described in detail in Chapter 6 in the Exploratory phase (see p. 157). They can be adapted for students in the Proficient phase according to their needs. For example, meetings may take the form of a committee, e.g. a committee set up to organise a dance or may take the form of small-group meetings with a specific responsibility, e.g. a group to organise entertainment for a class camp and another to organise a menu.

4 Now and Then

Now and Then is an activity that aims to compare and contrast the way attitudes, values and beliefs are shaped by and through language by comparing past and present situations. Prepare recordings of television situation comedies from the 1950s or 1960s. Involve students in analysing aspects of the television shows in order to compare and contrast some of the following ideas:

• Identify the language used that invokes sympathy or antipathy with the listener.
• Identify the viewpoints of different characters to uncover the values that are being promoted.
• Identify major themes in the text to compare general values, beliefs or attitudes.
• Identify the aspirations and expectations of the characters.

5 Communicating in the Community

Communicating in the Community is explained in detail in Chapter 6 in the Exploratory phase (see p. 156). This activity could be extended for students
in the Proficient phase by using some of the following ideas.

• What are some of the technical words used by hairdressers, doctors, sports coaches, librarians, surf shop assistants, clothing store owners and scout leaders?
• What do people say to make others feel comfortable when entering their homes or businesses?
• How do greetings differ between people who are familiar with each other and people who are not?

6 Speech Pyramid

Refer to Chapter 7, Consolidating Speaking and Listening Phase, p. 202. (See Figure 9.9).

7 Graffiti Groups

Refer to Chapter 8, Conventional Speaking and Listening Phase, p. 243.

8 This Is How They Saw It

This activity is designed to support students in reflecting upon the way in which people use language to describe from their particular point of view. A student or teacher collects spoken texts and uses them to facilitate a discussion about the way in which a particular situation is interpreted.

• Describe the activity to the students.
• Model the role of the facilitator in the first session. In the next session, students can work collaboratively to plan and facilitate.

Speech Pyramid

SPEECH SITUATION
Moving between classes

SPEECH EVENTS
School talk
Social talk
Organising talk

SPEECH ACTS

School talk – telling others what you just did, what homework you've done for the next class, what the teacher said, what happened.

Social talk – saying hello, telling others how you feel about the class, where you are going to sit, what you plan to do after school.

Organising talk – to find out what room you are in, asking what you need to take, reminding others of what to take to class, where you might meet for lunch.

Figure 9.9 Speech pyramid

- Present students with several taped or filmed spoken texts each constructed by different people who recount, describe, retell or report the same situation. When collecting the spoken texts, students should try to collect and record spoken texts from men and women, people of different ages, cultures or social groups. Situations for This Is How They Saw It could include:
  - everyday informal situations, e.g. the weekly shopping trip, a visit to the beach, going out to dinner, a bowling trip, having a barbecue, preparing dinner, reading the same story, watching the same show on television, attending a show, etc.
  - academic formal situations, e.g. news bulletins, current affairs, attending a lecture, attending a community presentation, meeting, interview, historical event, etc.
- Facilitate a discussion, focusing on the differences and similarities in the delivery of the messages, inclusion of the content and the importance placed on a particular feature of the event. When students facilitate they need to have some guiding questions or a

thinking framework prepared for the group, e.g. **What does each speaker include? Does everyone include the same information? Why?**
- Have students write their reflections in their journals.

How Might This Activity Be Used in Your Class?

- Use radio or television news for the spoken texts, especially talk-back responses.
- Consider how to support students in collecting their spoken texts. Consider setting some criteria, e.g. **the same people all playing the same game.**
- Introduce this activity to a small group of students using their stories about school. Each student could bring their recorded interpretation and compare it. It would need to be pre-recorded so that it is a personal account.

9 Time Machine

Refer to Chapter 7, Consolidating Speaking and Listening Phase, p. 203.

10 Presenting My POV (Godhino 2004)

This activity encourages Proficient students to think about and state their points of view.

Suggest students think about those interests or issues that they feel strongly about. Provide some examples, e.g. **favourite sporting team, special interest, local issue, etc.**

Allow students time to reflect. Explain that they must state their point of view along with one strong supporting reason that supports their point of view.
- Model the activity for the class, e.g. **My Point of View: I strongly believe that we should not be allowed to farm kangaroos. My supporting reason: I believe in animal rights.**
- Students can conduct the activity in pairs; at this stage, there is no time for extended discussion.
- Partners report each other's statements to the class.
- Record the statements onto a chart to use in extension activities.
- Extension activity: Have students express a point of view and give at least three supporting reasons for their opinion. Focus on using persuasive words, e.g. **strongly believe, firmly convinced.**
- Students can reflect on why it is important to justify their point of view with a strong reason and to think of the persuasive words they can use to express their view.

11 In Other Words

In Other Words is an activity that provides students with the opportunity to investigate the devices a speaker uses to persuade an audience. Prepare an audio recording of a persuasive text; this could be from a political speech or from a television current affairs program where someone is explaining their particular point of view. Ask students to record examples of idioms, similes, repetitions, exaggerations, etc. Ask students to note also how intonation is used to convey meaning to particular words.

- Students should record examples of devices used and then re-write what was said in their own words.
- Ask students to work in groups to compare their interpretations.
- Students could discuss the intentions of the speaker when using these devices.
- Allocate time for students to share their findings with the whole class. For example, discuss different interpretations of the use of different devices. Ask students to discuss the reasons behind different interpretations, e.g. **different life experiences, different expectations.**

12 Gender Issues

Gender Issues is designed to assist students in examining the way that gender is represented through television. Students are asked to analyse the verbal and non-verbal language used in advertising in order to make judgements as to how these representations are interpreted. In this way students develop an understanding of how stereotypes are constructed in society. Record a television advertisement that represents one particular gender. Students should watch the advertisement and record specific information to include in a discussion. Provide guiding questions to assist note taking, such as:

- Consider the way the male (or female) is represented in the advertisement. Ask: Who would this image appeal to? Who would this image not appeal to?
- How is the image constructed? List the language features used, e.g. **vocabulary, intonation, pace and pausing.** List the non-verbal features used, e.g. **stance, gestures and facial expressions.**
- Have students use these notes to discuss the way gender has been represented.
- Students could imitate the advertisement using a reverse role play, e.g. **a female student could represent the male part in the advertisement (or the other way round).**
- Students could discuss the way meaning would be altered if gender roles were exchanged.

CONVENTIONS

Major Teaching Emphases

- Support students to take responsibility for expanding, refining and using new vocabulary.

- Provide opportunities for students to compose complex spoken texts for known and unknown audiences.

- Teach skills needed to sustain and facilitate communication in unplanned and planned situations, e.g. to interrupt, intervene, recap or redirect.

- Teach skills needed to respond appropriately to the intellectual and emotional demands of different situations.

Teaching Notes

Teaching and learning experiences for students in the Proficient phase are organised under the following headings:
- Building Vocabulary
- Understanding the Conventions of Spoken Texts
- Conversations
- Understanding the Behaviours Associated with Speaking and Listening
- Understanding the Conventions of Listening.

Building Vocabulary

Students in the Proficient phase have an extensive vocabulary based on their experiences at school, at home, in the community and from the media. Students need to continue to develop subject-specific vocabulary in order to effectively express their understanding of concepts. A broad vocabulary is essential in order to manage a variety of social and community interactions confidently. To further develop and refine vocabulary, teachers can encourage students to analyse a variety of spoken texts, discussing vocabulary choice and the effectiveness of those choices.

Students could analyse texts from:
– political broadcasts
– television interviews
– radio interviews
– radio and television advertisements
– debates

– excerpts from movies or television programs
– interviews.

• Encourage students to keep lists of interesting words, or words
  that they aim to use for a particular purpose.
• Involve students in examining vocabulary. Ask: What effects were
  achieved? Is there a sense of balance or bias? What emotive words
  were used?
• Encourage students to reflect on their own speaking, noticing the
  types of vocabulary chosen for different purposes. Ask: Was the
  choice effective in making the meaning clear and precise for the
  listener?

Understanding the Conventions of Spoken Texts

At all phases of development it is important that students are
exposed to different examples of spoken texts so that attention can
be drawn to the structures and features of language composed for
different purposes.

The *structure* of a spoken text refers to the way information is
organised and presented in a text. These could include:
– complimenting another person.
– relating an anecdote within a conversation.
– giving precise directions.

The *language features* of a spoken text refer to the type of vocabulary,
grammar, tone and pace chosen. For example:
– using colloquial words or sayings when conversing with friends
– emotive language used to persuade in an advertisement
– stressing certain words or altering volume to gain impact.

Students in the Proficient phase can be encouraged to consider the
way language is used in the following ways.
• Involve students in discussions about styles of speech, e.g. research
  the way they speak when talking to friends, talking to known adults,
  talking to unknown adults, talking to those much younger or older
  than themselves.
• Ask students to compare different types of speaking used for
  different purposes, e.g. compare a news program to a documentary, a
  soap drama to a lifestyle program. Ask: What is Standard English and
  who uses it?
• Teach the conventions of formal speaking. Brainstorm and record
  purposes for formal speeches. Prepare audio or video segments
  that show examples of formal speech. Ask students to analyse
  the conventions used, e.g. vocabulary, tone, pace of delivery, use

of pauses, use of descriptive language or emotive language. Jointly construct frameworks or checklists to help students prepare their own formal speeches.

- Discuss the skills needed to extend discussions. For example, teach:
  - ways to extend a discussion by elaborating on the ideas of others.
  - how to give and justify an opinion.
  - how to offer viewpoints sensitively.
  - ways to include all the people in the group.
  - ways to interrupt when the discussion takes an unrelated direction.
  - ways to intervene, recap or redirect.

Conversations

Conversations are important in establishing and maintaining relationships through expressing feelings and sharing experiences. This type of unplanned speaking and listening not only develops self-awareness and interpersonal skills; it helps to build topic knowledge and processes for learning. Teachers can discuss likely issues with students and negotiate agreed behaviours for interacting during conversations. The following list of questions may provide a starting point.

- What are the implications of making 'personal' comments?
- How can differing opinions be stated in a respectful manner?
- How can likes and dislikes be expressed sensitively?
- How can confrontation and argument be avoided?
- How can everyone be included in the conversation?

Understanding the Behaviours Associated with Speaking and Listening

Students need to develop a critical awareness of the behaviours associated with speaking and listening and how it affects meaningful communication in a variety of contexts. Teachers can involve students in choosing appropriate speaking and listening behaviours through modelling, explicit teaching and discussion. Jointly constructing Y charts or T charts will provide meaningful reminders. The following list may provide some useful starting points when considering effective behaviours.

- Speak clearly and with enough volume so that everyone can hear and understand.
- Discuss body language when speaking, e.g. **appropriate eye contact, proximity of speaker and listener.**
- Discuss body language when listening, e.g. **nodding your head, proximity.**

- Discuss how to interpret body language for emotional cues.
- Provide opportunities for students to observe and reflect on the body language portrayed, e.g. watch an interview with the sound turned off.
- Discuss how an audience behaves, e.g. when listening to the teacher, when listening to another student, at assembly, at the theatre.
- How to take turns in a discussion.

Understanding the Conventions of Listening

Listening is an active, constructive process concerned with making meaning from verbal and non-verbal cues. By building an awareness of the conventions of listening, teachers assist students to develop and refine communication skills. Effective listening depends on the expectations and predictions about content, language and genre that the listener brings to the text (Gibbons 2002). The way in which we listen is also linked to the context of the communication. We listen differently during unplanned, spontaneous situations, e.g. in casual conversations, than we do when speaking and listening is planned and formal, e.g. in the classroom when instructions are being given. The structures and features of listening can be considered using the following framework.

Figure 9.10

Involve students in different types of listening for different purposes in some of the following ways:

• Provide time for students to engage in conversations.

• Provide opportunities for students to listen and respond to speech constructed for different purposes.

• Provide opportunities for students to respond to spoken texts through discussions, questions, journals, artwork.

• Provide opportunities for students to explore and analyse different types of listening. Use students' findings to clarify the conventions of listening needed for different purposes.

  – When is listening easy or difficult?

  – When do I change the way I listen?

  – How do I know when I should respond to a speaker? When should I stay quiet?

Involving Students

1 Workplace Talk

Workplace Talk focuses on the spoken language that is used in the workplace. Prepare students by discussing the types of part-time jobs they have or occupations that interest them. Generate a list of people that could be approached to visit the class. Alternatively, generate a list of people that students could arrange an appointment with in order to conduct an interview.

Students could work in pairs or small groups to compile a list of suitable questions. For example, students could seek information on:

• specific vocabulary needed.

• the different audiences expected, e.g. customers, clients, sales representatives, co-workers, senior managers, etc.

• how much speaking is one-to-one, in groups, or over the phone.

• specific phrases or patterns of language that need to be repeated, e.g. 'How may I help you?' or a particular phrase to be used answering the phone.

How Might This Activity Be Used in Your Class?

Students could brainstorm ways to share the information they gather. They could write a manual, a booklet, create a PowerPoint presentation or hold an information seminar.

2 Listening Investigations

Listening Investigations helps students to understand the different types of listening. Students become critically aware of the listening skills they need to access for different purposes. Ask students to form small groups to discuss the way listening changes in different situations.

Some guiding questions to help in responses could be:
- Think of a time when you needed someone to listen to you.
- Why was it important for someone to listen to you?
- How did you know that they were truly listening?
- How was that type of listening different to other types of listening?
- How did that type of listening help you?

Students could record ideas from the discussion in a reflection book. (See the Speaking and Listening CD-ROM, Proficient Phase — Conventions for an example of a recording idea.)

This activity is also suitable for the Conventional and Advanced phases.

How Might This Activity Be Used in Your Class?
- Students develop a format for sharing information about the importance of listening, e.g. create a brochure or poster.
- Students could role play writing an article for an 'advice' column in a magazine.

3 Radio DJ

Radio DJ provides Proficient students with an opportunity to examine the conventions used in broadcasting. Students investigate the role of a radio DJ and record the text types and conventions used in a broadcast.
- Have students (working in groups) listen to pre-recorded segments of a radio show (pre-recording allows a teacher to assess the suitability of the content). Choose different shows, e.g. from a variety of commercial stations, government-operated stations such as the ABC and Radio National and community radio.
- Ask students to record text types used, e.g. introductions, interviews, jokes, commentary, expressing point of view, explanations, etc.
- Ask students to choose one of the text types to investigate further to identify the conventions used; for example, some students may focus on the structures and features of an interview in order to make note of vocabulary used, types of questions asked, type of listening used, use of descriptive language or linguistic devices,

the use of colloquialisms, how the subject is changed, the use of volume and intonation, etc.

- Ask students to evaluate the segment using guiding questions such as: What type of audience is this show aimed at? What is your opinion of the DJ from the words and tone used in this segment? Can you see where this DJ might improve skills in ... (interviewing, introductions or farewells, telling anecdotes, etc.).
- Extend this activity by asking students to plan their own radio segment.

4 Barrier Games

Refer to Chapter 5, Early Speaking and Listening Phase, p. 123.

5 Jargon

Jargon develops the understanding of the use of jargon in spoken texts and how it can exclude many people. This activity encourages students to consider choosing words that communicate ideas clearly. It also encourages students to consider the needs of an audience when composing speech so that all members of a group are included.

- Prepare a recording of a spoken text that contains examples of jargon. This could be from a parliamentary broadcast, a political interview, a speech to shareholders, etc.
- Ask students to list words or phrases that could be considered jargon as they are listening. Compare and discuss these lists, asking students to consider factors such as:
  – Who is the intended audience?
  – Who is included in this spoken text?
  – Who is excluded in this spoken text?
- Students could make lists of words or phrases that could be more effective and inclusive of all members of an audience.

6 Pitch Variety

This activity develops understanding of the use of pitch and intonation and how it affects the meaning of spoken texts.

- Prepare sentences that can be said in ways where the pitch alters the meaning, for example, 'What time did you get home?' can be said crossly, kindly or suspiciously.
- Have students draw a line diagram to illustrate when the voice goes up, down, remains the same, or goes up and down. Students should label each diagram and compare their interpretations with others.

- Ask students to make a list of words, e.g. names, greetings. Work with a partner saying the words in different ways. Discuss what meaning is implied. Repeat the process with phrases or short sentences.

7 Active Listening — Group of Three

Active listening is an important skill to draw upon when someone needs to discuss a problem or a difficulty. The speaker is not necessarily seeking a solution but is hoping to develop a deeper understanding of an existing situation. This activity helps to develop an understanding of active listening. It allows students to practise the conventions and to receive feedback on their skills.

Discuss the purposes and behaviours associated with active listening. It may be useful to record the students' responses onto a chart or students could make personal records in a journal.

Students should consider the following elements of active listening:
- Purpose: active listening is listening with the intent to fully understand and to communicate understanding of both the content and the feeling being expressed.
- Verbal behaviours needed: ask clarifying questions, paraphrase to indicate understanding when needed.
- Non-verbal behaviours: attentive body language, appropriate eye contact.

A jointly constructed checklist could help to focus students' observations during this activity. Students will need to brainstorm suitable topics of conversation, e.g. a difficult assignment, a difficult customer encountered in a workplace, preparing for a job interview.

Students should form groups of three. One student is the speaker. This student should speak on a topic that is unfamiliar to the listener. Another student is the listener. The listener will practise the skills of attentive listening. The other student is the observer. This student will make notes in order to provide feedback.

Allow time for feedback to be given and for students to reflect, discuss and set goals for future improvement.

8 Inside/Outside Circle

Refer to Chapter 5, Early Speaking and Listening Phase, p. 122.

9 Telephone Talk

Refer to Chapter 5, Early Speaking and Listening Phase, p. 119.

10 Analyse a Video

Refer to Chapter 5, Early Speaking and Listening Phase, p. 127.

11 Radio Ratings

Refer to Chapter 8, Conventional Speaking and Listening Phase, p. 259.

12 Impromptu Speaking

Refer to Chapter 8, Conventional Speaking and Listening Phase, p. 257.

PROCESSES AND STRATEGIES

Major Teaching Emphases

- Teach students to select appropriate thinking strategies to explore complex concepts and ideas.

- Provide opportunities for students to engage in sustained conversations and discussions.

- Provide opportunities for students to adapt a range of processes and strategies to compose complex and challenging texts.

- Provide opportunities for students to interact responsively in contexts where they are required to facilitate discussion.

- Provide opportunities for students to identify and use prompts that anticipate and manage likely disagreements.

Organisation of the Processes and Strategies Aspect

There are several differences in the organisation of the Processes and Strategies aspect. Both the Teaching Notes and the Teaching and Learning Experiences (Involving Students) are in the *Speaking and Listening Resource Book* Chapter 4: Processes and Strategies.

The rationale for this difference in organisation is that the processes and strategies of speaking and listening are not conceptually hierarchical and therefore not phase-specific. In all phases, a variety of speaking and listening processes and strategies need to be introduced, developed and consolidated.

What varies from one phase to the next is the growth in:
- the number and integration of strategies used throughout the processes of speaking and listening.
- the awareness and monitoring of speaking and listening processes.
- the efficiency in the uses of the speaking and listening processes.
- the ability to articulate the use of the strategies used in the process of speaking and listening.
- the awareness of how the use of processes helps with composing and comprehending texts.

Supporting Parents of Proficient Speakers and Listeners

GENERAL DESCRIPTION

Proficient Speakers and Listeners have a controlled use of Standard English. They understand that the language needed to create certain spoken texts can be manipulated to achieve different purposes and effects. They assess whether certain kinds of speaking and listening are suitable for different audiences, purposes and situations. They draw upon a varied and complex knowledge of language in order to improve their communication.

Supporting Proficient Speakers and Listeners in the Home

Proficient Speakers and Listeners will benefit from a range of experiences in the home setting. Ideas for providing appropriate experiences are available on Parent Cards located on the *First Steps* Speaking and Listening CD-ROM. Teachers can select appropriate cards for each Proficient Speaker and Listener and copy them for parent use.

Parent Cards

1 General Description of Proficient Speakers and Listeners

2 Developing an Understanding About Different Types of Speaking and Listening

3 Developing an Understanding About Contexts

4 Developing Vocabulary

5 Listening

6 Family Meetings

CHAPTER 10

Advanced Speaking and Listening Phase

Unplanned	Planned

Unplanned

Teacher: What's happening with your job?

Philippa: Oh well, the job I had at [*retail outlet*] finished because that was really just for Christmas. I got to stay on a bit longer so that was good 'cos I really liked the people there, hmm. So now I've got to find another one. (*groans, laughter*)

Teacher: Any, any ideas …

Philippa: My friend works at [*retail outlet*] and she said that they were looking for people so I'm gonna try there. I'll look them up on the Internet, yeah, and find out some facts about their company. She said, my friend said, 'Oh go and buy a necklace or something and then you can say, oh yes, I'm ALWAYS buying things from here!' Have to get an interview first. (*laughs*)

Planned

(Philippa's planned speaking – extract from a description of 'How to edit a radio package')

Philippa: You hit the record button on that. You then go over to your audio deck or your mini-disk player, and select play, and as you're playing the sound through the mini disk, the computer will slowly be collecting all the information, and capturing all the sound, um, on a wave bar, so you will get louder sounds, and higher frequencies will make the bigger waves, and all that sort of thing. So you'll be able to see where speech and sound actually occurs along the audio bar. So if you allow, um, your, um, sound studio file to capture all the sound on the mini disk, depending on how much you've got. If you've got … if you're creating a piece, that's only five minutes and you've got twenty minutes worth of raw sound, just let it keep going, or you can always edit as you go, and only select the interview or the interview answers that you wish straight away. But if it is a shorter piece you can let it run out, and you can mark on the wave bar, with a special cursor, as to where one interview starts and ends.

Figure 10.1   Figure 10.2

Global Statement

In this phase, students show a sophisticated control of Standard English in a range of contexts. They understand the power and effect of spoken language, critically analysing factors that influence the interpretation of spoken texts. They use complex devices to modify and manipulate their communication for a range of purposes.

Advanced Speaking and Listening Indicators

Use of Texts

- ◆ Makes sense of a range of spoken texts, including specialised topics.
- ◆ Offers advice, extends views and presents ideas effectively in discussions with a wide range of audiences.
- ◆ Uses a wide range of unplanned and planned texts that achieve a variety of purposes.
- ◆ Analyses sophisticated and challenging information in a wide range of spoken texts.
- ◆ Uses Standard English in sophisticated ways.
- Analyses and manipulates spoken language to suit a range of contexts.
- Engages effectively in a range of complex topics and specialised areas.
- Analyses and substantiates different opinions.
- Evaluates and modifies the effect of own communication in relation to purpose, audience and text selection.
- Responds effectively to a range of spoken texts with critical awareness.

Contextual Understanding

- ◆ Makes deliberate adjustments in speaking and listening to suit a wide range of purposes and audiences.
- ◆ Interacts inclusively with a wide audience.
- ◆ Can critically evaluate spoken texts that represent differing perspectives on complex themes and issues.
- ◆ Selects and manipulates devices designed to establish a rapport, engage, persuade or influence an audience, e.g. anecdote, analogy, nominating others to hold the floor.
- Critically analyses the relationship between texts, contexts, speakers and listeners in a range of situations.

Conventions

- ◆ Draws upon a wide vocabulary to achieve planned effect.
- ◆ Controls and analyses language structures in formal and informal contexts.
- ◆ Uses speaking and listening behaviours to facilitate and maintain effective communication, e.g. intervenes sensitively, redirects.
- ◆ Selects listening conventions to suit a range of purposes.
- Uses language powerfully and effectively.
- Negotiates in groups where there are disagreements or conflicting personalities, managing the situation sensitively.
- When listening, identifies structures and features that implicitly and explicitly signal bias, attitude and opinion in complex texts across a range of purposes.

Processes and Strategies

- ◆ Draws upon an extensive repertoire of strategies to interpret and compose complex speech.
- ◆ Adapts processes and strategies to interact responsively and critically, e.g. monitors group to facilitate discussion.
- ◆ Adapts a range of processes and strategies to compose and improve complex and challenging texts.
- Students draw upon strategies to improve communication or repair miscommunication with audiences in formal and informal situations.

Major Teaching Emphases

Environment and Attitude

- Provide opportunities for relevant, challenging and purposeful communication.
- Create a supportive environment which values the diversity of students' speaking and listening.
- Encourage students to see the value of effective listening and speaking for community, school and family life.

Use of Texts

- Discuss and analyse a range of functional spoken texts.
- Provide opportunities for students to participate in authentic unplanned and planned speaking and listening.
- Support students to reflect upon and analyse their own use of text features and structures to suit a range of purposes.
- Support students to take responsibility for their own development in speaking and listening.
- Encourage students to use the metalanguage associated with speaking and listening independently, analyse, socio-cultural, ideology, world view, reiterating, deconstruct, regulate, critique, values, intertextual.

Contextual Understanding

- Provide opportunities that challenge students to carefully consider their choices when speaking and listening.
- Provide opportunities for students to reflect upon the way in which they interact with particular audiences.
- Support students to design their own speaking and listening opportunities.
- Provide support for students to contribute to discussions about matters of social interest or concern.

- Support students to take responsibility for developing critical awareness of spoken language.
- Provide opportunities for students to analyse a range of spoken texts.
- Provide opportunities for students to reflect upon and refine their use of speaking and listening devices.

Conventions

- Support students in taking responsibility for extending and developing their vocabulary.
- Support students to compose spoken texts to meet the needs of a variety of audiences, e.g. formal presentations.
- Encourage students to select speaking and listening behaviours that convey meaning and intentions with clarity.
- Involve students in a variety of situations that require sophisticated manipulation of conventions, e.g. job interviews, giving impromptu speeches.

Processes and Strategies

- Provide opportunities for students to compose spoken texts to meet the needs of a variety of audiences, e.g. formal presentations.
- Encourage students to take responsibility for choosing processes and strategies to compose a variety of spoken texts.
- Support students in taking responsibility for interacting responsively in a variety of situations.
- Support students in taking responsibility for adjusting communication in a range of contexts.

303

Teaching and Learning Experiences

Teaching Notes

Teaching and Learning experiences are not provided at this phase, as Advanced Speakers and Listeners are, on the whole, able to take responsibility for their own speaking and listening.

However, there will be occasions when students in this phase are faced with speaking and listening situations that are very unfamiliar, or which place high demands on their existing speaking and listening skills, e.g. job interviews, court and legal proceedings, workplace negotiations, financial transactions, buying expensive consumer goods, managing personal relationships, etc. To support students we have provided the major teaching emphases; the teaching and learning experiences can be obtained from the previous Proficient phase and adjusted accordingly.

Emergent Speaking and Listening Phase

Figure 11.1

Figure 11.2

Global Statement

In this phase, children use the sounds and patterns of language in which they are immersed. They verbalise and gesture to express their feelings, convey their needs and interact with others. Children may require adult support and interpretation to convey meaning.

Emergent Speaking and Listening Indicators

Use of Texts

◆ **Responds to spoken language in own personal way,** e.g. responds to familiar voices.
◆ **Produces first real words and begins to combine words.**
◆ **Understands simple and familiar questions,** e.g. *Where's Daddy?*
◆ **Imitates models of speaking,** e.g. babbles into the telephone or while turning the pages of a book.

Contextual Understanding

◆ **Recognises meaning from familiar phrases and tones.**
◆ **Recognises verbal and non-verbal behaviours in familiar contexts,** e.g. responds to a smile.
◆ **Communicates to meet own needs.**
◆ **Gestures, sounds and attempts at words are understood by familiar adults in supportive or predictable contexts,** e.g. pointing or saying *'dink'* indicates that the child wants a drink.

Conventions

◆ **Explores the sounds of home language.**
◆ **Uses favourite words,** e.g. 'no', 'mine', 'cos'.
◆ **Uses voice to attract attention.**
◆ **Responds to language games based on rhyme and repetition.**
◆ **Begins to follow rules of conversation,** e.g. uses name of person to attract attention before talking.
◆ **Is beginning to use social behaviours,** e.g. greetings, farewells, 'please' and 'thank you' in response to prompts.
◆ **Can follow simple directions.**
• Overgeneralises words to represent many ideas, e.g. *'dog'* may mean any animal with four legs.
• Uses some directional language, e.g. *'up'*.
• Uses single words and two-word phrases, e.g. *'go way'* – go away.

Processes and Strategies

◆ **Relies on copying and approximating to compose spoken language.**
◆ **Supports spoken texts with non-verbal behaviours,** e.g. *says 'Bye' and waves goodbye.*
◆ **Conveys lack of understanding through facial expression or body language.**

Major Teaching Emphases

Use of Texts

■ Immerse children in a wide variety of speaking and listening for everyday purposes.

■ Immerse children in songs, rhymes and games.

■ Talk to children often, responding to and encouraging attempts to communicate.

■ Model behaviours appropriate to speaking and listening for different purposes.

■ Interact with audio recordings.

■ Interact with video and television.

■ Allow children to participate in extended talk without constant adult supervision.

Contextual Understanding

■ Model how speech is modified for different purposes.

■ Encourage children to practise speaking skills with other familiar adults and children.

■ Read aloud often, discuss pictures, repeat favourite parts.

■ Provide opportunities for children to use speaking and listening for different purposes, e.g. play, problem solving, socialising, entertaining.

Conventions

■ Exploit daily routines, e.g. bath time, preparing meals to develop vocabulary.

■ Model language needed to describe emotions, interests and attitudes.

■ Model simple descriptive language.

■ Teach rhymes and finger plays, songs and chants to help children hear the sounds and patterns in language.

■ Model behaviours of greetings, farewells.

■ Discuss meanings of words and give definitions during discussions.

Processes and Strategies

■ Model question/response.

■ Extend simple responses and model alternatives.

■ Use toys to describe and explore the words for shape, colour and movement.

■ Model strategies to adjust speaking, e.g. volume, repetition.

Glossary

analogy   a comparison made to show a similarity in some way

appropriate   the suitable, fitting or right verbal or non-verbal language for a particular context

aspects   specific facets of speaking and listening that are categorised as Use of Texts, Contextual Understanding, Conventions and Processes and Strategies

clause   a group of words consisting of a subject and a verb that may or may not make a sentence

code-mixing   changing from one language or dialect to another during a spoken communication

code-switching   judging which dialect will best serve a speaker's needs in a given context

colloquial   everyday spoken language that may contain slang or idiomatic terms

conjunction   any word or group of words that join words, phrases or clauses, e.g. and, but, because, however

context   the particular audience, purpose and situation involved in a spoken situation

critical awareness   the ability to analyse and question spoken texts in order to detect bias, values or beliefs held by a speaker

culture   the ideas, beliefs, values and attitudes, values and beliefs that make up the shared basis of a group/s of people

deconstruct   a method of critiquing and dismantling a spoken text in order to locate various structures, features, cultural codes and ideologies in the text

device   a verbal and non-verbal feature such as making eye contact with individuals in an audience, using expressive speech, etc.

dialogic   interactive dialogue with participants having more or less equal input

dialogue   conversation, exchange of ideas, discussion, chats, etc.

discourse   the 'style' of language used to create an overall ideology or meaning of a spoken text

ESD   English as a Second Dialect

ESL   English as a second EAL Language

graphic organiser   a visual representation of concepts that enable a learner to visualise, record and retrieve information from a text, e.g. a table is a graphic organiser.

ideology   the values and beliefs held by an individual or an institution

interaction   spoken communication including non-verbal elements such as body language

interpersonal	interactions with other people
intertextuality	refers to the way in which a spoken text creates meaning through its relationship to other spoken or written texts
intrapersonal	understanding of self; knowing who you are and what you can do
language type	the language or dialect spoken
literary	fictional text, e.g. mythical, legendary, story or poetry
metalanguage	language used to describe and analyse language: language about language
monologic	a less interactive form of spoken language as one participant speaks while the other participants listen and construct meanings
PA	a public address system
presentations	the act of producing or performing formal or informal planned spoken texts
reconcile	using spoken language to repair miscommunication or misunderstanding
register	the type of vocabulary that we use in different contexts, e.g. formal speech, occupational words, casual words, family words
reiterate	to restate or repeat
socio-cultural	a combination of social and cultural factors such as economic status, geographical location, beliefs and values that exist in a group/s of people
spontaneous	unstructured, unplanned, spur of the moment
the Standard Australian English	the dialect that predominates in government, business, law, media and public life. It is predominant dialect of instruction used in Australian schools and tertiary institutions. Standard English is often described as the 'dialect of power' in Australia today.
variety of English	the different ways that spoken English is used

Bibliography

Alvarez, A., Del Rio, P. & Wertsch, J. (eds) 1995). *Sociocultural Studies of Mind*, Cambridge University Press, New York, USA.

Annandale, K., Bindon, R., Handley, K., Johnston, A., Lockett, L., & Lynch, P. 2003, *First Steps Second Edition: Linking Assessment, Teaching and Learning*, Rigby Heinemann, Port Melbourne, Victoria, Australia.

Anstey, M. & Bull, G. 2004, *The Literacy Labyrinth: Second Edition*, Pearson Education Australia, South Melbourne, Victoria, Australia.

Arnold, R. 2005, *Empathic Intelligence, Teaching, Learning, Reality*, University of NSW Press Ltd, NSW, Australia.

Australian Association for the Teaching of English Inc. 1999, *Oral Language and the Teaching of English: An Inservice Package*, Australian Association for the Teaching of English Inc., Norwood, South Australia, Australia.

Baker, C. 1991, 'Classroom Literacy Events', *Australian Journal of Reading*, 14 (2), 103–108.

Cahill, R., Collard, G., Haig, Y., Hill, A., Königsberg, P., Malcolm, I., & Rochecouste, J. 1999, *Two Way English: Towards More User-Friendly Education for Speakers of Aboriginal English*, Education Department of Western Australia, East Perth, Perth, Australia.

Campbell Rightmyer, E. 2003, 'Democratic Discipline: Children Creating Solutions', *Young Children*, 58 (4), pp. 38–45.

Campbell, R., & Grenn, D. 2003, *Literacies and Learners: Current Perspectives*, Prentice Hall, Frenchs Forest, NSW, Australia.

Collerson, J, March, P. PEN Notes (No. 12): *Talking and Listening*, Primary English Teaching Association, Newtown, NSW, Australia.

Collis, M., & Dalton, J. (1994) *Becoming Responsible Learners*, Eleanor Curtain Publishing, Prahran, Victoria, Australia.

Comber, B., & Cormack, P. 1995, *Cornerstones: Module 4: Frameworks for Critical Analysis of Teaching*, South Australia, Department for Education.

Cormack, P., & Bills, D., & Lucas, N. 1998, *Classroom Discourse Project. Classroom Perspectives on Talk: A report on collaborative research with teachers.* www.gu.edu.au/schoolcls/clearinghouse/1998_classroom/cd2.pdf

Costa, A. 2001, *Developing Your Child's Habits of Success in School, Life and Work*, Habits of Mind Website www.habits-of-mind.net/pdfHabits_of_success_parents.pdf

Cullen, J. 1998, 'What Do Teachers Need to Know About Learning in the Early Years?' www.edc.nz/publications/research/cullen.html www.edc.nz/publications/research/cullen.html

Curriculum Council, (1998) Curriculum Framework, Curriculum Council, Perth, Australia.

Cusworth, R. 1994, *What Is a Functional Model of Language?* Primary English Teaching Association, Newtown, NSW, Australia.

Department of Education and Training 2005, *English Outcomes and Standard Framework*, Department of Education and Training, East Perth, Western Australia, Australia.

Department of Education and Training 2003, *Pathways to Social and Emotional Development*, Department of Education and Training, East Perth, Western Australia, Australia.

Department of Education and Training. 2005, *Powerful Way: A Meta-Language and Literacy Development Project: Classroom Materials*, Department of Education and Training, East Perth, Western Australia, Australia.

Department of Education and Training. (2005) *Powerful Way: A Meta-Language and Literacy Development Project: Teacher Guide*, Department of Education and Training, East Perth, Western Australia, Australia.

Department of Education and Training 2002, *Ways of Being, Ways of Talk*, Department of Education and Training, East Perth, Western Australia, Australia.

Derewianka, B. (ed.). 1992, *Language Assessment in Primary Classrooms*, Harcourt Brace Jovanovich Group (Australia) Ltd, Marrickville, NSW, Australia.

Dickinson, D. & Tibors, P. 2002, Fostering Language and Literacy in Classrooms and Homes, *Young Children* Vol. 57(2), pp. 10–18.

Eades, D. 1993, *PEN Notes: Aboriginal English*, Primary English Teaching Association, Newtown, NSW, Australia.

Early Years Literacy Profile, Department for Education and Children Services, South Australia 1996.
www.earlychildhoodaustralia.org.au

Education Department of Western Australia 2004, 'Deadly Ideas' from the 'Deadly Ways to Learn Consortium', East Perth, Western Australia, Australia.

Education Department of Western Australia 2004, 'Deadly Yarns', from the 'Deadly Ways to Learn Consortium', East Perth, Western Australia, Australia.

Education Department of Western Australia, 1997, *First Steps Oral Language Resource Book*, Rigby Heinemann, Port Melbourne, Victoria, Australia.

Education Department of Western Australia 1999, *Solid English*, Education Department of Western Australia, Australia.

Education Department of Western Australia 1998, *Time for Talk Resource Park*, Education Department of Western Australia, Australia.

Ewing, R. *What Is a Functional Model of Language?* Primary English Teaching Association, Newton, NSW, Australia.

Freebody, P., Ludwig, C., Gunn, S. 1996, *Tackling Our Way Into Literacy*, Curriculum Corporation, Melbourne, Australia.

Freebody, P., Ludwig & C., Gunn, S. *Everyday Literacy Practices in and Out of Schools in Low Socio-Economic Urban Communities*, Curriculum Corporation, Melbourne, Australia.

Gee, J. 1991, 'Socio-cultural Approaches to Literacy (Literacies)' *Annual Review of Applied Linguistics*, Cambridge University Press, USA.

Gibbons, P 2002, *Scaffolding Language, Scaffolding Learning – Teaching Second Language Learners in the Mainstream Classroom*, Heinemann, Portsmouth, New Hampshire, USA.

Godinho, S., & Shrimpton, B. 2005, *Talking to Learn, Learning to Talk* [C- ROM], The University of Melbourne, Carlton, Australia.

Groves, C. (1999). *PEN Notes: Explicit Teaching: Focussing Teacher Talk on Literacy*, Primary English Teaching Association, Newtown, NSW, Australia.

Haig, Y., Oliver, R., & Rochecouste, J. (2005) *Tackling Talk*, Edith Cowan University, Perth, Western Australia. www.members.iinet/lingwa/TT/index.html

Hall, Kathy, 2004 *Literacy and Schooling: Towards Renewal in Primary Education Policy*, Ashgate Publishing

Hart, B., & Risley, T., *The Early Catastrophe: The 30 Million Word Gap by Age 3*, American Educator, Spring, 2003, 4–9.

Hill, S., & Hancock, J. 1993, *Reading and Writing Communities*, Eleanor Curtain Publishing, Armadale, Victoria, Australia.

Hill, S., & Hill, T. 1990, *The Collaborative Classroom*, Eleanor Curtain Publishing, Armadale, Victoria, Australia.

Jones, P. (ed.). 1996, *Talking to Learn*, Primary English Teaching Association, Newtown, NSW, Australia.

Katz, L. 1993, 'What can we Learn from Reggio Emilia?' Edwards, C., Gandini, L., & Foreman, G. (eds). *The Hundred Languages of Children: The Reggio Emilia Approach to Early Childhood Education*, Ablex Publishing Company, Norwood, New Jersey, USA.

Katz, L., & Chard, C. 2000, *Engaging Children's Minds: The Project Approach (Second Edition)*, Ablex Publishing Corporation, Stamford, Connecticut, USA.

Lake, V., & Pappamihiel, E., 'Effective Practices and Principles to Support English Language Learners in the Early Childhood Classroom', *Childhood Education*, June 22, 2003, pp. 200–203.

Lindsey, G. 1998, 'Brain Research and Implications for Early Childhood Education', *Childhood Education*, (75), 97–100.

Lyle, S. 1993 'An Investigation into Ways in Which Children "Talk Themselves into Meaning" ', *Language and Education Journal*, 7 (3), pp. 181–97.

MacNaughton, G. 2004, 'The Politics of Logic in Early Childhood Research: A Case of the Brain, Hard Facts, Trees and Rhizomes', *The Australian Educational Researcher*, 13 (3), pp. 87–103.

Bibliography

Migata, C, 2004, *Speaking Rules! Games and Activities for Creating Effective Speakers, Presenters and Storytellers*, Curriculum Corporation, Melbourne, Australia.

Murdoch, K. 2004, 'What Makes Good Inquiry Learning?' *EQ Australia, Talking Australia* www.curriculum-edu.au/eq/autumn 2004/article2.html

National Curriculum Council 1991, *Teaching Talking and Learning in Key Stage Two*, National Curriculum Council, York, England.

Phelan, T. 2003, *123 Magic: Effective Discipline for Children 2–12*, Parentmagic Inc., Glen Ellyn, Illinois, USA.

Prentice, R. 2000, 'Creativity: A Reaffirmation of its Place in Early Childhood Education', *The Curriculum Journal*, 11 (2), 145–158.

Radio National, *Life Matters*, [online] Accessed 26th August 2005, www.abc.net.au/rn/talks/in/stories/51445905html

Reid, J 2002, *Managing Small-Group Learning*, Primary English Teaching Association, Newtown, NSW, Australia.

Resnick, L. 2001, 'Making America Smarter: The Real Goal of School Reform', In A.L. Costa (ed) *Developing Minds: A Resource Book for Teaching Thinking* (3rd edition), Association for Supervision and Curriculum Development, Alexandria, Virginia, USA.

Rowe, G. 1991, *Making Time for Classroom Talk*, Primary English Teaching Association, Newtown, NSW, Australia.

Stevens, M. (ed.). 2001, *ESL in the Mainstream*, Education Department of Western Australia, Australia.

Tough, J. 1976, *Listening to Children Talking*, Ward Lock Educational, Heinemann, Portsmouth, New Hampshire, USA.

Wilks, S. 1995, *Critical and Creative Thinking*, Eleanor Curtain Publishing, Armadale, Victoria, Australia.

Zubrick, A. 1991, 'Oral Language Development in the School Years', *Australian Journal of Reading*, 14 (4), pp. 316–325.

First Steps Second Edition Professional Development Courses

First Steps Second Edition texts form a critical part of the *First Steps* professional development courses that promote long-term commitment to educational change. Together, the professional development and the texts provide a strategic, whole-school approach to improving student literacy outcomes.

First Steps offers a full range of professional development courses for teachers that are conducted at the invitation of a school or an education sector. Given the breadth of literacy, schools generally choose to implement only one strand of literacy at a time. A strand should be selected on a needs basis in line with school priorities. Schools can select from two-day courses in any of the following strands:
• Reading
• Writing and Spelling
• Viewing
• Speaking and Listening.

Each participant attending a two-day course receives:
• a Map of Development in the chosen literacy strand
• a Resource Book in the chosen literacy strand
• a copy of *Linking Assessment, Teaching and Learning*
• a course book of professional development reflections
• practical activities for classroom application.

Within each strand, a selection of additional sessions beyond the regular course will also be available to meet the needs of teachers in different schools and contexts. These sessions can be selected in consultation with a *First Steps* consultant.

For further information about or registration in *First Steps* courses, contact your nearest Steps Professional Development and Consulting Office.

UNITED STATES OF AMERICA
STEPS Professional Development and Consulting
97 Boston Street, Salem
Massachusetts USA 01970
Phone: 978 744 3001
Fax: 978 744 7003
Toll free: 1 866 505 3001
www.stepspd.com

UNITED KINGDOM
STEPS Professional Development
Unit 78
Shrivenham Hundred Business Park
Majors Road, Watchfield SN6 8TY
Phone: 01793 787930
Fax: 01793 787931
www.stepspd.com

AUSTRALASIA
STEPS Professional Development
ECU Churchlands Campus
Pearson Street, Churchlands
Western Australia 6018
Phone: 08 9273 8833
Fax: 08 9273 8811
www.stepspd.com

CANADA
Pearson Professional Learning
26 Prince Andrew Place
Don Mills, Ontario M3C 2T8, Canada
Phone: 416 447 5101
Fax: 416 447 3914
Toll free: 1888 867 7772
www.stepspd.com